Ethnic Routes to Becoming American

Ethnic Routes to Becoming American

Indian Immigrants and the Cultures of Citizenship

Sharmila Rudrappa

Rutgers University Press

New Brunswick, New Jersey, and London

Library of Congress Cataloging-in-Publication Data

Rudrappa, Sharmila, 1966–
    Ethnic routes to becoming American : Indian immigrants and the cultures of
citizenship / Sharmila Rudrappa.
        p.   cm.
Includes bibliographical references and index.
        ISBN 0-8135-3370-8 (hardcover : alk. paper) — ISBN 0-8135-3371-6 (pbk. : alk.
paper)
    1. East Indian Americans—Cultural assimilation.   2. East Indian Americans—
Politics and government.   3. East Indian Americans—Social conditions.
4. Immigrants—United States—Political activity.   5. Immigrants—United States—
Social conditions.   6. Citizenship—United States.   I. Title
    E184.E2R83   2004
    305.891'4073—dc22

                                                                    2003018864

British Cataloging-in-Publication data for this book is available from the British Library

Manufactured in the United States of America

Contents

Acknowledgments

The task of thanking the giants on whose shoulders I stand is never an easy one, for where do I begin? And what if I leave someone out? My mind, body, and soul have been nurtured by so many not just because I asked but because they sensed I needed it. This work would not have been possible without the women who came to stay at Apna Ghar. They have to remain unnamed but cannot remain unacknowledged. The endless evening hours spent over dinners, sharing more than just food, talk, and laughter made work at the shelter and the writing process years later bearable. My Chicago friends—Caryn Aviv, Tony Ganger, little Carlton Ganger, Shyni Muthyala, Jeff Root, and Umeeta Sadarangani—for the pizzas, ruglah, haleem, walks on Pratt Beach, dog care, and so much more.

My committee at the University of Wisconsin-Madison was more than just that. Jane Collins trusted me enough to let me take the directions I wanted. Yet, without those quiet questions she asked, this work would never have seen the light of day. Nina Eliasoph's enthusiastic engagement with my ideas and my talks with Paul Lichtermann as we walked round and round the block with little Leo in the stroller made writing more fun. Kirin Narayan—her compassion taught me to be kinder to people in my writings and in my life. Pam Oliver who taught me that the most obvious questions are always the most difficult to answer. Hemant Shah's careful notes in the margins made the book richer. And Nancy Worcester. TA-ing WS 103 "Women and the Bodies in Health and Disease" propelled me in directions I hadn't quite envisioned. Thank you, Nancy, for the tremendous emotional sustenance that you gave me over those last three to four years in Madison. And thank you, too, for bringing into my life

Araceli Alonso and Lisa Tetrault. I'm immensely grateful to Lisa for her love, warmth, and friendship.

Other UW-Madison folk—John Bruce at the Land Tenure Center, Bob Kowal in Botany, Sharon Dickson at the Center for South Asia, and Dennis Hill at the Memorial Library—thank you. Erik Wright put enormous effort in teaching me how to think. I owe much to Nikolas Kozloff. His comments on the shelter chapters were tremendous, and his friendship over these years, even more so. Friends made in Madison, many of whom are now elsewhere—John Antush, Chris Chekuri, Heidi Glaesel, Rosemary Griffith, Ibtisam Ibrahim, Shanti Kumar, Maneesha Lal, Tom Macias, Markos, Geeta Raval, Jean Yves Sgro, Jaspreet Singh, Diane Soles, and Peter Staudenmeier. They taught me how to make community. Thanks to Kalpana Prakash. Chinnie, your own work with mixed media has been inspirational in so many ways that I'm only beginning to learn now what all this means. And Nesara mudhu, in all of her fourteen years of worldly wisdom, recognizes that her aunt needs considerable editorial help.

I'd also like to acknowledge David Myers at Rutgers; though the first draft barely reflected the eventual direction the book took, he took my word for it. A first-time author could not find a better editor than Kristi Long at Rutgers, whose editorial interventions have only helped make this work stronger. I am also grateful to Mary Waters for her detailed input on the draft; her comments contributed to making this book more cohesive. Comments on the shelter chapters by Shamita Das Dasgupta were helpful. Jim Lee read the draft amid grading and winter break plans; his criticism was absolutely invaluable. Samer Ali, Mia Carter, Chiquita Collins, Gloria Gonzalez Lopez, John Park, Art Sakamoto, Gideon Sjoberg, and Christine Williams have all been wonderful colleagues in my two years at Austin. And of course, I am deeply indebted to Amma and Appaji who never fail to ask when the book is going to come out and why it takes me so long to write just one book. And to Tippoo, too, whose canine tolerance for my bad behavior is commendable. The world would perhaps be a better place if it did really go to the dogs, and the dogs were all as sweet as my Sultan.

Ethnic Routes to Becoming American

One

Introduction

Locating South Asian Americans

In the late 1990s, I lived in Roger's Park, Chicago, for just over a year. To get to the South Asian American battered women's shelter, Apna Ghar, where I worked thirty-six hours a week, I drove south on Broadway to the Uptown area at Lawrence. I went past boarded-up stores that proclaimed "the sale of the century" because they were going out of business. People who could potentially be shoppers in these stores now sat underemployed or unemployable, huddled on stoops of grand but decaying buildings as jobs flew out on the flight path of capital. Those ornate early-twentieth-century buildings were a dull gray from decades of traffic fumes. Sandburg's Chicago so lovingly celebrated as that "hog butcher for the world, tool maker, stacker of wheat, player with railroads and the nation's freight handler, stormy, husky, brawling, the City of the Big Shoulders" seemed so far from reality that it appeared a myth.[1] Instead, Uptown Chicago's shoulders hunched over with exhaustion, more resembling an overexploited, harried worker. I could not help but feel twinges of sadness for the city and its inhabitants; like those ashen buildings, we were unable to climb onto the bandwagon of globalizing capital. The gala parade had moved on, and we were left behind.

Yet, this sadness somewhat abated as I turned off Broadway onto streets such as Argyle. A whole new Chicago emerged there amid those pallid buildings. Signs of another kind of globalization, not in terms of large capital investments, but small immigrant shops owned and run by newcomers from Southeast Asia packed these side streets. Restaurants, bakeries, and grocery stores selling non-European foods abounded. People bustled in and out, bargained for better prices, and loitered by displays of foods that I had not seen

1

before. Ragged apartment buildings showed signs of habitation, this time not with Eastern Europeans but with new Southeast Asian arrivals. English was broken here. Former Vietnamese refugees had taken over this part of Chicago and were instilling nebulous life into it once again.

At other times when I was not working at the shelter Apna Ghar, I drove two or three times a week west on Devon Avenue toward the Indo American Center, located in what some people call "India Town." I worked as a part-time volunteer coordinator at the Center. Going west on Devon Avenue, away from Lake Michigan's idyllic Pratt Beach, I noted changes in the deteriorating urban landscape. People were not what I—a relative newcomer to the United States— expected to see. Interspersed among Blacks, Whites, and Mexican Americans were Russian, Ethiopian, Somali, Nigerian, Pakistani, and Indian immigrants like me, walking by stores that displayed goods not found elsewhere in the city. Besides English, I heard Arabic, Russian, Urdu, and Gujarati spoken on the streets. Devon was pronounced either "Divine" or "Diwan." Shortly, I reached the Western Avenue intersection and Devon/Divine/Diwan converted into Mohammed Ali Jinnah Way, proclaiming the predominance of Pakistani businesses. Three to four blocks later, Devon changed names again, this time to Mahatma Gandhi Marg, ostensibly attesting to the preponderance of Indian-owned businesses. In reality, Jinnah Way and Gandhi Marg supported both Pakistani and Indian businesses.

Brightly colored saris and the latest styles of *salwaar kameezes*, in bright reds, greens, blues, and yellows, all straight from the subcontinent hung outside shop doors like gaudy flags in the Chicago summer breeze. In other shops, tailors were busy at their sewing machines, stitching up sari blouses or tucking in oversized *kurtas*. Electronic goods stores displayed TVs, VCRs, and music systems. They also sold kitchen utensils such as steel pots and pans, blenders, juicers, and the ubiquitous pressure cooker that is essential to every South Asian kitchen. Huge suitcases stood outside these electronic stores in silent testimony to the constant travels of South Asians across the Atlantic to their sending countries and back to their present Midwest homes. Jewelry shops abounded on Devon, displaying highly ornate gold necklaces and earrings, studded with pearls, rubies, emeralds, and diamonds. At yet other store windows hung Indian movie posters, featuring red-lipped, voluptuous women leaning against bare-chested, brooding men in skin-tight black leather pants. These were invariably video stores confirming Bollywood's popularity among South Asian Americans. Loud filmi tunes resounded from these stores, proclaiming the proprietor's music and video wares.

One corner store claimed to be "America's first Indo-Pak Bakery." Meat stores advertised their stock of *halal* (kosher) meats for Devon's Muslim patrons. Amid all this were numerous restaurants with South Indian *idlis*, Punjabi *tandoor*, and Hyderabadi *nihari* on their menus. These restaurants vied with each other, advertising their buffet lunches as the least expensive or tastiest among them all. Inside, young South Asian men waitstaff hovered solicitously around their customers, while Mexican immigrants bussed tables, washed dishes, and cleaned floors.

The side streets perpendicular to Devon were packed with cars of every kind, with Wisconsin, Indiana, Michigan, and Minnesota license plates. South Asian immigrants from various parts of the Midwest converged here on weekends. The sidewalks were filled with husbands sporting mustaches, wives in salwaars, fathers-in-law stuffed in awkward suits, and mothers-in-law draped in saris, often with chubby babies in strollers. After a meal at one of the restaurants, they would almost invariably stop at Patel Brothers' Grocery Store, which was the first Indian store that had begun the flood of South Asian merchants into this previously declining Jewish business district. Today, one of the largest South Asian business districts in the United States has replaced this former Jewish business area.

Inside the Patel Brothers' Grocery Store sat the grand patriarch of the Patel grocery empire, presiding over his customers whose nostalgia for their Indian/Pakistani homes was temporarily alleviated by walking through aisles of *masala* mixes, pickles, lentils, hair oils, and incense sticks. The Northwater Market was another important pilgrimage site for South Asian shoppers, where they picked through vegetables such as *tindhi*, *bhindi*, *mulee*, *methi* and *baingan*. At times, shoppers might turn to other South Asians next to them—complete strangers—and exclaim excitedly over the availability of cherimoyas or jackfruits here in the United States.

On street benches older men and women, invariably dressed in clean, white *dhotis* and saris, lounged under the sun soaking in the sounds, sights, and aromas of raucous immigrant life on Devon. Traffic on Devon during weekends was noisy. Young boys cruised by slowly in their cars with windows rolled down to show off their collection of Bollywood music blasting over their effectively loud stereo systems. Gaggles of young girls sauntered down sidewalks, flicking their long, black hair frequently as they stopped to stare at window displays of the latest fashion item that had just arrived from the subcontinent. Every so often, they might glance shyly at the gangs of boys in their cars. Irate weekend shoppers honked incessantly in a frustrated attempt to negotiate the mad rush of people and traffic all chaotically mixing together on the street.

Like the thousands of other South Asian immigrants, I too made my pilgrimage to Devon over weekends to get our fill of ethnic goods. We returned home to cook our ethnic meals to last us over the week so that we could eat *parathas, bisi bele bath,* and *rasam* after a day's work in schools, hospitals, and offices. We sat back content, as we nostalgically thought of our past lives elsewhere. Devon met our yearnings for Bollywood, South Asian foods and groceries, and a public space that was predominantly South Asian, where people draped in saris, dhotis, and salwaars loitered around with no apparent self-consciousness of difference. Driving down Devon on weekends always excited me—I could not help but feel I was one with the noisy masses who swarmed there to shop for their ethnic essentials. There was something inexplicably gratifying in being part of the crowd, not particularly standing out one way or another. We South Asian immigrants bonded through our active participation in the crass, but lively commercial exchange of ethnic commodities that traveled from halfway across the world. Meanwhile, in the backrooms, Jose, Jorge, and Sergio refilled vegetable stalls and mopped grocery aisles. They scrubbed floors, cleaned tables, and washed dishes in those restaurants serving inexpensive buffets. Overworked and underpaid, they prepared Devon for the frenzied carloads of immigrant South Asians who would descend the following weekend, seeking out the best bargains to assuage their ethnic longings.

This was my Chicago, what used to be my home, globalizing in unplanned ways and in directions not quite expected. We were immigrants living out our everyday lives. Walking into Devon, especially on weekends, many of us could forget we were in the United States—except for the preponderance of Japanese-made cars. We flocked by the thousands on weekends into Devon. The ethnic commodities there and we ourselves in our brown skins and ethnic clothes became the central part of the spectacle for each other.[2] We bonded in our commercial engagements, satiating our nostalgia through buying, buying, and more buying.

Nostalgia for Authentic Homelands

This immigrant nostalgia for a life "back home" worry anti-immigration ideologues such as Peter Brimelow. They fear that non-White immigrants such as us on Chicago's Devon Avenue and our foreign ways are converting the United States into an alien nation. They project that within the next fifty years, the non-White population will be larger than the White population and alter forever an America they aspire for. Hence, they ask for a moratorium on or slowing down of non-European immigration.

Others, working within a more academic setting such as Christian Joppke, express the anxiety that immigrants are changing the cultures of American citizenship. As a cultural concept, citizenship refers to sets of practices citizens follow to constitute themselves as a nation. Joppke observes that nation-states are fundamentally constituted on the principle of sedentariness, that is, the fixity of a population in a geographical territory. Yet, immigrants challenge this principle of sedentariness and the idea of the geographically bound nation-state because they are transnational subjects. Their sending nations influence their everyday life, thus undermining the cultural content of American citizenship and posing a challenge to the American nation-state. In addition, immigrant groups push for multiculturalism. They ask for recognition based on their difference. Can a nation make itself based on diversity? According to Joppke, multiculturalism challenges citizenship by undermining "the American concept of non-ethnic, politically constituted nationhood . . . in its roots-orientated public exaltation of ethnic and racial identity, multiculturalism tears apart the future orientated, civic layer that had kept the fabric of an essentially 'new' nation together."[3]

So does the existence of ethnic neighborhoods, such as Devon, populated with individuals with inherited phenotypes and cultural practices so obviously not what we would think of as "meat and potatoes, apple-pie" middle-America threaten the making of an imagined American community? These questions become especially relevant in these days after the September 11, 2001, attacks on the United States. South Asians are frequently identified as Arab and are, therefore, automatically deemed terrorists and are targets of xenophobia in airports, streets, and neighborhoods. American civil society, with the state's tacit endorsement, has begun questioning anyone who displays the phenotype of being Arab. We are either with them or we are against them, we are told. What are we supposed to do to be with them? And what part of us is automatically read as being against them?

The Politics that Frame this Book

This book emerges from my year of work and research in the late 1990s in Chicago. What does it mean to be "them," that is, American today? What rights do we have because of our citizenship in this particular nation-state? Questions of citizenship and belonging invariably raise other questions—what cultural practices make us part of the imagined national community, allowing us access to becoming American? In this book, I examine two South Asian American Chicago organizations, Apna Ghar, a shelter for abuse survivors, and the Indo American Center, a cultural center, to illuminate immigrant race politics in late-twentieth-century United States. These ethnic organizations can be seen to endorse the development of a strong ethnic identity based on geographic origins—they work with primarily South Asian immigrants and are run by other South Asian Americans. They also receive state and private grants for their social work efforts among underserved populations. In other words, the state's multicultural agenda plays out in its support for these ethnic organizations.

The question arises—do these organizations, with the state institutions' blessings, contribute to the balkanization of the United States?

To even begin answering this question, we need to contextualize the work of these two organizations within the transformations witnessed in urban America since the 1970s. Given the changes we see in governance—the decline in welfare rights and the threats to affirmative action all pointing to a collapse in the social rights associated with citizenship; the burdening of nongovernmental agencies (NGOs) with the responsibilities of assisting those whom the state is unable or unwilling to support; the rise of multiculturalism that directs politics toward respect for "difference"—how do we make sense of ethnic nonprofit organizations? How do the social workers and volunteers engage in "community work" in these ethnic organizations? How is community defined through the process of active engagement in the various issues that people with similar geographical origins face? Does the celebration of ethnicity, especially in the context of multiculturalism, negate assimilation?

I examine these questions through ethnographies of Apna Ghar and the Indo American Center. I worked as a caseworker for a year in the late 1990s at Apna Ghar. In addition, I was a part-time volunteer coordinator at the Indo American Center for seven months during the same time. Apna Ghar, begun solely through the initiative of immigrant South Asian women, aims to do two things—provide battered immigrant women a safe space and politicize South Asian Americans on gender issues. And the purpose of the Indo American Center is to facilitate new Indian immigrants' assimilation into the United States. I explore the sociopolitical milieu within which these two organizations operate and delineate how the politics that we engage in are indelibly entangled with the cultures of American citizenship. Both intentionally and involuntarily, these two South Asian American organizations I show, articulate with the late-twentieth-century American nation-state in particular ways whereby race resistance is smoothly cleansed into ethnic assimilation.

While I frame my questions within the realm of American nation-building and the incorporation of non-White immigrants into the body politic, my larger concern—the metapolitics of this project—is the contextualization of Asian American "community" politics. Community emerges through our social engagements over the processes of meeting others, working out personal and public concerns, caring and being cared for, negotiating differences, compromising, and coming up with collective solutions. As racialized persons, we often like to think of our community organizations as autonomous spaces where we have authorial power; here in these spaces within civil society, we often believe, we can work an oppositional politics of racial justice. Yet given the reorganization of politics since the 1970s in the United States, can we unproblematically celebrate our actions and our organizations as resistance? The rise of the politics of "isms" in the United States, chiefly post-Fordism and multiculturalism, effectively effaces our resistance through benign incorporation. We are included in the polity, but it works as a politics of containment. While previously our very presence was a polemic against the American nation-state, we look around and come to the slow realization that we are undeniably part and parcel of the national project, deliberately and inadvertently bolstering the formation of the nation-state in its altered racial and economic structures.

The Nation-State's Post-1970s Configuration

To understand the South Asian American organizations Apna Ghar and the Indo-American Center, it is crucial to locate them in the larger structures of change within which they operate. These two organizations under scrutiny here certainly exercise their autonomy and power in making choices regarding their particular political routes, but their decisions make clearer sense when we contextualize them within the larger sphere of politics. Governance and the meanings of citizenship in the United States irrevocably altered by the end of the twentieth century, and it is within this backdrop that we need to understand how these two organizations operate. Economic recessions; the reorganization of capital from Fordism to post-Fordism; the collapse of communism; the globalization of manufacturing through subcontracting; the influx of non-White immigrants from Latin America and Asia as refugees, braceros, or techno-braceros; social movements such as the civil rights movements; antiwar agitations, especially vocal in college towns across America; second-wave feminism; and the rise of White ethnicity over the 1980s all have impacted two aspects of American politics that are inextricably tied together: (*a*) they have heralded new structures of urban governance, and (*b*) they have impacted our notions of citizenship rights.

The mid-1970s marked a transition from Fordism to post-Fordism, which changed the face of American economies, politics, and cultures irrevocably. While Fordism consisted of heavy manufacturing, assembly line production, and centralized trade unions, post-Fordism entailed flexible modes of production with an adaptable industrial infrastructure, an accommodating workforce hired on a short-term contractual basis, just-in-time production, and the growth of subcontracting that tie production regions around the world. Within these changed economies, David Harvey notes that a particular sort of postmodernist culture has arisen, one that "seeks some kind of accommodation with the more flexible regime of accumulation that has emerged since 1973. It has sought a creative and active rather than a passive role in the promotion of new cultural attitudes and practices consistent with flexible accumulation,"[4] which Jameson calls the cultural logic of late capitalism.[5]

In contrast to the Fordist mass consumptive patterns, today we see in post-Fordism flexible and permanently innovative methods of consumption, where customers actively seek difference in the market so that they may accrue symbolic capital. Whereas the cultural discontents of the 1960s at various levels rejected standardized accumulation and mass culture,[6] today these very discontents themselves are being marketed. In these times, counterculture has become a basic capitalist tenet to meet a new kind of consumerism that aggressively pursues uniqueness. Our very dissent is commodified, and our thirst for transgression is "perfectly suited to an economic-cultural regime that runs on ever-faster cyclings of the new; its taste for self-fulfillment and its intolerance for the confines of tradition now permitting vast latitude in consuming practices and lifestyle experimentation."[7] Hence, commentators such as Michael Piore observe that capitalism since the 1970s has become much more tolerant of diversity and supports varied lifestyles.

Not only is counterculture normalized, but also, cultural differences that were unacceptable in mainstream America not too long ago, are now familiar items. From the private arenas of consumptive practices where White Buddhist converts sit in contemplative silence sipping chai tea in chic cafes, suburbanites eat sushi dinners with warm sake in restaurants at strip malls, and Volvos with bumper stickers that claim "Kali is my co-pilot" to public affirmation of difference where schools across the United States have "multicultural days," universities institute ethnic studies programs, and even the 2000 Democratic and Republican conventions doffing their hats at diversity, difference talk in the United States has become endemic. Anyone walking into the nation would believe we have entered an era of not just acceptance but revelry in racial difference. Indeed, multicultural politics claims to do exactly that in a pluralist America where, ostensibly, all cultures are accorded equal respect.

Paralleling all these changes, we notice a transformation in state authority. The global deflations of the early 1970s demolished older forms of governance especially at the local level, and by the 1980s, urban governments in the United States were backing away from their earlier welfare distributive functions to making their cities investor friendly to a flexible, mobile, globalized capital. The welfare state has slowly given way to the workfare state, which acts to "promote product, process, organizational and market innovation in open economies in order to strengthen as far as possible the structural competitiveness of the national economy by intervening on the supply side."[8] The focus under these regimes is flexible responses to globally mobile capital and work training programs for citizens in lieu of social policies that we witnessed in an earlier era.

The American nation-state, both culturally and in terms of governance, is not what it used to be. We are witnessing the rise of a radically different kind of politics that has an overtly cultural focus, with little or no attention to deep redistribution. Even as social security is privatized, AFDC has given way to TANF, and overall welfare benefits for needy communities are shrinking, we see a cultural turn in politics where "ethnic" differences are accorded respect, and communities of color are ostensibly allowed a place in public spheres as I show in this book. The very nature of the political beast has metamorphosed from when state institutions were understood as structured along abstract, universal lines, to present forms where difference is acknowledged through multicultural politics. I argue that these changes do not mean we have a racial democracy and neither does it mean that state power has dissipated. It only means that the nation-state—chameleon like—has altered its cultural and governing form. The state's bark is muted, but slip through the cracks, and you will find it biting hard at your heels as you desperately hang by the skin of your teeth in a considerably altered economy.

The Meanings of Citizenship

In an everyday sense, American citizenship is all about getting permanent residency and eventually receiving an American passport. Yet, citizenship is more than a matter of passports. When we examine its contents we see that citizenship is centrally about the rights that accrue to us because we have this national membership. T. H. Marshall's famous 1950 essay notes that as citizens we have civil, political, and social rights. Civil rights give us access to free speech and equal justice. Political rights provide us the privileges and responsibilities of participating in politics, running for elections, and voting for candidates of our choice. And lastly, social rights entitle us to "economic welfare and security to live the life of a civilized being according to the standards prevailing in the society."[9] Citizenship, therefore, implies a set of juridical, political, economic, and cultural practices that define us as competent members of a polity, which consequently shapes the flow of resources or allocation of rights to us as individuals and the social groups to which we belong.[10]

The allocation of rights is not universal or ahistorical, but as Rogers Smith observes, laws regarding our rights as citizens are shaped by political elites who "require a population to lead that imagines itself to be a 'people.'" The ways that people imagine themselves are crucial because these imaginations facilitate leadership by aspiring political elites. Political needs drive leaders to "offer civic ideologies, or myths of civic identity, that foster the requisite sense of peoplehood, and to support citizenship laws that express those ideologies symbolically while legally incorporating and empowering the leaders' likely constituents."[11] The distribution of rights is one mode by which nations—the United States in this instance—imagine themselves into being. Citizenship, points out T. H. Marshall, "requires a bond of a different kind, a direct sense of community membership based on loyalty to a civilization which is a common possession. It is a loyalty of free men endowed with rights and protected by a common law. Its growth is stimulated both by the struggle to win those rights and by their enjoyment when won."[12] Hence, we see that the exercise of our rights are central to integrating us as valid members, but more than this, our access to the social rights of citizenship are far more crucial to incorporating us as constituents of the nation-state. Public schooling, for example, is central to nation-building. T. H. Marshall thus notes:

> It was increasingly recognized, as the nineteenth century wore on, that political democracy needed an educated electorate, and that scientific manufacture needed educated workers and technicians. The duty to improve and civilize oneself is a social duty, and not merely a personal one, because the social health of a society depends upon the civilization of its members. And a community that enforces this duty has begun to realize that its culture is an organic unity and its civilization a national heritage.[13]

Through the extension and exercise of citizenship rights in the United States, inchoate masses of mostly immigrants are ordered into an established national polity who do not belong to this or that sending nation but who imagine themselves as a singular people, as Americans. These imaginings are not broadly cast, however; they are shaped by graded exclusivity. Some members are seen as more deserving of some rights than other members are. Working-class individuals have very different rights, especially social rights such as welfare, unemployment benefits, and so forth than do middle-class individuals. Or for that matter, African Americans have very different kinds of civil rights in comparison to Arab Americans. Men from both groups may be profiled because they threaten an imagined American nation, but their presence is deemed threatening for very different reasons. The reasons for profiling African American men are cloaked as law and order issues, and Arab American men since September 11, 2001, have suddenly turned into potential terrorists, plotting away in their sleeper cells. Hence, citizenship rights are not evenly distributed; instead, individuals' geographic origins/race/religion/gender/sexuality/class matter in how they are perceived and the kinds of rights or responsibilities that accrue to them.

Social movements seek to expand these citizenship rights and might in fact be successful in pushing for social change; however, laws regarding distribution of rights and responsibilities often tend to bolster the racial/gender/class status quo. Laws concerning citizenship rights build on social beliefs and practices that are already in place. It is not as if laws are racially discriminatory for the sole purpose of perpetuating prejudice; instead racialized modes of distributing rights both make and sustain the imagined national community. They are structured as well as structuring principles in a nation's social life. Laws are structured because they are underpinned by existing ways of racial thinking. Equally, they are also structuring principles because they reinforce extant racial ideologies. In this sense, they contribute to making racialized communities, fixing where we live, what we can own, what jobs are open to us, and whom we can rightfully marry. These laws are, as Omi and Winant say, racial projects that order the ways in which race is understood, experienced, and lived.[14]

So we see that in spite of its espoused liberal traditions, race has been central to the distribution of citizenship rights in the United States. A cursory glance at the civil rights movements, for example, reveals the ways communities of color struggled to gain acceptance as full members of the American polity who justly deserved an array of civil, political, and social rights associated with citizenship. It is no startling revelation when Rogers Smith notes that if we take into account immigration, naturalization, and voting rights that

> for over 80% of U.S. history, American laws declared most people in the world legally ineligible to become full U.S. citizens solely because of their race, original nationality, or gender. For at least two-thirds of American history, the majority of the adult domestic population was also ineligible for full citizenship for the same reasons. Those racial, ethnic and gender restrictions were blatant, not "latent."[15]

This book closely examines two realms of citizenship that are inextricably tied together—the cultures of American citizenship and the social rights associated with citizenship. By cultures of citizenship, I mean a set of social practices that people follow to recast themselves as a common citizenry. While we may visualize American citizenship as purely legal matters concerned with passports and bundles of rights that are differentially distributed, we cannot help but notice that citizenship is underlined by cultural contents as well. This culture not only plays a role in ordering redistribution, but also a common culture, a national habitus, makes a cohesive polity. Culture is crucial in making a common citizenry whereby people imagine themselves as sharing destinies, embracing identical value systems, and upholding collective goals for their polity. Lisa Lowe points out that "the legal and political forms of the nation have required a national culture for the integration of differentiated people and social spaces that make up 'America,' a national culture, broadly cast yet singularly engaging, that can inspire diverse individuals to identify with the national project." The nation's culture, "the collectively forged images, histories and narratives that place, displace, and replace individuals in relation to the national polity—powerfully shapes who the citizenry is, where they dwell, what they remember, and what they forget."[16]

The social rights of citizenship, as defined by Marshall, had essentially meant welfare rights and education. However, at present, social rights have come to include persons' rights to be recognized for their difference. Increasingly nation-states are realizing that citizenship rights can not be premised solely on the notion of an universal individual but that group particularities need to be accepted, which in turn leads to differential interpretations and applications of laws so that all citizens can access equal rights. Equal rights do not mean just economic benefits but also cultural rights, so that persons who are racially/sexually different may lead a life of dignity. It is within this context that we see the rise of multicultural politics.

To give multiculturalism its due—as this book critiques it so relentlessly—it is a means by which we acknowledge difference. It is a politics that admits that whiteness, discussed in detail over the course of these pages, has the power to name, describe, and categorize any deviations from the racial norm. Such naming, describing, and categorizing often lead to misrecognition, which Taylor notes, imposes negative images on the oppressed, leading them to internalize demeaning notions of themselves. *Mis*recognition is a form of injustice because classes of persons such as women (due to patriarchy), African Americans (due to racism), or gay men (due to homophobia) are induced to internalize their oppressions and denigrate themselves. They are condemned to suffer the pain of low self-esteem, and they become the worst instruments of their own subjugation. Therefore, "due recognition is not just a courtesy we owe people. It is a vital human need," and liberal democracies today try to offer their citizens due recognition, leading us into an era of multicultural politics.[17] Multicultural policies work at two levels—recognition and redistribution. At purely the recognition level, these policies attempt to inculcate respect whereby, for example, school and university curricula are diversified to acknowledge and value the histories, cultures, and contributions of communities of color. At another level, multicultural policies comprise redistributive or allocative measures such as affirmative action in educational institutions and hiring, grants for underrepresented groups in the arts, or state funding targeting ethnic NGOs such as Apna Ghar or the Indo American Center.

This turn in politics to multiculturalism has aroused many criticisms. While some, taking a conservative stance, see it as a dangerously balkanizing politics, others arguing from the left are concerned that multiculturalism weakens progressive politics through its focus on culture and identities, rather than "real" class-based social inequalities that grow almost exponentially today. I will revisit these themes as the bulk of this book engages with multiculturalism.

The Reconfiguration of Urban Governments

Paralleling the growth of multicultural politics, we see that urban governance has been restructured over the latter half of the twentieth century in moves to accommodate globalization of capital. Since the economic recessions of the 1970s, urban governments are allocated increasingly smaller and smaller amounts of resources from their central governments to meet their social costs, but conversely, these local/regional governing bodies have greater direct negotiability with global capital than ever before. The growth of post-Fordism, with its rapid movement of globally mobile capital, flexible labor needs, and diversification of consumptive practices has progressively transformed central governments into lumbering dinosaurs that are incapable of responding quickly and in a flexible manner to the changes all around. Hence, we have grown increasingly dependent on the abilities of regional/urban governments to negotiate deals with multinational capital for their business. Governments have to be leaner and meaner for two reasons. First, they have lesser resources for accommodating the social rights of their urban citizenry. And second, whether these urban governments are left leaning or inclined to the right, they have no option than to become "entrepreneurial cities" that subordinate social policies to economic policies. Mayer comments: "[T]he pressures exerted by the economic restructuring and mass unemployment on the one hand and by shrinking subsidies from central government on the other and the willingness to accord priority to economic development policies have pushed into the background one of the formerly central functions of local state politics, namely the provision of social consumption goods and welfare services."[18]

Under these situations, local governments are gradually drawing more and more on a range of private and semipublic actors to facilitate governance. Some people see these as positive developments because they believe that we are increasingly experiencing nonhierarchical modes of government whereby local authorities merely facilitate cooperation among communities or organizations and businesses, all for the good of the city. These new arrangements are perceived as making "the welfare state more flexible through less rigid bureaucratic forms" and enlarging "the sphere of local political action."[19] Devolution, or the sharing of responsibilities with community organizations, is believed to foster greater democracy by pulling more and more actors into governance. These political developments are glowingly described as "replacing the overbearing, hierarchical state with a more pluralistic, and, in some ways more egalitarian version."[20] Rather than a top-down approach, devolution is idealized as building horizontal government, where people share power with state officials. However, in the face of such optimism, David Harvey soberly notes:

> [M]uch of the vaunted 'public-private partnership' of today amounts to a subsidy for affluent consumers, corporations and powerful command functions to stay in town at the expense of local collective consumption for the working class and the impoverished. Second, urban governments have been forced into innovation and investment to make their cities more attractive as consumer and cultural centers. . . . Inter-urban competition has thus generated leap-frogging urban innovations in life-styles, cultural forms, products and even political and consumer based innovation, all of which has actively promoted the transition to flexible accumulation.[21]

Moreover, the third sector, that is nonprofit organizations, is increasingly being weighed down through the restructuring of urban governance. Urban governments throughout the 1980s have been successively restructured through the privatization of city functions; the dismantling of institutions through outright elimination of programs; or through devolution, wherein government operates through establishing hybrid programs in "social, environmental and urban renewal policy domains . . . while burdening non-profit (third sector) organization with the delivery and implementation of urban repair or social service functions."[22] Church groups, ethnic associations such as the ones described by Park and Miller and by Breckenridge in early-twentieth-century Chicago, and other social movement organizations have always provided services to women, immigrants, youth, and the unemployed; but city governments since the early 1980s have begun screening these organizations and entering into partnerships with them to deal with long-term unemployment and marginalization of entire sections of their urban polities. Social welfarist functions, previously met by state institutions, are increasingly delegated to the private sector, and more and more to the third sector. George W. Bush's present policy of encouraging church and other faith-based organizations to meet the citizenry's needs is only a speeded-up continuation of the processes set in motion earlier.[23] Notions of community, familial love for each other, and other such forms of gemeinschaft are deployed to make the argument that these organizations are far better equipped to deal with human needs than cold, impersonal state bureaucracies. I will return to these matters of new governance in the concluding sections because they help us recast Apna Ghar and the Indo-American Center.

The Cultural Turn in Politics

Given the rise of multiculturalism alongside the restructuring of governance in contemporary politics, we see a bizarre contradiction in the evolution of citizenship rights vis-à-vis the state; we discern that social citizenship is very curiously expanding and shrinking simultaneously. At one level, social rights are expanding through a multicultural push for recognizing difference. Multiculturalism ostensibly allows for difference because communities of color have a space to participate in the public sphere, but at the same time, social welfare is being systematically dismantled with the growth of post-Fordist modes of production, accumulation, and governance. T. H. Marshall had idealistically held that class disparities created in capitalism would dissipate through the gradual increase of social rights, whereby a welfarist state would provide education and universal health care to all citizens. Instead, we see the opposite in current economic/political climates. What do we make of this simultaneous extension and contraction of social rights, other than noting that rights are increasingly coming to mean regard for culture with little regard for the hard realities of poverty?

American politics has taken a cultural turn. It is in this cultural political context that I raise questions regarding the cultures of American citizenship, institutionalization of our ethnic organizations, and contemporary race politics through my ethnographies of Apna Ghar and the Indo American Center. The bulk of the book deals with ethnographic details, after which I return to matters of reconfigured citizenship in the concluding section of the book. While my work may provoke the ire of some, I want to note that I launch into my descriptions of the two organizations as an insider who worked within the folds of these groups. I am an essential part of the very communities that I describe. In no way am I saying that we should do away with these organizations, but I am solely asking that we contextualize our immigrant race politics within the cultural turn we see in the larger sphere of American politics. Given the retreat of the state from welfare, the growth of multiculturalism in formal and everyday politics, as well as the institutionalization of social movements, can we still look at our activism or activist organizations as stances of resistance? Or to ask ourselves the far more alarming question—is our resistance itself the basis for our assimilation?

These are important queries for us whether we are academics, activists, or average Janes living out our average American lives. It is perhaps no startling revelation to various activists that we cannot nostalgically relive our experiences of race politics in the 1960s. The very kinds of things that were radical back then have been incorporated into mainstream politics through affirmative recognition in acknowledging cultural difference and affirmative redistribution through funding underrepresented community organizations. These developments do not mean that the racialized polity in the United States has dissolved, or even better, has been radically democratized. All it means is that the political fields in which we operate today are fundamentally metamorphosed, and we need more effective ways for organizing our immigrant race politics.

Ascribing and Asserting Race

A central part of our immigrant race politics is about how we define ourselves and our communities. Race/ethnic naming has two aspects—one is ascriptive, that is, how we are named. And the second aspect is assertive, that is, the manners by which we define ourselves through our words, actions, and coalitions. In this book I use *South Asian American* as an ascriptive term to indicate a larger racial grouping of persons from Bangladesh, India, Nepal, Pakistan, and Sri Lanka. Afghanis were included in this category, but their inclusion has become more disputed after September 11, 2001, with their being classified as "Arab." There is, no doubt, animosity between Indian Americans and Pakistani Americans, which is a reflection of South Asian regional tensions. However, regardless of politics between India and Pakistan, for example, immigrants from South Asia are racialized in similar ways upon their arrival into the United States. Various progressive South Asian American organizations, such as Trikone or New York Taxi Workers' Alliance, intentionally structure themselves as South Asian American organizations to overcome regional conflicts on the subcontinent and build a larger coalitional racial identity here in the United States. And various domestic violence organizations in the United States such as Saheli or Sakhi were begun for South Asian American women at large and not only for Bangladeshi or Nepali Americans, for example.

Nevertheless, it has been pointed out that even if *South Asian Americans* is meant to include all persons from South Asia, Indian Americans' experiences are used as proxy for all other South Asian Americans. Hence, in this book I use *South Asian American* when I speak of Apna Ghar because the shelter fashions itself as a pan-South Asian American organization and *Indian Americans* or *Indian immigrants* when I mean to indicate persons from only India. The Indo American Center is composed of all Indian Americans; hence, when I speak of events that transpire there, I can only write of Indian immigrants.

Like the term *South Asian American*, the idea of community is contested. In line with the framework I have outlined so far, I do not define "the South Asian American community," for community politics are the assertive aspect of race whereby definitions only happen through the process of doing. Community—who is included and who is written out—is delineated only through our social engagements. Therefore, I do not take "the South Asian American community" to be natural or a pre-given, but instead, I examine the ways by which communities emerge in the spaces of Apna Ghar and the Indo American Center. I look at contestations over definitions of community and what these contestations can inform us about how these new non-White immigrants want to be perceived by the world around them and how they wish to articulate with the American nation-state.

Apna Ghar and the Indo-American Center

Both Apna Ghar and the Indo American Center are located in Chicago and were begun in 1989. Apna Ghar, the shelter, is a space where private familial discord and dysfunctionality is aired. The shelter attempts to address how one leaves an abusive spouse and manages as a single parent and as an immigrant. On the other hand, the Indo American Center solely focuses on the adjustments immigrants need to make to fit into public American life. They teach new immigrants the external accoutrements—through English lessons, helping children with homework, teaching adult computer classes—that make one an American citizen.

During my stint at Apna Ghar, two Pakistani American women volunteered there, and some of the shelter's residents were of Pakistani origins, but most workers were first- or second-generation Indian Americans. The Indo American Center had only first- and second-generation Indian Americans. Both the shelter and the Center are those rare spaces where mostly Indian immigrants of different class backgrounds, different regional origins, varied religious backgrounds, first and second generations congregate. In my descriptions of the Center and the shelter, the reader will recognize that these spaces hold the potential for interclass dialogue among South Asian Americans. However, this potential invariably evaporates into thin air, and the relationships established in both sites, but especially at the shelter, are almost always of service provider and client. In this dialogue, working-class immigrants constantly contest the normative disciplines imposed on them, indicating the tensions that deeply mark this community-building process. In both places, the social work rhetoric, where the middle class attempts to "rehabilitate" the working class, reveals how immigrants try work out ways in which to belong to an imagined national community. Through examining these efforts, I illuminate the logic by which they understand the cultures of citizenship in the late-twentieth-century United States.

South Asian American Domestic Violence Services

At present there are easily more than twenty domestic violence service organizations around the United States for South Asian women.[24] These organizations attest to political activism among South Asian feminists, but they also alert us to the high levels of domestic violence prevalent among South Asian immigrant families. The emergence of these spaces that potentially provide alternative gender paradigms are crucial developments in Asian American communities. Yet, a large number of the Indian immigrants view domestic-violence-related organizations with suspicion. Activists such as Shamita Das Dasgupta, Purvi Shah, Annanya Bhattarcharjee, and Sujata Warrier note that any organization that threatens an idealized notion of the Indian American community, but especially those that provide alternative gender/sexuality paradigms, are treated with suspicion by many community leaders.[25] Domestic violence organizations are perceived to be "home-breakers" that intervene in matters that should not be made public but should be left alone within the private walls of the home.[26] These authors write that many Indian Americans believe shelters encourage women to leave homes instead of advising them to be good wives and stay on in marriages and make them work. Shelters are alleged to be detrimental to family togetherness and consequently, community solidarity. Shelters, therefore, are made out to be destroyers of "Indian culture."[27]

There is yet another perspective among Indian immigrants regarding domestic violence organizations. Some immigrants believe that immigration destroys "good" family values, resulting in violence. Becoming "ethnic" once again is seen as the best antidote to abusive family structures that arise from adopting western values, and ethnic shelters are seen as restoring desired family values. Instead of viewing shelters as cultural destroyers, some Indian Americans view these spaces as repositories of ideal cultural values where battered women can be restored to ethnic wholesomeness once again. For example, Caitrin Lynch says the shelter Apna Ghar is well accepted by Indian Americans in the larger Chicago area. Community leaders do not protest the shelter's presence, she says, but they are suspicious of the radical messages that women's groups might pass on to abuse survivors, along with services.[28] In her view, places such as Apna Ghar are celebrated as bastions of Indian culture that restore family values into dysfunctional immigrant women's lives.

In my initial work at Apna Ghar, I saw that the shelter was well accepted by Indian Americans in Chicago. The shelter was allowed to run an information booth during the celebrations for India's independence in Grant Park, Chicago. The Club of Indian Women had given them a gift of $7,500. Apna Ghar had, I observed, successfully negotiated acceptance within the larger Indian American community. At Apna Ghar, I came across a third perspective regarding domestic violence. Many workers at the shelter did not see domestic violence as solely an Indian or American phenomenon but believed that violence was rampant in families with "poor" cultural values and low levels of education.[29] Interestingly, poor cultural values are purportedly not seen in Hindu families but only in Muslim and Pakistani immigrant families. Arati, a caseworker at Apna Ghar, explained "Abuse depends on the class of society they come from. If they are from upper classes abuse is emotional. If they are working class, there is physical abuse too. Pressure builds up for these uneducated, lower class people. They start drinking and abuse begins. It depends on culture and training. Pakistani families have more abuse. We get more women from Pakistan." Yet, upon enumerating Pakistani and Indian shelter residents, Arati and I counted more Indians than Pakistanis. Arati was convinced we had missed counting all Pakistani women—"there surely cannot be more abuse among Indians!" she exclaimed. She then justified that Indian women suffered only emotional abuse but not physical battery. I pointed out this was not accurate because Indian battered women had also spoken of physical abuse. The dichotomy drawn, then, is between working-class versus middle-class values and good Indians (code word for Hindus) versus Muslims who ostensibly ill-treated their women.

During my fieldwork period, all shelter residents were working-class women. However, this does NOT mean that abuse happens only in these families, because I have heard of numerous stories of domestic discord and violence recounted by doctors' children and engineers' family friends. It is harder to get to these stories of violence because middle-class immigrant women often do not end up in shelters as do working class women. Their class locations provide them with very different exit options from an abusive marriage.

Questions of class differences invariably raise questions on race; whenever I present my work, I am almost without fail asked if domestic violence is more common among South Asian Americans than among other Americans. In this book, I do not provide any statistics on the prevalence of domestic violence among South Asian Americans because such information is only tangential to the questions of multiculturalism and assimilation that I ask here.[30]

Apna Ghar

Apna Ghar, a Hindi word that translates to "Our Home," is a small shelter that supports a maximum of six women and their children at any given time. Indian American women living in the greater Chicago area began the shelter, and today the board of directors consists mainly of first-generation Indian and Pakistani women. The executive director of the shelter, when I worked there, was a White woman, and almost all the other paid staff were of

Pakistani or Indian origin. The one counselor who was not paid, but interned at Apna Ghar, was White as well. The shelter today predominantly serves women of Asian descent but is open to women of all racial backgrounds. Apna Ghar also runs a hotline for domestic violence, a child visitation center, provides legal advice for women requiring orders of protection, and helps women initiate divorce proceedings.

Apna Ghar was an interesting location because it was a place where the public-private divide implodes. Board members and workers view Apna Ghar as a "home outside a home" for abuse survivors. Yet this home survives only because of public funding. The state intervenes actively on the behalf of battered women. Though the shelter is a public space in the sense of not being bound within the confines of the nuclear family, it is a uniquely female-centered space where men are not allowed. "Outsiders" are not told the location of the shelter.

In addition, I wondered how class issues work into immigrants' understandings of race. This question especially intrigued me because even as I was beginning fieldwork, a controversy had erupted in Sakhi, a domestic violence organization in New York City. Sakhi had refused to serve domestic workers, that is, middle-aged women who have been brought in from India to work as maids for upper-middle-class families. These domestic workers earned less that $400 per month and often lived in exploitative and abusive situations in middle-class Indian American homes. In the late 1990s, Sakhi's board of directors unilaterally dissolved its Domestic Workers' Committee (DWC) and the Steering Committee and dismissed Nahar Alam, the DWC Coordinator. Sakhi justified its actions by saying it was not abandoning its fight for the rights of exploited workers, it was merely going through "important programmatic changes to enhance their efficacy."[31] The DWC went on to form Workers' Awaz, or Workers' Voice. Would I see similar class ambiguities in Apna Ghar?

Indo American Center

Indian Americans in the larger Chicago area established the Indo American Center to serve the growing needs for legal aid with immigration procedures. Today the Center runs a legal clinic, provides free medical services once a week, immigration advice, classes for citizenship training, English as a Second Language (ESL) classes, computer classes for adults and children, and child tutoring. The Center has two full-time paid staff and two part-time employees. Most of the services provided are through volunteers, almost all of whom are professional Indian Americans. For example, the Network of Indian Professionals (NetIP) has a cadre of dedicated volunteers who arrive at the Center once a week.

As volunteer coordinator at the Center, I was in contact with both the middle-class volunteers and the "clients" who were mostly new working class immigrants from India. The Indo American Center was a crucial research site because it held citizenship classes for Indian immigrants and a couple of Pakistani immigrants. Other than teaching potential immigrants who is the American president, what is the national anthem, and how many stars are there on the flag, command over the English language was seen as an important part of becoming American. As one of the volunteers said, "we want them to learn English not just to pass the citizenship test, but they should be able to read notices, ask for directions at the bus stop, and interact with people outside the community." The Indo American Center was a space, I thought, which would starkly reveal how we learn to become American in the public sphere. How does the middle-class train the working class to become citizens? What practices are crucial to becoming American in the perceptions of the middle class?

Apna Ghar and the Indo American Center as Free Spaces

Apna Ghar—ostensibly sensitive to South Asian women's unique cultural needs—aims to function as a place where women who experience abuse can recover a sense of an ethnic, gendered self once again. Battered South Asian immigrant women arrive here, hoping to find a safe space where they can retain a sense of "ethnicness" as they find their feet in an American world. The Indo American Center, on the other hand, helps new immigrants adjust to the public world in the United States.

While restructured urban governments no doubt sees benefits in working with these ethnic civic organizations, Indian immigrants too perceive Apna Ghar and the Indo American Center as arenas in which they can establish a uniquely ethnic presence. Nonprofits such as Apna Ghar and Indo American Center have the potential to intervene, creating a niche for immigrants where they are able to make their non-White presence felt in the urban landscape, claiming a piece of public space for their own. Apna Ghar and the Indo American Center have the potential to be free spaces where Indian immigrants can exercise autonomy in expressing a non-White racial identity.[32] Free spaces are public arenas that exist between private spaces and large-scale institutions. The appeal of the term *free space* in social movements literature lies in the fact that it offers a conceptual as well as physical space in which subalterns are able to resist dominant paradigms—racial stereotypes, typecasting and so forth—in remaking themselves. Apna Ghar and the Indo American Center are perceived to be two such safe havens, ethnic public spaces, in which Indian Americans come together to identify the issues their communities face, to come up with collective solutions autonomously, beyond external influences. Indian immigrants perceive that their organizations are not controlled by dominant groups, are voluntarily participated in, and generate the cultural challenge that precedes or accompanies political mobilization.[33]

Yet, contrary to what the volunteers and social workers at Apna Ghar and the Indo American Center believe, my ethnographies reveal that they do not provide alternative paradigms or ways of thinking about race to their constituents in remaking themselves. Through ethnographies, I demonstrate why these two organizations are not removed from prevailing gender/race ideologies and do not necessarily provide the cultural challenge that precedes political mobilization.

Given the existence of nonprofits such as Apna Ghar and the Indo American Center where the expressions of non-White ethnicity are celebrated, even abetted by the state (through funding), can we say that today we are entering a new mode of race relations, where the incorporation of immigrants into the body politic is *not* assimilation but instead there is tolerance for difference, even a revelry in the racial diversity of the nation's citizenry? Many non-Whites might answer this question in the negative. For example, many South Asian Americans say they conform to whiteness in public, and in the privacy of their homes, they revert to their "ethnic" selves.

White in Public, Ethnic at Home

Though multiculturalism allows for difference to enter into the public sphere, many South Asian Americans speak of how they are unable to bring their ethnicity—a part of what they think is their true self—into the public sphere. Sayantini Dasgupta, a second-generation Indian American, describes her childhood in words that could be said by any of the second-generation South Asian Americans with whom I have spoken in this decade I have been in the United States. She says:

> I was brought up in a predominantly White, Germanic suburb in the heart of the Midwest, the only daughter of two Indian immigrants who came to this country for graduate studies. . . . I was always different, particularly due to my ethnicity. There were times I longed to be "just like everyone else." It seemed that social acceptance hinged upon having blond hair, blue eyes, and a name like Julie, Kimmy, or Nancy. . . . I experienced every day, the feelings of exclusion and foreign-ness, the pressure to assimilate to a White cultural norm.[34]

In yet another essay titled "Passing," another second-generation Indian American woman, Amita Vasudeva, describes her childhood: "I guess I've always pretty much passed as White. Not White in color; White in culture-outwardly only. Why was it so easy to pass? Because I made an effort not to deny or refute any assumptions people had about me. I never really talked about my heritage . . . there is always that ever-present fear in children of not being accepted, or even harsher, of being cast out, ignored, ridiculed."[35]

Amita Vasudeva and Sayantini Dasgupta, like many Indian immigrants I have spoken with, are crucially aware of the racial order in which they find themselves, and in fear of being cast out, they assimilate to a White cultural norm. In quiet—though unnamed—recognition of the whiteness of American society, Vasudeva and Dasgupta became "White." People of all other racial categories disappear in their dialogues with Americana, because for them, all that is around in them in their neighborhood, school, on television is "the white bland mass of non-color."[36] As she grew older, Vasudeva says she learned to accept her difference and preferred to be "recognized as distinct from the white bland mass of non-color and homogeneity" around her.

The constant reminders of their outsider status pressures these non-White immigrants to assimilate into a dominant cultural norm and even try pass as European "ethnics" in public spaces. Yet simultaneously, at home, especially young women are constantly reminded of their cultural heritage by their parents. Dasgupta says she became familiar with

> the corrosive effects of being Indian on the weekends and American during the school week, the cultural juggling act that each second generation Indian American must learn to perform. . . . The effect was exacerbated for Indian American young women, who felt the pressure of a White beauty standard at school and the pressure of being a dutiful, very "Indian" daughter at home. It depresses me still to remember how many of my lighter-skinned Indian sisters tried to pass themselves off as Italian or Greek during school, while dancing in *bharata natyam* recitals and going to *pujas* on the weekends.[37]

R. Radhakrishnan writes that the second-generation Indian Americans he spoke with "felt they could not escape being *marked* as different by virtue of their skin color, their family background, and other ethnic and unassimilated traits. Many of them recited the reality of a double life, the ethnic private life and the "American" public life, with very little mediation between the two."[38] The excerpts I use above indicate ways by which second-generation Indian Americans, in various parts of the United States, cope with being persons of color. These are sentiments expressed by immigrants other than Indians as well, wherein they recognize that in spite of multiculturalism there are only certain "ethnic" things they can do in public, and most others they need to reserve for the privacy of their homes.

Similar sentiments have been expressed countless times by the second-generation South Asian American students who take my classes here in Texas. In their eyes, the east is east, the west is west, and they are wedged in between.

In an effort to make sense of their lives and to reconcile their peculiar racially bifurcated dilemma, they speak of trying to make the best of both worlds; that is, take what their "ethnic culture" gives them to enrich the opportunities their "American culture" provides. They then go on to describe to me in detail what Indian-ness means to them—family, language, food, Bollywood movies, relatives who visit from India. Contrarily, they are unable to pinpoint what whiteness means to them. They say they need to conform to whiteness in public yet are unable to establish what this conformity actually entails. What exactly do the Julies, Kimmys, and Nancys in Dasgupta's world do that makes them White women? And what do our Amitas and Sayantinis do to become more like them?

Two questions rise in me when I read or hear about these feelings of bifurcated existence—first, why do these non-White second-generation individuals feel conscious about their "difference" in these multicultural days when we honestly believe that diversity is celebrated? And second, why does silence surround whiteness? To answer the first question, that is, their anxieties about their difference, we need to examine the contents of multiculturalism itself.

Multiculturalism allows for diversity, but the kinds of difference that we are can deploy is tightly contained within the parameters of whiteness. We may have some authorial control over how we present our difference, but the choices we make are constrained by the cultures of American citizenship. What these constraints are and what is allowable difference will emerge over the course of this book through the ethnographies of the shelter and the Center.

And to get to the second question—why does silence sit as a shroud around whiteness? We could speculate on two reasons; the first one is that Indian immigrants are outsiders to a normative White culture and therefore cannot name its practices. On the other hand, they are insiders to Indian culture and can, therefore, describe the smallest details regarding their own ethnic practices. Or conversely—which I think is more the case—Indian Americans normalize whiteness to such a degree that it is hard to name the practices associated with it. As the normative standard, whiteness is self-evident and does not warrant any explanation. Conversely, all other cultures are deviations from this norm, and their differences have to be explained. Indian Americans accept whiteness as the normative standard against which they measure the degrees of their racialized differences. Hence, they are unable to say what whiteness means to them; on the other hand, Indian-ness is so deviant from the cultural norm that its differences need explaining. And having explained what Indian-ness means repeatedly, they have necessarily developed a descriptive vocabulary around their difference.

I thought at Apna Ghar and the Indo American Center I would learn about what non-White immigrants thought of as their ethnic and White practices.

The shelter believed it provided a safe haven within which women could recover within a culturally familiar space their ethnic selves once again. Here, I thought, I would witness social practices that entailed ethnicity. The Indo American Center, on the other hand, explicitly stated that it wanted to help newcomers assimilate, and here I thought I would see what it meant to become White and conform to a public norm. Yet, my initial presumptions were all wrong. At Apna Ghar shelter, staff attempted to train women out of their ethnicity. Ethnicity was seen as the root cause of women's problems because it exaggerated feminine passivity and masculine aggression. Conversely, the Indo American Center, so intent on assimilation, was curiously caught up with defining authentic ethnic culture. As new non-White members, they could never speak as generic, plain Americans. But in these multicultural times, their ethnicity provided them a platform from which they could launch themselves as participatory members in their new home nation.

Through providing ethnographic details from the shelter and the Center I argue that Indian immigrants—in spite of what they say—are not really White in public and not really ethnic at home. In this story, what emerges is that these non-White immigrants routinized "American" practices into banal everyday acts, and "Indian-ness" was a ritualized display of well thought-out, ostensibly unique ethnic cultural practices.

Outline of the Book

Jean Bacon (1996) documented 107 Indian American organizations between the years 1990 and 1991. Some of these associations are defunct now and no doubt new ones have emerged. For this book, however, I choose to focus on service-oriented organizations to explore the twin issues of assimilation and community formation.[39] Just because South Asian Americans come from a particular geographical region does not automatically constitute them into a natural community. Making community is hard, political, and often gendered work—it takes our imaginations, our longings of how we want to be perceived in the United States, the reworking of collective and personal histories in particular directions, casting out individuals and drawing in members, and reinventing traditions to stand as authentic ethnicity. Community is always in the making, materializing in our imaginative powers and our engagements with each other. How then does making "ethnic community" enmesh with nation-building efforts?

Following this introduction are the three ethnographic chapters on Apna Ghar and the Indo American Center. In chapter 2, I describe the kinds of programs the shelter instituted for its "clients" and how the shelter staff went about teaching life skills to the residents. Apna Ghar purports to be a community space for battered immigrant women who need a safe place where they can retain a sense of "ethnic-ness" as they recover from abuse. Instead, women are counseled to move on and forge themselves anew into intrepid individuals in a brave new free world. Apna Ghar embraces an early-twentieth-century American high modernist tradition where individuals are urged to forget communal belonging, group particularities, and embeddedness in racially specific networks. Much of Apna Ghar's efforts went into Americanizing its residents, in the sense of initiating them into a consumer, market-driven mass culture where success and upward mobility is mythically attributed to individual efforts alone. In the end analysis, the only thing ethnic about Apna Ghar shelter is that most of the clientele, and almost all the workers, are of South Asian origins. Though workers may understand the cultural specificities of abuse, the model for survival is not necessarily culturally specific.

Chapter 3 is a description of the effects of the institutionalization of the shelter on its workers who engaged in emotion labor. Through participant observation and informal interviews, I draw out why South Asian American women sought involvement at Apna Ghar. Participation in movements such as domestic violence intervention is an expansion of their traditional caregiver roles, but South Asian American women's participation also emerges from their dissatisfaction with the gender paradigms prevalent in their racialized communities. They take part in these organizations to change these genderings. Yet, the institutionalization and concomitant commercialization of care work depoliticizes domestic violence intervention, leading to feelings of alienation among those involved at Apna Ghar. The workers' anomie arises because they are unable to translate their everyday caring into "radical caring" they deem central to changing gender paradigms in their communities. Thus, their reasons for getting involved at the shelter are rendered redundant. Apna Ghar, begun with the best of intentions, is often unable to meet its concomitant goals of service to abuse survivors and politicization of workers.

A few words on my two Apna Ghar chapters—while I am critical of the kinds of social work pursued at the shelter, I still think such spaces are crucial developments on immigrant America's landscape. Shelters might impose draconian measures on women's lives all in the name of recovery, but they are also places to which women can escape so that their lives can be free of physical violence. Some women are able to use shelters in getting their lives together so that they may move out of emotionally devastating and physically dangerous homes. Moreover, shelters such as Apna Ghar still retain their potential for politicizing young women, because here they learn that violence against women emerges through an interpellation of larger social structures. These young women can learn that if we want to effective intervention strategies against violence, we need to tackle issues such racialized economies, legal questions regarding citizenship, and patriarchies that operate in everyday, covert ways.

I am not opposed to the existence of Apna Ghar, but I am only casting a critical eye at the social work that goes on there for the "good" of the battered individual. Shelters are necessary, but I ask that we think carefully about the ways in which we go about intervening in women's lives, as they are disciplined into standards of perceived normalcy. The institutionalization of advocacy to end violence, the pressures to raise money from both public and private sources to run the shelter, relationships with other social service organizations that compel the shelter to institute certain rules just so that they can access these other services and so forth all affect the ways in which we do shelter work today. My intentions are to point out how, even a site we understand to be a free space, is deeply marked by race and class.

Chapter 4 is about the Indo American Center. The Center's openly stated mission is to facilitate the assimilation of new immigrants, yet my fieldwork reveals that assimilation was fundamentally premised on proving themselves as good non-White immigrants who would be moral Americans if only given the chance. At the Center, they constantly tried to establish that their purportedly superior cultural proclivities made them laudable Americans. The Center held neighborhood tours for tourists visiting Chicago, workshops for teachers on how to include India into their curricula, and facilitated school trips for students from Chicago schools into the South Asian American business district. Hence, I witnessed they focused their energies on defining who is an Indian, and concomitantly, there were endless debates regarding authentic ethnicity.

In Chapter 5, "The Politics of Cultural Authenticity," I explore why non-White immigrants feel the compulsion to become "authentic ethnics." The search for authenticity arises for South Asian immigrants because they want to be full participants in American civil society. As non-Whites, they are never accepted solely as plain American subjects but are compelled to be authentically ethnic. They repeatedly invoke details of their "superior" culture as evidence of their personal worthiness. Authentic ethnic culture allows them too to become bona fide Americans during these multicultural times.

Chapter 6, "Becoming American: The Racialized Content of American Citizenship," examines early-twentieth-century Americanization programs and the rise of White ethnicity along with newer theories on assimilation posited since the 1980s to describe non-White immigrants' experiences in the United States. I lay out the historical development of what Lowe terms the "terrain of national culture," fundamentally drawn along racial lines, in which South Asian immigrants develop a national subjectivity.

In the concluding chapter, I locate Apna Ghar and the Indo American Center within the larger sociopolitical changes that we see in the United States that I've outlined in the preceding pages. Given that the nature of social citizenship is altering in front of our very eyes, that is, we are witnessing the rise of multicultural recognition with the simultaneous shrinking of deep redistribution, what can these ethnographies reveal about present-day immigrant race politics? I show that multicultural politics in no way contribute to the balkanization of the United States but, instead, bolster governance of immigrants and discipline them into the cultures of American citizenship. In these multicultural times, our very resistance is the basis for our assimilation. Immigrants may think of their organizations as safe havens where they have sole discretion on how to deploy their difference in accordance with their sending nation's "traditions and customs," yet these alleged safe havens are sites for Americanization in the late twentieth century.

Notes on Fieldwork

My motivations for working at the shelter and the Center were not out of cool analytical interest. Instead, I sought these organizations out because I wanted to be a part of them, as I considered them an irrevocable part of me. Under these circumstances fieldwork and the subsequent writing process became agonizing. In the first instance, my co-workers never considered me a researcher. I never hid the fact that even though I was a worker in both places—caseworker in Apna Ghar, and volunteer coordinator at the Center—I was also a researcher. Yet in spite of my repeated attempts at establishing my researcher status, no one took me seriously. How could they, when I got involved in almost every controversy? I felt more real to them as a co-worker than as an academic. Their beliefs about me were only bolstered by the fact that I myself wondered whether my research would come to fruition.

I was constantly immobilized by questions of what right I had to write about South Asian Americans. Upon whose invitation had I walked into the shelter and the Center and begun researching these organizations? How did I need the battered women, working-class immigrants at the Center, and middle-class South Asian Americans to sustain my writing process? My political passions and belonging wedged between the haves and the have-nots, I often ask myself who appointed me the Muse? My fieldwork aroused a sense of powerlessness in me; I wanted so badly to transform what I saw but felt it all way beyond my abilities. Then I would stop short and ask myself why I thought I had all the answers, and why I assumed those around me operated under flawed presumptions. Moreover, I was a transient worker at Apna Ghar and the Indo American Center, and after my year there, I would move on. Launching critiques at the shelter and the Center, I have come to realize, is far easier than staying on and working concertedly toward social transformations in these particular settings.

The more embroiled I became in the shelter and Center politics, the more I tried to disconnect from them. For instance, I write in a subsequent chapter how I try to hide behind my camera during the Apna Ghar fundraiser. Or, I deliberately dressed in jeans and hiking boots at Indo American Center events when other women arrived in Indian clothes. I tried to set myself apart, even when there is no denying I was written into the communities that I theorize about. I frequently got into heated discussions with my supervisors and co-workers, which in Apna Ghar, resulted in public reprimands and disciplinary action that cut my work hours. Alone at home after work, or sitting with my dog at Pratt Beach on northern Chicago's Lake Michigan shores, I questioned if it was my place to become so deeply involved. After all, I was a researcher. Was it my responsibility to raise these questions while I did fieldwork? My decreased hours meant one shift less at the shelter and, therefore, lesser fieldwork. Moreover, reduced hours translated to $84 less per week, which had significant repercussions on my ability to cover rent, buy groceries, and pay utility bills. As an international student with no funding—a resident alien with no paperwork for laboring outside my academic discipline—I had no option other than working at the shelter and the Center for $7 per hour. So I stuck on, motivated by the dictates of having to make a livelihood, the compulsion to complete my research, and mostly, my very real desire to reconnect with other South Asian Americans and engage in political questions regarding who we are and what our actions mean in the racial cartographies of this nation to which we had arrived.

Through reproducing chunks of my field notes in the three ethnographic chapters that follow, I reveal the degree to which I was hopelessly entangled in the various debates around me. For example, at the Indo American Center I got drawn into protracted discussions on Hinduism and "Indian culture." Even as I cast a critical eye on ethnic authenticity, the reader will discern my repeated attempts to establish my own authenticity so that I too would be validated in my speech. And in the Apna Ghar chapters, I recount details of how my supervisors reprimanded me because my transgressions sometimes complicated work for all involved. I frequently appear in my own field notes along with others, and with them, I am complicit in the efforts at making community as we clashed on numerous occasions on how to interpret our culture(s), our politics, and our locations in the racial hierarchies extant today.

Much of my field note excerpts are underanalyzed. For instance, throughout the Apna Ghar parenting classes the shelter residents giggle or express boredom in the proceedings. In various ways, they refuse to accept the discipline imposed on them. I describe their actions, but I do not analyze these moments of resistance. In addition, I materialize very intrusively either as shelter worker or as representative of "the Indian American community" at the Center in various field note vignettes. It will become apparent that I am part of the processes that I write about, and there is no real separation. My own complicity in the shelter and the Center, and my own search for political authenticity, is palpable in these field notes. My actions too are grist for the sociological mill, but these instances remain unanalyzed.

I reproduce large chunks of my field notes not just to indicate the untidy ways by which ethnographies get produced, but more crucially, I want you as the reader to analyze the various actors'—including mine—reactions and make this reading your own. I ask you to reflect on what draws you to read these words- and why you may have the reactions that you do. I call upon you to be reflexive about why you may embark on particular engagements or disengagements (as the case may be) with this body of work. In other words, think about how you make a sense of your own place in the events I describe and analyze. I ask you as the reader to see how you too are caught up in the pursuits for communal kinship, making viable communities, and your own quest for authenticity. This book emerges out of my emotional and political investments in Apna Ghar, the Indo American Center, and in Asian American communities in general, and part of my engagement is to invite you as the reader to see how you too are implicated in the political projects of making communities.

Two

Finding Our Home in This World

Abuse Survivors in Apna Ghar

Introduction

The Fund-raiser, late 1990s.

Yesterday was the day of the Apna Ghar fund-raiser and also the day I went back to volunteer at the shelter after a hiatus of almost a month. I'm emotionally rested, and ready to volunteer once again, I told myself. In addition, I thought the fundraiser would be a pleasant event where I could spend a few sunny hours chatting with my co-workers before I returned to my twelve-hour shift at the shelter. At 11:00 A.M., Nellie, the shelter supervisor, and her husband, Abraham—both originally from the western Indian state of Goa—came to pick me up from home. Armed with my camera, I set off to the Apna Ghar fundraiser, the Chicago South Asian American premier charity event of the year. Apna Ghar. Our home. Like all homes, Apna Ghar too is wrought by contradictions; the public performance of fairy-tale model minority existence at the fundraiser, and the private hell of alcoholism, abuse, and bruised souls residing in the shelter, and sometimes, employed as shelter workers.

We arrived at the Cuneo Museum grounds at noon among Chicago suburbanites, strikingly beautiful in their saris, salwars, and Saabs. Middle-class professional South Asian immigrants had paid $65 per ticket for a nicely catered meal with champagne. After speeches, drinks, food, and more drinks, the entertainment began on the lawns at 3:00 P.M. First arrived dancing White women dressed in rayon Victorian gowns of the brightest hues imaginable. They bowed, danced, and skipped along with White men dressed in black long-tailed coats. This was not what I had expected in a fundraiser for domestic violence. I had an overwhelming urge to leave, so I got busy, trying to adjust angle, light, and compose pictures within the eyepiece of my camera. Next on the entertainment agenda was a "horse" dance performance by little White children dressed like white horses. They had horsetails stuck on their backs that swung this way and that as they lightly stepped little baby steps. What did this have to do with domestic violence, I thought a bit desperately now, as I shot even more photographs. To give myself distance from what unfolded before me, I viewed the whole spectacle through the lens of my camera. Perhaps my little black box could hide me. The entertainment then segued into the grand finale of the dancing-prancing, white Viennese horses. Our master of ceremonies explained to us that these horses are usually born dark and turn white with time. How appropriate, I thought nastily; these horses are a perfect metaphor for the South Asian American middle class.

Yet, as hard as I tried to hide that day, I could not deny that I, too, am like the others gathered that day, undeniably South Asian American. As much as I looked at my fellow middle-class South Asians with disdain, could I be anything else but that myself? So I viewed it all through the distorting lens of my camera, not quite a willing participant, but undeniably a part of the whole scene.

The most bizarre part of the entire day was yet to come. I had a night shift of twelve hours at the shelter later that evening. After picking up Tippoo, my dog, from home, I headed toward Apna Ghar, located in the uptown area of Chicago. The house was a three-story white building with purple trim. Though pretty, the building was in disrepair. The basement had sprung a leak, and we needed approximately $6,000 to fix the plumbing. The fenced-in yard around the house was clean, though weeds that had been mowed down around the edges struggled to reemerge once again. As soon as I entered the house, I found myself in the familiar hardwood-floored foyer. The foyer had a couple of notice boards, announcing the schedules of various sessions that women residents must compulsorily attend—individual counseling, group counseling, communication classes, parenting classes, art therapy. The weekends belong to the women. Also pinned to the two notice boards are various job announcements:

> Indian family living in Winnetka looking for domestic help. Prefer older woman with no children. Competitive pay scale. If interested, call 847-000-0000.

> Another announcement reads:
> Indian family with two young children are looking for help. Prefer Muslim woman, who is good with children. Pay negotiable. Call 847-111-1111.

I entered the foyer at 5:45 P.M. and turned left to the shelter office, which was cordoned off by glass doors. A huge officious desk dominated the room, imparting an aura of impersonal authority to anyone who sat behind it. On the desk lay various files, phones, papers, pens, pencils, and paper clips. Behind the desk, on a swivel chair, sat Ruth, the shelter worker. Around her, at edges of this office, were five to six maroon upholstered chairs. When a shelter resident—called "client"—wants to speak with the shelter worker, she sits in one of these chairs. The desk provided a suitable distance between the worker and the client. When the shelter supervisor arrived in the mornings, the worker would rise from behind the desk and occupy one of the maroon "client" seats. She ceded her authority to the shelter supervisor.

I walked into Apna Ghar to relieve Ruth who'd been at work since 6:00 A.M. We worked twelve-hour shifts at least three times a week. As Ruth, a Malaysian Tamil woman in her thirties, and I exchanged pleasantries in the office, Ok, a Korean resident entered the main office. She was visibly upset as she sat on one of the maroon chairs. Her husband is a very bad man, she explained, because he's taken up with another woman after eighteen years of marriage. But what really hurt her was that her thirteen-year old son was thrown out of the house, and he now slept on a mattress on the floor at the family store. He had nowhere to go. She asked us how could she stand aside and watch this happen to her son?

Later that evening I met Nancy, a Thai woman, for the first time. In her early forties, Nancy claimed she's met Mahatma Gandhi as a child (Gandhi's been dead for over fifty years). This Thai woman from the Midwest had been on Prozac for two years for depression and suffered from vertigo. She had a very severe asthma attack earlier that morning and returned from the hospital at 2:00 P.M. After Ruth left for the evening, Nancy had a panic attack. I held her tightly for almost half an hour, talking to her softly, trying to calm her down. She eventually curled up on the living room floor. She did not want the couch because she worried she might fall out. Nancy fell asleep holding my dog, Tippoo.

I settled behind that officious desk with a novel. One more person had to return to the shelter, and it was already past the curfew hour of 9:00 P.M. Outside the doors, I heard drunken Chicago denizens wander up and down the streets. Angry screams, some laughter, and at other times slurred speech soaked with alcohol. Interspersing the sounds of traffic swishing back and forth were police car sirens wailing into the night, in an endless surveillance of those who populated street corners and alleyways. Suddenly, the doorbell rang. I jumped in my skin and my Tippoo began to growl softly. I peered outside the window and saw a frail, light-haired White woman standing hunched at the door, rocking on her feet, and hands jammed in her jacket pockets to keep the cold away. I turned off the alarm system and opened the door. The woman staggered in. She wore blue jeans and a denim jacket over a white tee shirt. Fumes of alcohol enveloped her in an overpowering embrace. I had just met Sherri. My watch said 12:45 A.M., way past the 9:00 P.M. curfew deadline. She shoved an unlit cigarette in her mouth, and it dangled dangerously, almost falling off her face. I told her she couldn't smoke inside the house. There was silence. I repeated myself, and suddenly she turned at me, screaming, "You fucking don't understand!" I kept quiet. She stumbled into a chair. There was an uneasy silence. I asked her if she was all right, and she screamed back, "You fucking don't understand. I was robbed." I reached out to hold her hand and she burst into tears, saying she was scared. Two Black women jumped her just a block away, threatening to beat her. They let her go minus $10 and her pack of cigarettes. I led Sherri outside to the back porch so that we could talk without waking Nancy who slept on the living room floor.

Sherri cried outside. She didn't want to speak of the robbery attempt but showed me the bruises her ex-boyfriend had given her. Black eye, cut eyebrow, black-and-blue thighs. The worst thing he'd done, according to her, was that he'd taken a pair of scissors and cut up her blonde hair. Her hair was so ugly that she had to get it all buzzed down. Her hair grew out, she said as she reached out and touched my black hair gently, but it grew out dark. She hated it dark, so now colored it a lighter shade of brown.

Her left ear was infected. "You won't believe the stuff that comes out of it," she kept repeating, as she dug her long-nailed fingers into her ears. "I lose my balance, and people think I'm drunk. I'm not a dirty person, you understand, but my body is falling apart. It's all falling apart." This mid-thirties woman had been drinking since she was fourteen years of age. "But I'm not an alcoholic," she reasoned. "Its just that my ear leaks and I lose my balance." Finally, at 2:15 A.M., I helped her change out of her alcohol-sodden clothes. As I tucked her under the blankets, she held my arms tight and pleaded with me not to leave until she slept. She did not want to be alone because she was scared.

I begin this chapter with an excerpt from my field notes as a worker in Apna Ghar. Though none of the shelter residents I speak of in the above excerpt are South Asian, all the workers and almost all the attendees at the fundraiser are South Asian Americans. I reproduce my notes to convey to the reader the bizarre nature of shelter work in the late twentieth century—as the welfare state shrinks, organizations like Apna Ghar increasingly turn to civil society to raise funds and garner support from wealthier citizens for abuse survivors. The kinds of entertainment at the fund-raiser have nothing to do with domestic violence. I felt disjointed because I arrived from the public presentation of a wealthy and benevolent South Asian American "community," into the dysfunctional privacy of the shelter. It seemed as if the immigrant middle class needed the working-class abusers and abused to feel like they were making a difference, contributing to a cause larger than themselves, even as they bought $65 tickets, wore silk saris and chiffon dresses, sipping champagne as they watched dancing white horses. Domestic violence activism had been converted to an act of consumerism. It became an occasion to people-watch and let people watch you. Yet, in the face of a shrinking welfare state, battered women needed liberal middle-class consumerism to sustain shelters and counselors and shelter workers who sometimes cared and often did not because they were burnt out.

Background on Apna Ghar

Though the shelter was begun in 1989 to serve South Asian immigrant women, because the shelter receives state funding, it cannot reject "clients" on the basis of their racial origins or sexuality; when I began working there in the late 1990s, Apna Ghar served women of all racial origins. The board of directors and social workers, however, were primarily first and second-generation Indian and Pakistani women. The executive director was a White woman.[1] Apna Ghar ran a twenty-four-hour hotline for domestic violence. During the day, the hotline stayed in the shelter, and the caseworker fielded calls from battered women. In the evening, the hotline was forwarded to one of the volunteers. A cadre of volunteers, mostly second generation Indian/Pakistani women volunteered once a night every month to take over the hotline in case someone called with an emergency. In addition, Apna Ghar ran a child visitation center, where abusive fathers spent time with their children under staff supervision. Apna Ghar provided other services such as legal advice for women desiring orders of protection and assistance for women in initiating divorce proceedings and obtaining child support or custody. Translators of various Asian and Middle Eastern languages facilitated immigrant women's interactions with various state institutions. The shelter provided individual and group counseling and communication/assertiveness/mediation skills. It conducted workshops on building self-confidence and self-reliance, parenting classes, and twice a week art therapy classes were held so that women may "express feelings and goals in a nonthreatening, non verbal medium."[2] In addition, women and children were provided with one-on-one counseling with counseling psychology interns from academic institutions such as the University of Illinois-Chicago. These women were often White women, and their work at the shelter was part of an unpaid internship for which they received academic credit. Apna Ghar's informational brochure said that it assists women with finding housing, job training/placement, literacy, and financial aid. The brochure also claims to help battered women obtain medical attention, transportation, and child day care, but these services were largely unavailable during the time I worked there because of lack of funding.

Apna Ghar comprised two units—the main office and the shelter residence, which housed battered women. The main office was on the fifth floor of the very ornate Uptown National Bank building at Broadway and Lawrence. At the main office sat the executive director, the accountant, child visitation staff, the volunteer coordinator, and the legal consultant. The shelter supervisor spent much of her time there preparing various reports. The other Apna Ghar building, the residential unit that housed battered women, was concealed in a neighborhood close to the main office. The address of this building was kept a secret to keep at bay abusers who might be stalkers. Almost all of what I write in these next two chapters, except the various evening classes, transpires in this house. Eight to ten caseworkers—almost all Indian or Pakistani first- and second-generation women—worked in twelve-hour shifts at the house. These women, and I was one of them, were the lowest paid Apna Ghar staff. We worked just under forty hours and received no benefits. Of all the workers at Apna Ghar, the shelter residents saw us most frequently. We were "frontline" workers, dealing with battered women and engaged daily in emotion labor.

Contextualizing Apna Ghar's Domestic Violence Intervention Strategies

A perusal of the literature on domestic violence suggests two modes of addressing domestic violence; in the first mode, social service practitioners focus on the distressed *individual*, targeting her with all kinds of psychological testing and counseling interventions. Various activists and academics note that such intervention individualizes something that is essentially a larger social issue. The failure of social service agencies to "incorporate these social factors into clinical practice has contributed to the process of 'blaming the victim.'"[3] On the other hand, the second mode recognizes that domestic violence is a *social* issue and focuses on the group in which the woman is a member. This is a standard approach among social workers with a more feminist stance, and this is precisely the approach Apna Ghar took. They recognized that social, cultural, and political factors are central to an interpretation of gendered violence. They were very conscious that violence did not result because of a woman's psychological characteristics; instead, they problematized power disparities between men and women. In their reading, violence occurred because of social institutions that both overtly and implicitly endorsed values and norms regarding women, marriage, and family. Hence, Apna Ghar focused on two intervention strategies; first, they attempted to foster social change among South Asian Americans so that gender norms may be altered within communities. Second, they encouraged women to leave abusive networks and empower themselves on a personal level.

I address these two domestic violence intervention strategies in these two chapters. In the following chapter, I write about the first type of intervention, that is, how Apna Ghar attempted to foster social change among South Asian Americans through addressing gender dynamics. Central to this strategy was the politicization of women workers and volunteers. I look at why the volunteers and workers came to Apna Ghar and what happened to them over the course of their stint at the shelter. In this particular chapter, I explain the kinds of interventions into battered women's lives the shelter instituted. There were certain skills Apna Ghar deemed necessary for a woman's healing process. I explain what these skills are and how the shelter staff went about teaching these skills to battered women. Nowhere in these pages do I reproduce gory details of violence that the shelter residents narrated to me. If there are any stories of violence at all, they were repeated to me by shelter workers. Rather than reproducing descriptions of battery, I instead examine shelter workers and the ways in which they intervened into women's lives.[4] Moreover, though emotional abuse is far more pervasive in relationships, I speak only of survivors of physical violence because when I worked there, Apna Ghar had a policy of accepting only those women who were battered physically and not victims of emotional abuse.

Outlasting Violence, Emerging as Abuse Survivors

Survivors of trauma frequently remark that they are not the same people they were before being traumatized. As a survivor of the Nazi death camps observed, "One can be alive after Sobibor without having survived Sobibor." Jonathan Shay, a therapist who works with Vietnam veterans, has often heard his patients say, "I died in Vietnam." Migael Scherer expresses a loss commonly experienced by rape survivors when she writes, "I will always miss myself as I was." What are we to make of these cryptic comments? How can one miss oneself? How can one die in Vietnam or fail to survive a death camp and still live to tell one's story? How does a life-threatening event come to be experienced as self-annihilating? And what self is it who remembers having had this experience?[5]

Our sense of self is partially derived from our bodily integrity. Not only does our material body signify where our physicality begins and ends, but also the corporeal reality of our sex, skin color, hair texture, and sexual pleasures all affect our conception of our self. However, though our physicality gives us a concrete reality, we are not aware of our bodies in a self-conscious manner as we live out our everyday lives. Instead, for the most part, we take our bodies for granted. For example, we may not think, act, or perceive ourselves as women every single waking minute of the day because our gendered reality becomes a backdrop for much of our everyday lives.[6] However, when our attention is called to our being women—either through pleasurable associations, bodily functions of menstruation, or the humiliation of derogatory cat calls—the materiality of our body enters our consciousness and alerts us to how it makes us gendered beings.

When a woman is abused, her conceptualization of her body, and subsequently her self, undergoes considerable alteration. As a victim of violence, her body is called to her attention in ways that it never has been before, and her understanding of her body and self change. Her body becomes the site of her vulnerability on two accounts; in the first instance, she is victimized precisely because of her gendered/sexed body.[7] And second, her body itself is the site for violence. The pain inflicted on her makes her aware of her flesh in ways never before. For example, speaking of the time she was beaten, raped, strangled, and left for dead, Susan Brison writes that the pain her perpetrator inflicted reduced her "to flesh, to the purely physical. . . ."[8]

Her notions of self are completely erased because her abuser reduces her to a mere object. "It is as if the tormentor says with his blows: You are nothing but a body, a mere object of my will—here, I'll prove it."[9] Almost any agency she has over the situation is wiped out, and her "subjectivity is rendered useless and worthless."[10] This loss of agency and control over the situation, and consequently who a woman wants to be in relation to others, shatters her conception of her self. Though she survives physically, her self-identity is destroyed.[11] Her past self is dead.

The immediate psychological responses to trauma such as sexual assault are terror, loss of sense of control, and intense fear of annihilation. Long-term effects of trauma are hyper-vigilance of surroundings, heightened startle response, sleep disorders, depression, inability to concentrate, lack of interest in activities that once meant a great deal, and no sense of future. These symptoms, commonly termed as posttraumatic stress disorder (PTSD), occur when a person's normal responses to danger preparing her to fight back or flee the situation are rendered useless as she is traumatized by violence, and "each component of the ordinary response to danger, having lost its utility, tends to persist in an altered and exaggerated state long after the actual danger is over."[12] Immediately after the violent episode, the victim of trauma often cannot narrate the violence perpetrated on her; instead violence exists as an "experience that reoccurs, either as full sensory replay of traumatic events in dreams or flashbacks, with all things seen, heard, smelled, and felt intact, or as disconnected fragments."[13] The victim loses her narrative voice, and the helplessness that she felt under the original experience is "replayed in the apparent helplessness to end or modify the re-experience once it has begun."[14]

Her sense of agency is annihilated through physical violation. Yet, the individual's personhood does not remain destroyed forever but reasserts itself in ways that it did not exist before. This reassertion of personhood occurs within a community of sympathetic listeners. With "the help of understanding listeners, the survivor begins not only to integrate the traumatic episode into a life with a before and after, but also to gain control over the occurrence of intrusive memories."[15] Narrating the incidence of trauma helps a victim master the event, give direction to her life, and emerge as a survivor. Whereas the actual violent episode and the intensely physical memories she has of it might lay outside her control, the narration of the events are within her authority, "re-mastering of the traumatic memory involves going from being the medium of someone else's (the torturer's) speech to being the subject of one's own. . . . Saying something about a traumatic memory does something to it."[16]

To emerge as a survivor, the victim has to learn to control her emotions and her environment and reconnect with humanity. These achievements are highly dependent on the empathetic listening of a community of people. Therefore, while a person can destroy a woman's sense of self through violent objectification, her self can also re-emerge through her reconnection with people who give her back her life by listening to her testimony. A new self emerges through the caring of others; "the right sort of interactions with others can be seen as essential to autonomy."[17] Speaking from her own standpoint as a rape survivor, Brison remarks that "the self is both autonomous and socially dependent, vulnerable enough to be undone by violence and yet resilient enough to be reconstructed through the help of empathetic others."[18] A woman's capacity to survive violence depends on a community of sympathetic listeners.

Battered South Asian American Women and Survival

Brison, whom I cite extensively in the previous section, writes of her recovery from being assaulted by a stranger. How is violence different when perpetrated by someone in your family? In addition, how does one find a safe space when the home itself—a crucial space for emotional *and* racial rejuvenation for immigrants—is the territory of trauma? How do these immigrant women, non-White and often without language skills and American citizenship, reconfigure their lives to emerge as survivors from violence in their homes?

The process of immigration—the movement from a nation where a person is the norm, to a nation where she is a colored minority—radically ruptures the way she conceives of herself. As a new immigrant, she needs to reinvent her self and think of new ways to make community. Taken-for-granted life practices do not seem natural anymore but become high maintenance rituals crucial for remaining "ethnic." The family and home lose their naturalness and reveal themselves not to be a priori sites; instead, they are produced actively in the everyday practices of speaking the mother tongue, cooking and eating familiar foods, and raising children according to norms and values central to an "ethnic" imaginary.

Simultaneously, even as the family and home are actualized through everyday practices, they embody her. They are meaning-giving contexts, structuring a woman's self and giving her a sense of grounding. The family is a familiar unit in which the immigrant makes a home for herself within an alien world. The familial location gives her a sense of connection and continuity with her previous life in the "homeland." Instead of extensive kinship ties that existed before, all the immigrant woman has is her nuclear family to provide her access to larger racial networks. The home and family, therefore, become an anchor for rejuvenation of self for the new immigrant. As a new arrival in a "White" country and in an unfamiliar cultural context, she acutely feels the need of a home and family where she can be "Indian" once again.[19]

Yet, when the home, where her racial self is anchored, is precisely the place where violence is perpetrated, the immigrant woman can feel wholly violated. Violence within her home potentially destroys her *racial, gendered* self. She has no home within her body as well as this material world. As a non-White immigrant in a White world, she can feel that no one will understand her origins and the daily rituals she holds so central to every day living. She may feel isolated in an alien culture with little or no means to negotiate what she perceives to be, at best, an indifferent outside world. Leaving an abusive situation, then, is that much harder for her than for an American-born woman. How does one walk out of the home, even one that is abusive, when it is the only space that provides connections to a life world left behind? Yet, how does she persist in a situation where she is being slowly but surely destroyed?

As with other women of color, the notion of self for immigrant South Asian women is inseparable from the group.[20] Many feel a strong sense of wanting to be within a cultural space that is comprehensible to them. When victimized by violence, many women need a safe space where they can recover a *racial* bodily integrity to their selves. In other words, they want to recover in ways that are comfortable and culturally familiar, all within their control. Ethnic shelters such as Apna Ghar are spaces where battered South Asian American women can potentially recover a sense of a racial, gendered self once again. Women who have experienced domestic violence arrive here, hoping to find a safe space where they can retain a sense of "Indian-ness" as they recover their selves.[21]

Who are these battered women who come to Apna Ghar? When I first began working there the residents were Lola and her five-year-old and three-year-old boys, all of whom were African American. Kanwar and her teenage son were from Punjab, India. Diana, Cindy, and Cynthia were all White, midwestern women. Soon Salma from Pakistan, along with her three children all under five years of age, arrived at the shelter. The women usually resided in Apna Ghar for a maximum of two months, during which we assisted them with finding housing, public aid, and if possible, jobs. They also had numerous counseling sessions, art therapy, parenting classes, meditation classes, and so forth every evening that they had to compulsorily attend. In spite of the two month stay Apna Ghar allowed, however, women residents were often asked to leave the shelter for breaking some rule or the other; major transgressions were arriving at the shelter past the curfew time of 9:00 P.M., leaving children unattended and unruly, getting drunk, or missing the various sessions held in the evenings. Of the women residents when I first began work, all except Kanwar were asked to leave the shelter before the completion of their two-month stay. Therefore, we constantly had women coming to and leaving the shelter. When I finally discontinued work a year later, the residents at Apna Ghar were Akosia and her daughter from Nigeria. Sameera hailed from Pakistan. Hansa, Zubeda, and, Tabasum and her two daughters all came from India. So Apna Ghar saw women of all racial backgrounds, not just South Asians, enter its portals. All women, though, were working-class individuals.

Apna Ghar was tremendously helpful to some women in providing a space for reconstituting their lives. Parvati who now works in the shelter, for example, thinks she could not have emerged as a survivor if not for this particular shelter. "Whoever started Apna Ghar, I thank them a million times. I tell you, really!" exclaimed Parvati in our interview. For others such as Najma, of whom I speak in the next section, the shelter was more detrimental than helpful. In this book, however, I do not evaluate the shelter's effectiveness in providing assistance to women's recovery processes; instead I examine how the shelter attempts to shape women's identities as they reconstitute their lives. The ways in which we shelter workers listened, our reactions to survival narratives, counseling and parenting classes, indeed proscribed ways of conducting oneself in everyday situations, all reveal the ways in which racialized citizenship is engendered in this immigrant space.

South Asian Immigrant Women's Dependence

Parvati, who now works at the shelter, spoke of her situation two years previously in her ex-husband's home. She described how she needed to fill in her income tax forms:

I told my husband that I need to do a joint file with him for income tax. He agreed. And you know my mother-in-law started—you have [a] lot of the friends, you can go to them for help. Why are you asking my son to do this for you? Then she started to ask for dowry. For money. For everything. Everything, you know, was coming out from her mind. And my husband was alcoholic. He started to beat me. Very, very badly. If you want to see the picture, I have the picture of me, all beaten.

Parvati then proceeded to pull out a Polaroid photograph that showed her face swollen and covered with bruises. Her front tooth was chipped and bleeding. Her hair was pulled out in clumps. The skin on her neck was black, blue, and bleeding as a result of her husband's attempts to strangle her. Parvati said her mother-in-law was the instigator of the violence in her marital home.[22] I spoke with Naseem, a long-time shelter worker, about whether violence is different in South Asian immigrant women's lives (tape recorded interview). Naseem identified the extended families common among South Asians as a potential source of strength and support for women, but

> sometimes that family network can be suffocating for her. The family, which should be helpful, can become her deathbed. Ah . . . it's common. Domestic violence is as common in the Indian communities as among Whites. The only thing that makes it different is that I think the reason why violence occurs. In the west [western societies], violence mainly occurs due to alcoholism, maybe. Ninety percent of the time people lose control at that point and then the abuse starts. But in India the reasons could be very varied [by extension Naseem is making references to Indian Americans as well]. For example, the marriages are arranged so it could be because the person is not interested. Marriages are conducted for business or dowry reasons like a gain or a profit and things. If expectations are not met, that could be the beginning of violence. Or the issue of reproduction can also be the starting point of violence. The in-laws always expect the daughter-in-law to produce a son so that he will be the name bearer of the family. And if this woman cannot bear children or doesn't have a first-born son or doesn't produce a son at all, then her problems can start. So apart from this there are all the other reasons like economic reasons and alcoholism too in certain communities in India.

Naseem elucidated that the issue of citizenship compounded the occurrence of violence among immigrant South Asian families: "All the cultural reasons regarding abuse exist for Indian women here—like your mother didn't give this, we didn't get this in dowry, etc.—but here the other reason is the possession of the green card or legal status. A boy marries a girl to get a green card. It could be a marriage of convenience. The violence can start because that convenience is over now, and the relationship will break. So some people will outright divorce a person. Some don't. They prolong it by all this misery."

Besides, being in an unfamiliar cultural context isolated immigrant women. Naseem continued:

> Another reason why violence escalates here, or it's so profound, is because there is no support system for the woman. Support system in the sense of a system that she recognizes and can trust. She doesn't know who to trust here because sometimes she might have come from a place in India where she is not so, ah, aware of what is happening in the world. She might come from a village. Or she might be from a smaller town where there isn't much education. People know that America is an advanced country, but there isn't education about women's organizations or what help can be available. Or trusting the police. Because we have seen that in certain parts of the world, and I'm ashamed to say India is one of them, the police don't protect the peo ple as much as it should. People are very, very wary of the police, and they think a known abuser is better than an unknown policeman. So they continue to live with abuse. So all these reasons make her case more profound. Now the person might also—add a bit of illiteracy—this adds to the violence because literate people might find a way out faster. Or might see the signs of it coming and stop it altogether. But for an illiterate person violence may escalate.

I asked, "Is it because they don't have jobs and they won't be able to leave the home?"

Naseem corrected me:

> No, that's economic dependence. Illiteracy in the sense of, they really don't know what to do with their time here. In India their time passes very well because there is a neighbor to drop in, there's shopping to do, there are things they do in the community. But here she is alone. She doesn't have much to do. So she is depending on her husband to take her out, to meet peo- ple, to take her shopping or whatever. She is housebound. This man is going out to his job. All the time she has built up a case to present before him. When he comes, he's tired. He has no time to give her and that causes some friction between them. So if she finds something useful to do—if she knows there are libraries, and these libraries are free of charge she could go and spend two or three hours there. If she knows they are within walking distance from the house. If she knows that there is a lot of voluntary work she can do, ah, if she is capable of that, then that could also be so satisfying for her as well as *make*

her a better person at home to be with. So in some ways if she's literate about these things, she might be better off. She might not fall into the domestic violence cycle. (My emphasis.)

I interviewed Naseem because she had been working in Apna Ghar for the longest period in comparison to all other workers. She was respected among South Asian Americans in Chicago, and families often turned to her to mediate spousal disagreements. She draws contrasts between the United States and India; in the latter, she said women have more access to female-centered spaces to interact with other women. In this country, as immigrants, non-White women have almost no access to such public spaces. Naseem identifies this lack of public space as contributing to the woman's isolation and complete dependence on her husband. I had blithely presumed that Naseem would tell me illiteracy causes economic dependence because an illiterate person has fewer job opportunities. What she told me, however, is something different. She postulated that an illiterate woman does not have the wherewithal to use the new forms of public space in the United States. The alienation a new immigrant feels, in Naseem's perspective, is her own fault. Instead of being a "better person at home to be with," she becomes a nuisance, thus inviting abuse.

I questioned Naseem about whether South Asian women were more prone to keep silent about domestic violence compared with other women. She nodded in agreement and replied:

> The Indian girl is brought up to keep whatever is happening to herself. We are not so open about our feelings, whether they are feelings of love or hatred or whatever. Like, a little child here might constantly say "I love you" or "I hate you." They are two very easy things for people [here in the U.S.] to say, and they connote it with all the things that are happening in their lives. But in India a little child doesn't say these things so often. And he not told "I love you" so often. So in India these are—these types of feelings are within you and you don't broadcast them. So it follows that if there is domestic violence or something is happening to you, then don't broadcast it. Try to bear it. In fact, girls are taught to leave their homes as a bride and enter the in-laws' house as bride and leave as a dead body. So they have no choices or options available like divorce him, or come back to your mother's house, or do this or do the other. So they think that well, if this is the life I have, or it has been planned for me, then I'm going to stick it.

I expressed skepticism at this generalization, "Hmm. This is the way a woman's life is?"

"Yes," Naseem replied, "most people are told when you are a woman you are bound to suffer. But I think that young women now do not identify with that. Then they get called rebellious."

I concurred, "Yeah. I mean, in India as well as here I think young women don't identify with the notion of complete docility." Naseem nodded and continued:

> India too has changed much since the time we were there and you feel that more people are not submissive. It doesn't mean that people have become openly disobedient to the elders. They still retain that. But if the elders cooperate, then the woman can be an obedient daughter-in-law. Like recently we had client here who told me over the phone that she has an in-law household. She's married into a household now. The husband is one person, but there are five other people in that house. And she is the person who is cooking and cleaning for them. She is doing all that for quite some time now. She is working outside too. Whereas there is a healthy mother-in-law who is at home who will not move a pin in the house. This mother-in-law waits for her to come and do the housework also. This woman said "this is OK; I can bear it. Because I know mothers-in-law will make you work so I can bear it." But what she cannot bear is that her husband is so quiet. He doesn't speak to her at all. That he has no feeling of being married to her. They don't have any companionship. She says, "I'm alone. There isn't anyone to talk to. It's only—get up, do the housework, go to your job. Finish your job, do the groceries, come back. Do the housework. Go to bed." She has basically nobody to talk to. She says doesn't mind the work, but this feeling of loneliness is killing her. And I asked her, isn't there any help? She says no. "Nobody does anything. I do it. It's OK. I don't complain. It's OK, because I can manage it. I'm expected to do the housework."

Naseen concluded that Indian women are patient, "they can bear more. They can suffer more without complaining."

In addition to being reserved about their emotions, Naseem's perception is that Indian women are more tolerant of exploitative conditions. They are willing to do all the housework for their extended families, and all they ask in return, as this hotline caller does, is for companionship. Naseem added that this particular hotline caller was chosen as a bride only because she was healthy, educated, and could work well at a job.

All this talk about marriage, extended families, and the proclaimed docility of Indian women inevitably leads us to talk about arranged marriages. Naseem began, "People ask me whether I believe in arranged marriages. I do. I do. They are the ones that are most successful. And, given the changing ideas of men and women, they are the ones that last longer. I don't mean to say that no arranged marriage ends in divorce. Maybe some of them do end in divorce. But there are better prospects for a successful arranged marriage."

I asked, "Is it because there are no false expectations in arranged marriages?"

"Yes" she replied, understanding my question differently:

There is no individual expectation. The expectation is subject to the family's outlook. So you always think that if my family believes in education, then I'm going to be married to an educated person. Naturally, if they want education for you, they'll not marry you to a person who's uneducated. If the family is a business family, then the expectation is that you will be married to a business partner. Something to further the business alliance, maybe. So, in this way, the businessman's daughter expects to be married to a businessman or a businessman's son. That's how your expectations get colored by what is happening with the family. But as people have here, or people wherever marriage is free, think about–Oh, I like this person. I want to marry him. That liking process comes to the Indian girl after her arranged marriage. That, I'm married to this person, and this is the person I've got to like. And I think love grows after that.

Naseem said that for Indians, and especially women, the notion of an autonomous individuality does not exist outside family. A woman's self emerges through her adjustments to her parents' expectations and then to her husband and his family's expectations. Her own wants arise within these familial contexts. Her ideals, interests, and expectations are all fundamentally tied to her family. We then spoke of Naseem's eighteen-year-old daughter's marriage.

I asked, "Your daughter just got married recently, right, this past year?"

Naseem answered, "Uh hm. And it was an arranged marriage."

I questioned, "Is she in Chicago, or . . ."

Naseem replied:

For a while she was here. Originally we'd planned that she would be here with us for two years until she finishes her college education. Her husband concurred. He had said that she should do her undergraduate degree. And then she plans to study law. So they'll take it up later. But now that he has been married for nine months, my son-in-law would like her with him. So he has asked her whether she will continue her studies there with him in Louisiana. He's an international student. He can work off-campus and will take up a job only if she can come and join him there. And, ah, being the parents, we want her to be happy. Her education will follow. This is what we have told her, that she has to look out for her happiness, which I think people in the West will laugh at. But I think they can bond very well if they are together and she can pursue her education later. She is an A grade student. She has received a lot of awards and so, which she recognizes too. His family too is educated. All the girls are educated. So, we told her it might be tough on you because you might have children and . . . but you have to cope with it. And I think she's up to it. The way I've brought her up, I think she'll manage. So now she's going out. She would have been there already, but because of my husband's health, she'll leave next month. Probably the 4th of July. But it was a totally arranged marriage.

Naseem did not seem to see the similarities between her eighteen-year-old daughter's life and the earlier hotline caller's situation we spoke of earlier. That lonely woman on the hotline who had no one to speak with, was, according to Naseem, selected for marriage solely because of her economic potential. Why was Naseem's daughter selected for this marriage, I asked myself? In her earlier descriptions of violence among Indian families, Naseem specifically pointed to women's lack of education leading to their isolation and abuse. Yet, her own daughter has interrupted her own education to be with her husband, following the very pattern that Naseem thinks can lead to domestic violence.

She continued to describe the conditions of her daughter's marriage and why perhaps her daughter was chosen for this marriage:

My American friends were very surprised about this arranged marriage. They were asking me whether she has met the boy. She didn't get to meet him. She just, ah—*he* got a glimpse of her. He saw her, but it was in a group of people. My brother took my daughter to just wish his uncle, and that's the time the boy saw her. He didn't have any chance to talk to her, but he wanted to ask her one question. He said he was still a struggling student and that he would not be able to provide lots of luxuries for her. He had a small car. And a very small house. Could she manage living like that for a couple of years? The boy's aunt conveyed to us that he would like to ask our daughter this question. I replied, "this is not done in our family. We take the responsibility for that; our child is not going to ask you for anything that you cannot afford to do for her. She has been brought up like that. And we guarantee that she is not going to trouble you saying change your car and buy a new house. I want this. I cannot move without this." And I also told him "I don't think my daughter will be able to tell you—yes! OK, I'll accept. She'll just nod her head to whatever you say. So there is no point in this conversation with her. She doesn't know you. And she's not used to talking to people about what she wants and so on. But she's been brought up in such a way that she'll not tell her husband why do you have a small car." Ah, we think that that's how she's going to behave. And so we accept that responsibility. We tell you that she'll not mind what kind of house you have and so on. And you have to take our word for it."

I gathered her daughter's silence results either because she is raised in a "decent household," that is, well-brought up girls do not voice their needs. Or, Naseem's daughter's self is irredeemably tied to her family. Naseem's eighteen-year-old had not even met her prospective husband but agreed to get married to him solely based on her parents' wishes. The young woman will not talk with an unfamiliar man, yet she is willing to marry him. So implicit is her trust in them, and so intricately linked are her and her parents' interests, that there is no issue of her wanting anything different. She is so embedded within her natal family that her needs and interests are assumed to be in complete synchrony with the rest. Is the eighteen-year-old's compliant nature what makes her an ideal partner in marriage? Not as yet having openly articulated interests of her own, her husband's interests can become hers as well? She will comply as she always has and not question any expectations that may be imposed on her?[23]

Naseem still thought of her eighteen-year-old as a child, yet she was old enough to bear the responsibilities of marriage. "Do you miss her?" I inquired. Naseem's face immediately changed, and her voice became choked, "Oh yes. It's terrible without her. But we couldn't help it. Ah, for our sake we can't hold onto her." She added that her daughter would probably miss them too. Naseem herself had been married now for twenty-five years: "I've lived for so long away from my own mother. But even now I always think of my mother's house as my home. I'm sure my daughter's going to miss it [her maternal home] too. But we don't let on that we miss her. We are encouraging her to buy the things she needs to set up a house. We encourage her to go away. But we miss her." Naseem added that she and her husband long to call their daughter in Louisiana everyday, but "my husband tells me we have to let her be with her in-laws and so on. Yet, in the mornings he asks me, 'have you called her?' And afterwards he asks, 'did she speak? Have you called her?' So we . . . we long to talk to her."

Naseem, who works at the shelter, does not question the gender norms in South Asian families. Naseem points out that lack of education and the culturally prescribed ideal of reticence in women potentially lead to violence, but yet she fails to recognize that her eighteen-year-old daughter's life has all the parameters that set her up for an abusive situation. However, abuse within her home is incomprehensible to Naseem because she believes her family has "good" cultural values. Naseem and her husband accept full responsibility for their daughter, because they've raised her in culturally prescribed ways and she will meet the cultural expectations of her marital home. Naseem does not love her daughter any less; she and her husband are doing only what their extended family expects of them. By their own standards, they have done their best for their daughter. Now, if anything happens to them, they will know she ensconced within a family similar to the one in which she was raised. They have fulfilled their parental obligations toward her as all good parents should, and they can only hope that she will do her part in being a good daughter, wife, daughter-in-law, and mother.

American Women's Dependence

In my interview with Nellie, the shelter supervisor, I asked her whether South Asian battered women were different from other battered women. She answered, "The Americans are too dependent on the system. They know that if everything else fails, the system will take care of them. So they tend to become lazy." The South Asian clients were different because "you see, it's in their culture. They know there is no support network, so they try very hard to make things work out."

I changed my line of questioning to our work at Apna Ghar, "Are we successful in the work we do?" I asked Nellie. She shrugged her shoulders. "In some cases we are—look at Zina, Ginny, and even Kathy. They have all left their husbands and are trying to manage on their own. With Indian women, we have lesser success. These people just make use of us," Nellie said. She explained further: "They don't really want to leave their husbands, but they just come here so they can bargain with their husbands. See Jayashree—even though she was here she always called her husband. She told him she would stay here until he promised to change. These people are not really serious about leaving and getting their lives together. They only use us." She then invoked the example of Heena, "She not only went back to her husband, but she's pregnant now. She called the cops on him twice, but now she's pregnant with his child!" The exasperation in Nellie's voice indicated that to her, Heena's pregnancy could have resulted only through consensual sex.

In addition, Nellie thought South Asian clients came to Apna Ghar not because of abuse but because of abandonment. South Asian women, she expressed, never knew when to leave an abusive marriage. "Sameera is a good example," Nellie said, indicating a young Pakistani woman. Sameera's husband beat her endlessly. Finally, she had taken an overdose of sleeping pills. He apologized and she returned to him after four days in the hospital. Eventually, he sent her off to Pakistan. Sameera returned to the United States with the help of her family in Pakistan, but once in Chicago, she had nowhere to go. Nellie's understanding was that Sameera's decision to come to Apna Ghar was not because of abuse but only because of homelessness. I became confused; didn't being driven out of one's home constitute abuse, I asked. Nellie remained unconvinced.

Deciding to work along with *her* definition of abuse, that is, physical battery, I countered, "OK. But Zubeda came to Apna Ghar because she was beaten." Nellie disagreed, "Zubeda's husband asked her get out of the house, so she left. She said she was scared what he would do if she stayed on, so she left." More confused now, I questioned, "Is the threat of abuse not enough?" Nellie nodded reluctantly, but reiterated that South Asian battered women left their homes not because of abuse but only because of expulsion. The only reason they came to Apna Ghar was because they had nowhere else to go. However, once at the shelter, "they try very hard to get jobs, and all the other things. Americans are not like this. They are too dependent on the system."

Various studies show that women's economic dependence and emotional commitment to their abusers make it very hard for them to leave. Strube and Barbour, for example, note that a large number of women return to their abusers; citing earlier studies, they reveal that a large percent of battered women lived with their abusers.[24] Of a study conducted in 1981 in Detroit with 119 women, only 13 percent indicated that they would return to their abusers when they were interviewed upon their arrival at the shelter. However, at discharge, 34 percent indicated they would return and follow-up interviews between six and sixteen weeks after their having left the shelter revealed that 60 percent of those contacted had returned to their abusers.[25] The dynamics of violent relationships are remarkably complex. Working with a sample composed of predominantly working-class White women, Strube and Barbour note that women's prior exposure to violence, the lack of a supportive network of people, and their emotional and physical well-being all contribute to their tolerance of abuse and their ultimate decision to leave the abuser.[26]

Yet, Nellie is unable to comprehend how or why immigrant non-White women—who have been raised to never even consider leaving their homes, who do not have extensive networks here in the United States, who can barely speak English, who have difficulty finding employment—stay on in abusive relationships. Nellie is blaming the women for being victimized by violence. They are asked to assume personal responsibility for an issue that extends far beyond themselves, an issue that emerges from the values on which they have been raised within extended families, and an issue that is cultivated by state institutions, the cutting back of welfare, and worsening economic situations that further foster their economic and emotional dependence.

Speaking of the residents led Nellie to the topic of South Asian American workers. She found first-generation shelter workers very different from second-generation Indian American women. "They [the second-generation] expect their parents to take care of them. We are not like that," said Nellie.

> Also, I've noticed they tolerate stress very poorly. They complain a lot. They want more sympathy. They want to be taken care of. Whereas, people like us who have been raised in India can bear a lot more stress. We are stronger emotionally. Take, for example, this girl. She worked day shifts but would get so scared because of the clients she would call me in a panic. A couple of times she got so scared she even wanted to call the cops! So silly, you know. I mean, what is there to get scared?

As she talked, I recognized that Nellie is not aware she is drawing similarities between first-generation workers and South Asian battered women; the shelter residents tolerate abuse in homes, and the first-generation workers tolerate difficult conditions at work. Whereas "South Asian reserve" makes battered women difficult to work with—they are stoic about abuse, they do not leave homes unless thrown out of the house—these very same qualities makes for a better worker. First-generation workers are interpreted as having endurance and forbearance, the qualities that are deplored in battered women. Simultaneously, Nellie describes both second-generation shelter workers and American women as being more in touch with their individual self; American women walk out when abuse begins. They will not tolerate any violation of body and spirit. These are good qualities that shelter staff *wants* battered immigrant women to emulate. Yet, in Nellie's views these very same qualities— articulating wrongs directed at them, asking for emotional support—make substandard workers.

American women, however, are criticized for their dependency on the state. This sort of dependency, in Nellie's eyes, is far more insidious and destructive because the nation is left with a whole cadre of battered dependents who will not assume responsibility for themselves or their children. On the other hand, Nellie believed that Asian culture made a person hard working. Battered immigrant women had to learn independence from their families, but once they achieved this autonomy, they were far better than American women because they also became independent of the state, leading their lives as self-reliant individuals in an America world.

Rehabilitation Work at Apna Ghar

Naseem's daughter whom I spoke of earlier, as far as we know, is not in an abusive marriage, but many others are not as fortunate. Women called Apna Ghar everyday, asking to come in. Anyone who wanted to stay at the shelter had to obtain a police report against her batterer. Her police report proved that she truly was a victim of domestic violence and not homelessness alone. In addition, this policy of requiring women to file a police report against their abusers proved to us that the women were serious about leaving their abusive home. Only with police reports in hand would they be admitted to the shelter as bona fide victims.

The problem with the stipulation of a police report is that it recognizes only physical abuse and not emotional abuse. A victim of spousal abuse is someone who is deemed as having bruises on her body and broken bones. Moreover, some researchers and activists point that pressing police charges and obtaining orders of protection are highly individualistic tools for combating domestic violence.[27] First, the onus of vigilance against violence becomes solely the victim's responsibility. Second, there are numerous reasons why she may not call the police when the order of protection is violated. She may lack language skills and confidence to deal with the police. Continually reporting on her abuse is a tremendous responsibility to bear, which becomes harder if she has children who may have affection for the abuser. Others in her extended communal network may intervene, sometimes convinced by the abuser's remorse and confessions to having reformed his ways. Her filing a report or calling the police when he violates the order of protection then marks her as an unreasonable wife, and any support she has among her network can erode further. In addition, there may be other reasons—the spouse may be an undocumented worker; he may be the sole income earner, which is especially crucial when she is not a citizen and does not speak English. Or, she may worry that she may lose her children to the Department of Children and Family Services for child abuse and neglect. Nevertheless, Apna Ghar insisted that women who arrive at the shelter have a police report in hand.

In addition, Apna Ghar pushed women to walk out of their abusive homes. They developed this stance because of the ways in which they understood violence; they recognized that violence was not an individual woman's psychological problem but arose within their social networks. Therefore, the first step toward surviving a violent domestic situation was to step away from the abuser. As a result, though the shelter recognized culturally specific forms of violence, the model for recovery from abuse was uniform for all women—they urged women to leave their abusers, their families, and real and fictive kinship networks so that they may sustain themselves in a violence-free world.

Apna Ghar pushed women to leave, but the women often wanted to return to their abusers. Contrary to the shelter's expectations for them, and much to the shelter staff's disapproval, the South Asian battered women often expressed a desire to negotiate with their abusers in the presence of extended family and community members. Hansa was one such person. She was a mid-forties Indian American widow who was abused by her son. When her oldest son, in his twenties, threw her out of the house, she moved in with Fauzia and Nasser, a younger couple she knew. Because this couple lived in a very small apartment and could not accommodate her, Hansa arrived at Apna Ghar. She did not want to file police charges against her son. Meanwhile, the abusive son had been calling Fauzia and Nasser, remorsefully asking them about his mother's whereabouts. Fauzia and Nasser were convinced the son was serious about altering his ways, and they tried to convince Hansa to return. They promised to act as intermediaries so that the son would not abuse his mother again.

Hansa was torn. The son had abused her four times previously; all four times she had left home but returned when he expressed regret. This fifth time, once again, he apologized. If she did not return home now, people of her community would regard her as a stubborn, unreasonable person. She would bear the stigma of having left her son's home. "Boys will say things in anger, and we are supposed to just accept that because boys will be boys," she explained to me, shaking her head. Hansa was angry but saw no alternative. Should she take on her community's disapproval, or should she return, knowing she may be abused once again? Finally Hansa decided not to return to her son right away but instead negotiate a position that would give her more power in her relationship with him. She stayed in the shelter for a couple of weeks and met her son on a regular basis to work out an agreement with him.

Making Shelter Residents Emotionally Independent

The shelter staff often expressed frustration with the South Asian American battered women, because like Hansa, they used the shelter to negotiate the terms of their return to their abusers. Whether the survivors wanted it or not, the staff pushed women to lead independent lives divorced from familial/community ties. While the ideal of autonomy is desirable, Apna Ghar staff often imposed their own ideals of autonomy on their clients based on what they thought was the best route for their residents to recover a life of dignity. However, the kinds of independence battered women sought were qualitatively different. They did not want to jeopardize their acceptance in their communities and tried various compromises with their abusers. Apna Ghar staff instead saw these negotiations by battered women as counter-productive to the goals the shelter set for the women. The shelter staff rarely attempted to put themselves in the positions of the battered women and ask why family and community—though they may be structured along restrictive, patriarchal lines—were so important to battered women. Instead of working within the gendered proscriptions that the abuse survivors held, shelter staff imposed their own narrative of what an ideal abuse survivor should be. Any deviations from the ideal type were frowned upon.

Donileen Loseke, for example, notes that many shelters have a "homogenous service goal—to help clients become independent and self-sufficient."[28] When a woman arrived at the shelter, the staff set her goals for her, regardless of her wants. These goals include individual emotional strength and social independence, premised on a resolute determination not to return to the abusers. Yet, in spite of pushing women to make independent decisions, "it seem[ed] that social service ideals of clients' rights to self-determination stopped when *workers believed* that their courses of action were self-destructive. . . . It seem[ed] that social service ideals of client self-determination [were] . . . put into practice . . . only when, clients agree[d] with the organizational image of the problem and the resolution."[29]

Workers—not just at Apna Ghar but in other shelters as well—often come up with a singular solution to battered women's violent realities. Apna Ghar workers understood differences between South Asian women and American women, as indicated in Naseem's and Nellie's words reproduced earlier. Yet, in spite of this understanding, they pushed all residents to become "ideal" survivors. When battered women left the shelter after their two-month stay, they were to be self-reliant and independent in ways the workers deemed right. If the battered women wanted qualitatively different kinds of independence or if they decided to return to the abusive relationship, the shelter staff—ostensibly working for the self-determination of women—intervened with a velvet-gloved iron hand, guiding women onto the path deemed appropriate for survivors.

This path to self-determination was premised on a particular kind of autonomy for battered women that asked them to be divorced from their problematic histories, social realities, and cultural contexts. Apna Ghar's workers' urged women to leave their homes precisely because they did not pathologize violence. That is, they did not blame the individual but instead recognized that domestic violence had social origins. Abuse arose within certain kinds of values, customs, and practices prevalent in extended families. Apna Ghar recognized that certain traditions, patriarchal structures, and gender norms extant within South Asian American communities implicitly endorsed violence against women. Women, therefore, were not safe in their social networks and had to create newer, safer spaces for themselves. As a result, they were urged to move on.

The Importance of Family for South Asian American Women

My fellow caseworkers and I had many conversations on how family, community, and individuality were intertwined for South Asian Americans. I asked twenty-two-year-old second-generation Reena, "Why is family important for us South Asians? I mean, is it more important than for others?"

Reena began with a stutter, "You gotta keep . . . you got to keep the family together. I think there's a lot of pressure to do that, as opposed to non-south Asians, specifically ah . . . like White or . . . or Black families for that matter. There is not as much pressure to keep . . . to keep the family together in American culture. I mean, divorce is really high."

"Why" I asked, "is it important to keep families together?"

Reena began even before I finished my sentence, "Because families like, I mean back in India, family was the main unit. Even if they come as a nuclear family here, it's still important that they keep those ties. I think when I . . . when I grew up, the thing was that you always used to be . . . you needed a support system to be here."

I then asked, "Why do we need more of a support system?"

Reena was silent for a while, and then, "Hmmm. Us, like me? Second generation?"

"Or first generation."

Reena's thoughtful frown on her forehead cleared and she explained, "I think it's different for first generation (said very emphatically). They need to like . . . my mom has her sisters up here. They need each other because, they're, I'm mean, like its nice to communicate with somebody who, like, who you can just be free with. And just say everything to. And speak the same language to. And they know your hometown, and everything. It's just. . . ."

"They know your history?" I finished enquiringly.

Reena answered:

Exactly! I mean like, everything like, that. And I think (silence) . . . that, ah . . . also some of it, like for me, I know I always want to . . . I'm not exactly the closest with my cousins. I have cousins right here through my mom— through her brothers and sisters right here in the Chicago area. But for me, I want to . . . I'm Gujarati. I want to go to *garbas* (all said very quickly and with more emotion), and I feel like I have to do this with my family. If I want to keep up a lot of the things that I do, it feels like I have to do it with my family. You know, like, being the Indian part of myself (some silence; laughter). So cheesy! (More embarrassed laughter).

Families not only loom large in everyday lives in India, but upon arrival here, family takes on an even greater significance. First-generation Indians, like Reena's mother, feel that their extended families are the only social unit that can understand them. Their Indian American relatives and friends form the core of their support system as they try make homes and raise families here, in this new country. Second-generation Indian Americans—like Reena—may not have close emotional ties to their extended families, but an essential part of their self is actualized within the context this kinship network. They practice their race, "become Indian" if you will, within the context of these familial networks.

Reena's and my conversation then shifted to the topic of domestic violence among Indian Americans. I asked her whether domestic violence was different for South Asian women than for American women. Reena thought for a while and then replied:

> I think for South Asian women leaving is not an option. And for a non-South Asian woman leaving is *the* option out there. South Asian women just don't think of it. When you get married, you get married for life. I feel like it [marriage] was never about love anyway. It wasn't like . . . ah, I love him. I can't leave him. I love him, I can't leave him. Instead its like . . . oh . . . my family. What are they going to say? Who am I going to turn to now? Its not like, its not about . . . its not this kind of ah . . . emotional . . . you know what I'm saying?

Having heard Naseem speak in a similar vein, I nodded. Reena pointed out that while these large family networks can be a useful support system in disciplining an abuser, extended family can also pressure a woman into remaining in an abusive situation, trying to make things work against all odds. Or often, women may remain in a marriage for the sake of the children.[30] In addition, Reena described the veil of silence that covers abuse. It is harder for an Indian/Pakistani woman to talk about abuse freely because the larger community endorses muteness in private, familial matters. Women fear that they may be ostracized if they make their situation public. Their ethnic community might see them as somehow deserving the beatings and blame them, instead of blaming the abusers.[31]

As a result, battered women may stay on in the relationship because if they leave, they cut all their ties not just to their nuclear family but also to their community. For the average American woman in an abusive relationship, the issues of power and control are exacerbated precisely because of the ways by which they are isolated in their relationships with their abusers; the abuser may monitor her interactions with kith and kin or he may screen her telephone calls, thus making it harder for her to reach out to others who may be supportive. Hence, walking out of an abusive situation can potentially end an average American woman's isolation. However, for South Asian American women, walking out of an abusive situation can *lead* to their isolation. Not only do they walk out of the abusive home, but by walking out of community—the context out of which arises their histories, a group of people who speak the same languages, hold similar values, and so forth—immigrant battered women can potentially be isolated further because they remove themselves from the social networks they may have once had.

Reena and I talked about the exit options for an abused South Asian woman. Reena thought that when domestic violence occurs, "the South Asian woman is worse off because she just doesn't have the resources to get out of it." Shelters such as Apna Ghar help:

> If they [battered women] know about it. It helps them . . . ah . . . I don't know, I mean it helps them get a job only if they are willing to. You know, it's really hard to change somebody's cultural perceptions. I think that's something we could work at. I mean, we are a South Asian women's shelter. I remember we had this one client who was South Asian. She'd only been in the States for about a year. I had to explain to her that she's not in India anymore. She can do a lot more here than she can there. She could get a divorce. She could get a job. And she didn't have to listen to everything her family said now because they are so far away. They're not here. But it's so hard to get her to stop thinking in those terms I guess.

A contradiction develops in our conversation; while Reena previously acknowledged the importance of family and rootedness in community for herself, she expresses her frustration with South Asian abuse survivors who convey the same sentiments. When speaking about herself and her mother, Reena *knows* that as a woman of color in the United States she cannot be who she wants to be. She recognizes the need for a familial network to give her the context for developing her racial self. Contrarily, she urges a battered woman who's been in the United States for only one year—and hasn't had as much time in the United States or the class advantages that Reena or her mother have—to step out of her home. She questions why a working-class battered South Asian woman cannot give up the only social capital she has and begin afresh with absolutely no networks.

Apna Ghar Residents and Wage Work— Making Them Economically Independent

Immigrant women who are not American citizens are not eligible for welfare. The Personal Responsibility and Work Opportunity Reconciliation Act (PROWRA) signed by Bill Clinton in 1996 tied public benefits to citizenship. Documented noncitizens, and many of the Apna Ghar immigrant residents fall under this category, cannot receive Supplemental Security Income (SSI) and Food stamps unless they have proof of having worked for forty qualifying quarters or have been refugees in the United States for less than five years. They are eligible only for emergency medical assistance.[32] They do not receive TANF or medical assistance. Nonemergency medical assistance is especially crucial to battered women, who have recurring emotional and physical problems because of abuse. Many Apna Ghar residents' children, however, are citizens. As a result, they might receive food stamps for their children but not for themselves.

Having left the marital home, then, a battered immigrant woman has no option for supporting herself other than entering a shrinking labor market with low or no English language fluency and limited job skills. As with numerous other Americans, Apna Ghar residents' only option to make ends meet was to work at a minimum wage job in the service sector. So, they worked as cleaning staff in large hotels and motels; manned counters in ethnic clothing stores; or worked as O'Hare airport staff, cleaning floors, bathrooms, or pushing airport transients in carts from one terminal to the other. In addition to all these service jobs, South Asian women had one other job option not available to non-South Asians at the shelter. Middle-class suburban South Asian housewives sought to employ them as live-in maids or baby-sitters. I include an excerpt from my field notes about a call I received requesting a live-in maid.

February 25th, late 1990s.
I'm on shift this cold morning, and the hotline keeps ringing nonstop almost all day long. A woman calls on behalf of her Vietnamese friend who had been battered the previous day. I called the Vietnamese woman back, but she is not interested in coming to the shelter. Apparently, this has happened before. Numerous times people intervened to help her, but she usually backed out the last minute, too scared to stay with the abuser but petrified by the prospects of leaving him. The hotline rang twice more. Both calls are from homeless women looking for overnight shelter. I gave them a list of phone numbers to call and also the DHS phone number. The DHS sends out a van to pick them up.

Amidst all these calls, the phone rings once again. Another distress call, I think, wincing inwardly. Only this woman's distress is different. Her trauma is caused not by abuse or homelessness but instead by housework that lays undone. She is Kirin from Westchester, who wants household help for four days per week, to do five hours of cooking and cleaning per day. She is willing to pay at the going rate. "What is that?" I ask. "The amount other Indian families pay their maids," she replies discreetly. I then asked Kirin where she'd heard about Apna Ghar, and how she knew she could get maids here. She replied that she'd known of us for about three years now. Usha Singh, an abuse survivor, had three years earlier worked for her. Kirin would love to have Usha back in the house, but if that couldn't be done, she would settle for any other Indian woman.

What shocks me is that a domestic violence hotline should serve as a potential maid service, catering to middle-class women's housekeeping needs. More than any other job, live-in servitude is especially structured for fostering exploitation and abuse on the shop floor, that is, the households in which workers live and labor. The treatment of live-in maids is so bad that in New York City Workers' Awaaz was begun in 1997. Nahar Alam writes that live-in maids work up to fourteen hours per day, are isolated from others, and are wholly dependent on their employers for food and shelter. Often their employers seize their passports as a way of keeping the workers hostage in homes. Employers are known to intimidate workers by telling them they cannot seek outside help because they are illegal workers and will be deported.[33] The Samar Collective in New York City conducted interviews with domestic workers. One woman says of her experience: "I arrived in 1992, as a domestic worker or nanny, and I was promised $200 per month. I agreed, not knowing what was going to be the case. She treated me worse than a slave. No proper food, and always saying insulting things like, 'you are my servant.'"[34]

Alam described Tara's situation, another live-in maid's life:

There were two children—a four-year-old and a fifteen-month-old. Tara did the cooking, cleaning, and babysitting from 6:30 in the morning to 10 o'clock at night (and even later when they had parties), seven days a week. Her employers had agreed to pay her $800 per month in rupees to her family in India, which she found out was not being paid regularly. They gave her a room in the basement, did not allow her to talk on the phone, and only permitted her to leave the house in their company. Isolated, frightened, and depressed, she had to contend with the threats of being thrown out of the house or being reported to the police. She was constantly verbally abused by her employers and occasionally physically hit. When she said she wanted to return to India, she was told that she would need to work for one year without wages to pay for her ticket to go home. She had no money at all, and her passport was being kept by her employer.[35]

While all cases of live-in maid service may not be as abusive as the one described here, Alam warns that these are not isolated instances either. What is especially disturbing is that a battered women's shelter hotline should also double as a live-in maid service "hotline," where working conditions can lead to similar patterns of power and control as in spousal battery. In an attempt to make women economically self-sufficient, Apna Ghar may have inadvertently contributed to situations that had the potential to make women vulnerable to violence all over again.

However, even live-in servitude was not an option available to all women. Middle-class families do not want maids with children. What, then, happens to these mothers who cannot find jobs? An excerpt form my field notes reveals the case of Najma.

February 25th, late 1990s.
Kathy, our only White caseworker, relieved me at 6:00 P.M. We talked about the staff meeting held the previous evening that I could not attend. Only Nellie, Janet (the ED), and two caseworkers—Kathy and Vandana—were at the meeting. The meeting began with Nellie, the shelter supervisor, complaining about Najma, our Afghani resident. Najma, her husband, and children came to the United States as refugees. Now, seven years later, and with three children in tow, she had left her abusive husband. She was not eligible for benefits because she had been a refugee for over five years. She was Apna Ghar's difficult case because she did not speak English. She had never worked outside the home. The kids were deemed unruly and undisciplined. In two months time, she was supposed to learn English and get a job. All caseworkers complained constantly about Najma and her children, and Nellie was no different that evening. Janet finally had a helpful suggestion to make our work easier, "Well then, perhaps we should just send her back to Afghanistan." The other staff members became furious. Janet insisted that hers was the only viable solution.

April 5th, late 1990s.
Najma's stay in Apna Ghar had come to an end, and Nellie and Janet asked her to leave. We had not found housing for her, and Najma had nowhere to go. I climbed the staircase to her third floor room where she packed to say good-bye. I knocked and Alam, her oldest son, opened the door. I walked in and the middle child, Nausheen, began to cry. Quiet sobs racked her body, as she clung to my waist, with her face burrowed in my stomach. I clung to her too, not wanting her to see my face. She couldn't talk but only nodded at my empty words. I then turned to Najma. She burst into tears, as I stood there helplessly watching her face. She apologized for her children's raucous behavior in the shelter, "Sometimes I know they bother you. Sorry," she said tearfully. She had done everything Apna Ghar asked her to do, "You tell me take English class, I take. You tell me put baby in day care, I put." But now Apna Ghar was unwilling to find her housing. She tried finding housing in the vicinity of the shelter, but without a job and no money to make the security deposit, she had been unsuccessful. She cried some more and said, "Thank you for everything Sharmila. You and Sita have helped so much. Thank you very

much." And she began to sob. She stood at her doorway, crying. I turned and quietly walked down the stairs, feeling utterly helpless.

Najma was that "unworkable case" who was not eligible for welfare. She had no job skills and had never worked outside the home. In addition, Apna Ghar staff thought her three boisterous children were badly behaved. We had explicit instructions not to find subsidized housing for Najma. She was a "bad client" and would bring disrepute to Apna Ghar, which could result in other service agencies rejecting all our referrals, and we would not be able to find suitable housing for any other Apna Ghar resident. So we were not allowed to make any calls for Najma.

Najma would have taken any job she got. But that was not the case with Alushka, Apna Ghar's Bosnian refugee resident. Alushka wanted to pursue an education so that she may develop the skills needed for a better paying job. She had converted to Islam two to three years previously. She claimed that she fought in the war, yet never divulged what she did or when and how exactly she got to the United States. All we knew was that her four-year-old son Mikey was born here, and he was a citizen. When at the shelter, she attended Truman College for a course on psychology. She wanted to get an undergraduate degree. She did not want a job but instead wanted to concentrate on getting an education. Alushka wanted to educate herself with state aid.

Alushka's ambitions for herself and her strong determination, however, led her into many clashes with the Apna Ghar staff, and she was a "problem client." She had differences with the executive director, Janet, who always instructed Alushka the proper way to raise her son Mikey. Alushka had her own methods and countered Janet with her own parenting tips. Eventually, Janet came to think that Alushka had a borderline personality and needed institutionalization. She even investigated mental facilities so that Alushka might be admitted there. As Alushka's case manager, I was supposed to convey the news to her. I refused. Yet, Janet had made up her mind. She wanted to write Alushka up as a borderline personality in her file and throw her out of the shelter on that basis. In addition, Janet wanted the Department of Child and Family Services to investigate Alushka because she was ostensibly a bad mother to Mikey. The Apna Ghar staff collectively refused because we were unqualified to make psychological assessments. Eventually, Nellie, the shelter supervisor, and Janet, the director, arrived at a decision that suited them; Alushka would not be written up as a borderline personality, but she had to leave the next day. We would call Department of Human Services to pick her up.

Najma and Alushka were examples of problematic clients. They were perceived as such because of the lack of symbolic capital they carried, that is, speaking English and having worked outside the home and therefore already familiar with the double shift of work inside and outside the home. Najma especially had a difficult time in terms of adjusting to becoming a working mother, with three children the youngest of whom was just under three years of age. Moreover, the child had never been away from his mother, making his transition to day care especially complicated. In addition, both Najma and Alushka were seen as difficult clients because of their personalities—both women were seen as not complying with the rules set by the shelter. They were seen as incapable of maintaining a modicum of cleanliness in their bedrooms; unable to keep up everyday schedules; tardy in attending various workshops; and worse, being argumentative or incapable of taking "advice." They were also construed as having poor mothering skills. Bad clients were not only difficult to work with, but other agencies were sometimes known to have been displeased with being sent such women. They felt overburdened in these days of shrinking budgets.

Apna Ghar's Parenting Classes: Making Them American Mothers

Battered women were construed as having poor mothering skills. So Apna Ghar decided to have weekly, hour-long parenting classes. Whether they had adult offspring, or whether they were mothers or not, women had to compulsorily attend parenting classes. Any absences from the parenting classes had to be explained. Or, they needed advance permission from the director if they were going to miss a parenting session. I reproduce here details from the parenting classes.

June 17th, late 1990s.

Parenting Classes: Raising Children Without Violence.

The residents of Apna Ghar have been counseled since 5:30 P.M., and now at 6:30 P.M., they gear up for parenting classes that will last another hour. I meet Janet, the executive director, running back and forth between her office and the Xerox machine. She's trying to send off a grant proposal and mutters frequently that next time she will hire a grant writer. As I make small talk, Janet suddenly squints up at me and asks, "Now, did I give you permission to observe these parenting classes?" I'm startled by the suddenness of the question. "Yes. Three weeks ago you said it was fine by you. And besides, I've gotten Kathryn Hill's permission to observe her parenting classes."

"Yes. That's right. I don't want too many people running around Apna Ghar, but we'll make an exception for you."

Kathryn Hill, the White woman who runs the parenting classes, is petite and exudes tremendous energy. She arrived at the office even as I was waiting. Kat wore a light blue dress that ended at her knees. She formalized the outfit with a navy blue cotton jacket. Just under her messy, blonde hair glistened silver cat earrings. The pin on her lapel matched—it was one fat silver cat. "With a name like Kat its hard to avoid cat jewelry," she shrugged her round shoulders.

Today Janet has decided to sit in on Kat's classes. The women feel uncomfortable in her presence. In spite of Kat's attempts to ease the atmosphere with jokes, there's stiffness about the room that was not evident in previous sessions. Kat begins, "I'll merge two topics today. We'll talk about raising children without violence and raising children in a different country." She then goes to the board with a marker and asks women to list the differences between their own childhood and the lives of children today. She makes two columns—Then and Now. The women begin listing items, and soon the list looks like this:

Now	*Then*
1. Lack of respect	1. Respectful
2. Rowdy/independent	2. Quiet/obedient
3. Grow up fast	3. Stay child-like
4. Undisciplined	4. Disciplined
5. More responsibilities (or "more burdened" says Janet)	5. Carefree and protected
6. Aggressive	6. Passive

The women have drawn from memories of their own childhood to write up the past. Their childhood is idealized. As children they were respectful, quiet, obedient, and stayed child-like. They were disciplined but had no concern for the present or the future, because they were protected.

"In villages, hundreds of years ago, parenting was easy," Kat says. "You had your nuclear family and then you had a village full of relatives and other very close friends, and they all helped with raising kids. Things didn't change much too. What your father did for a living, your kids would do too. And so the rules of parenting were easily apparent." She notes that things began changing with technology. And societies began changing too. For example, she says, an older person might draw something very beautiful painstakingly by hand. He had the knowledge to reproduce a painting. "But with technology there are Xerox machines. A younger person might have this knowledge, and he would come and say 'why waste your time; just put the original in the Xerox machine and make copies faster and closer to the original.'" She explains that older, traditional ways of doing things become obsolete with technology, and while the younger person's suggestions might be construed as disrespectful, young people are only making sense of the world according to a new reality.

Kat continues that the world in America changes so fast that the parents cannot keep up with the changes themselves. So good child rearing, then, entails not imparting knowledge, but instead children should be taught skills on how to cope in a rapidly changing world. In her parenting skills classes every Wednesday, she would teach mothers how to work with their children. The old countries from where the women arrived were right in their own way, but in a new context, things had to be done differently. "And soon you will be raising good citizens," added Kat, as she closed off her introduction to today's classes. With this background Kat moves to the details of American parenting.

"In America, the baby sleeps alone in the crib, often times alone in its own room. Mother hears the infant through a listening device. And when the baby begins to crawl, it is allowed to roam and is not carried constantly." Janet and I are the only ones furiously taking notes. "This doesn't mean American mothers love their kids less, but instead they're training kids to become INDE-PENDENT," emphasizes Kat. "They don't carry babies, but instead they childproof the room so that the child can explore safely." In other countries, Kat adds, children are carried constantly to keep them out of harm's way. This maybe crucial for safety, but the child does not learn autonomy and become an independent thinker.

"In America people are taught to have a healthy disrespect—skepticism." Kat then points to the first item in the column marked "Now" on the board. The word is "disrespect." Kat says that the kids nowadays are not being dis-respectful; they're only expressing skepticism, which is a good American quality. "People have to think about new ideas or they can be taken over and lose their business. So kids need to be taught to be skeptical of ideas. Good parents know that questioning is thinking creatively." Kat pauses once again, and I try write down her words furiously. I know I've missed certain choice sentences, but this is all good material, I think, as my pen moves rapidly across the paper. "Creativity. Clear thinking. And implementation of ideas. This is the recipe for success in American society. Now lack of respect may just be a child having an idea, so don't get angry. Work with the child. A kid who gets hit doesn't learn anything. Kids need guidance. They need parents. They need discipline."

Kat asks us, "What is discipline?" After some silence Sameera says, "How to behave in society, at work or wherever." "Being responsible" adds Akosia. Then rapidly, more answers from all of us—correct behavior, teaching right from wrong, reward/punishment. Kat writes all these responses on the board. "Sometimes when people talk about discipline they're talking about punishment," says Kat. "But discipline means focusing and regulating behavior." She repeats these words once again, "focusing and regulating behavior. Punishment is only one way to focus and regulate behavior." The child should be taught self-discipline. Self-discipline is "finishing a job even when you don't want to," explains Kat. "Many of *us* are physically punished as children or as adults. Some of *you*, even if you hate it, have hit your children."

Kat explains the pros and cons of spanking: "spanking interrupts bad behavior, and it helps express anger. But you also hit in anger and you can very easily lose control." Janet interrupts, "Oh, you can spank without anger." The battered women in the shelter have told repeatedly, again and again in their various counseling sessions that beating is wrong, yet now the shelter director in the parenting classes tells them that spanking without anger is acceptable. Kat quickly adds, "Spanking should be done only if the kid is in danger. I mean, its better she's hit by you than hit by a car!" She explains that when hit, children learn to control behavior in the presence of their parents, but all hell breaks lose when their parents are not around. "Kids also learn that the parent strikes only because he or she is bigger which sends them the wrong message, and they can learn bad behavior." Kat adds that kids who get hit at home might get bullied more easily at school, or if they are big kids, then they might turn in to bullies themselves. With that Kat thinks she has gotten the final word. "Instead of spanking, reward good behavior," she ends.

Janet interjects, "Yeah, but what about asking the child to choose his own punishment? I remember when I was a child and I'd been bad, my mother would ask me to choose my own punishment for what I'd done wrong. I think that's very effective."

Kat disagrees, "The child may think that his actions were so wrong that he may give himself a punishment that far exceeds the crime."

"Yes, but don't you think the child develops an understanding of his wrong-doing?" challenges Janet. Kat doesn't pursue this, but continues her lecture.

Rewarding too, however, had its problems. "Children begin to expect bribes for their good behavior. So punishments and rewards are not effective tools for disciplining." What then, is a mother to do? Kat recommends what she calls "logical consequences." Every action has a consequence, and the parent lets the child know that there will be consequences for his or her bad behavior. So, the child has the option to follow up to avoid the consequences. Kat gives an example; you can tell the child that she has thirty minutes to pick up the toys, or else you will take away the toys and the child will not have those toys for the next twenty-four hours. Tami jumps in, "Yeah, but what if the kid keeps bugging you all day, asking you for those toys? How do you put up with it?"

"You don't give in," says Kat. "Focus on a single task. Choose a consequence. The consequence may be natural—for example, the child loses her gloves, then she has cold hands—or the consequence may be something we impose. Tell the kids the consequence. Be clear. Don't waver." Kat looks around the room once again, and makes her final point, "We ACT on the plan if the child does not do its job."

Janet doesn't look too happy. "Wait a minute now. I think this is fine, but how about giving the child some choices? You can either put away the toys in thirty minutes all by yourself, or have mom help you, or you don't get your toys at all for the next twenty-four hours? How about something like that?"

"Yes" agrees Kat "but you have to be careful that mommy doesn't put away all the toys and the kid doesn't do any work. The work has to be divided equally. Also, you have to be very clear about the choices. Sometimes when the child has too many choices it confuses him."

Even as Kat is finishing her words, Janet looks at her watch, and says, "It's past 7:30 P.M., and I think its time for all of us to leave. Can we end now?" The women immediately gather their things, and I don't fully catch Kat's concluding words. I walk back to my car with Akosia and Tami. I pack Tippoo into the car and drive down to Caryn's Rogers' Park apartment. I'll be in Madison by 8:00 A.M. Friday morning.

I see why Kat has merged together what I think are two vastly different topics—raising children in a new culture, and raising children without violence. A parent needs to teach the child self-discipline that is crucial for creativity, but this discipline should not be violent. Throughout her talk, Kat emphasized the "rugged" individual who will conquer the constantly changing modern world through self-generated new ideas alone. Gone are notions of cooperation and embeddedness in the social world—American society apparently does not require such commitments for individual success. All an individual needs is independent thinking, and she will be able to creatively pick out the choices a rapidly changing world throws in her direction.

Each time Kat described how children are raised in America, she implicitly juxtaposes the cultures of the women's countries of origin. These other cultures are ALL alike, standing in stark contrast to American Culture. The key difference is that Americans are creative, whereas others are not. The United States is constantly changing, requiring all of us to mold our selves to this constantly altering world. Kat assumed the Apna Ghar residents come from rural backgrounds instead of recognizing that these women mostly grew up in densely populated Asian cities.

This construction of the battered women's sending cultures and the women themselves as economically and culturally backward is not a new phenomenon; we see similar descriptions of Jewish, Italian, and southern European immigrant mothers. Elizabeth Ewen writes about immigrant Italian and Jewish women on the Lower East Side of New York City between 1890 and 1925. Social workers, she says, "complained of the old-world imprint on the ways in which mothers dressed, did house work, organized their days, gave birth, nursed children, went shopping, or participated in community life."[36] Social workers intruded into working class immigrants' lives to improve their social and economic conditions through Americanization. Americanization, as discussed in the penultimate chapter, implies the exchange of an originary nationality for a new one but was also something more. Americanization was also the initiation of people into an emerging industrial and consumer society.[37] These early-twentieth-century immigrants often came from agricultural backgrounds or small-scale industrial towns in Europe. Upon their arrival in the United States, they found themselves in a new universe, driven by large-scale production and mass consumerism. From leading agricultural lives patterned along rhythms established by nature, the logic of the New World was established by the industrial clock and the need for hard cash—clocking in and clocking out at textile mills, piece work at home, or work by the hour that went hand in hand with the expenses of purchased foods, manufactured clothes, and monthly rents.

In Apna Ghar, too, the logic of social work was not as simple as replacing a South Asian self with an American self, so much as aiding women to cope with late capitalism in the United States. Most Apna Ghar residents do not come from agricultural backgrounds as did early-twentieth-century immigrants. These late-twentieth-century immigrants arrive from thriving metropoles in South Asia. Here in the United States, they are inserted into the logic of late modernity that is qualitatively different from that which exists on the subcontinent. Hence, much of our efforts went into Americanizing Apna Ghar residents, in the sense of initiating them into a consumer, market-driven mass culture where success and upward mobility is mythically attributed to individual efforts alone. Kat implicitly described to us how we are inserted into late modernity in the United States. New ways of life, new ways of doing things, endless American highways on which endless streams of cars move back and forth. And numerous numbers to memorize—street addresses, telephone numbers, social security numbers, bank account numbers. Numbers and machines drive everything.

The parenting session begins to disintegrate as Janet and Kat develop differences on parenting. The executive director believes in corporal punishment, Kat does not. Though both women disagree, they are in complete agreement over the notion of choices. Even in disciplining, the American child has a range of options. The American child is taught, even through punishment, about free choice.

In Kat's world, American children are raised to deal with a rapidly changing world so that when they grow to be adults they have the capacity to cope with modernity. Conversely, does that mean immigrants are raised to be obedient, uncreative, and to "go with the flow"? Why does Kat cast these women as tradition-bound or unadventurous, despite the fact that they have traveled halfway across the world, leaving behind familiar worlds, willing to start anew? Given the life choices they have made, how can she still posit that they are raised in a "choice-less" world where they do not question tradition?

I came to realize that these parenting classes were not about raising American children; instead they were lessons about leading fundamentally different lives in an American world. Let me provide more details from the parenting classes.

American Life and the Importance of Time Management

How, Kat asked, does one make the time to do all the multifarious tasks that all Americans perform everyday? The answer, she said, lay in time management. I write about the first time I attended the parenting class, where women were taught about the importance of time management. The American world was driven by time, and as recent inserts into the American economy, immigrants needed to learn to structure their lives accordingly.

June 11th, late 1990s.

Parenting Classes: Time Management.

Kat's parenting classes began fifteen minutes late—around 6:45 P.M. She first introduced me to the women. Except for Zubeda and Sameera—the Indian and Pakistani Muslim women—I'd met all of them in the shelter before. Today's topic is time management. Kat paired the women—Zarina and Carol, Tami and Akosia, Sameera and Zubeda. Kat and I were observers. She then gave each of us two sheets. One was a blank sheet divided into twenty-four rectangles, each little segment representing one hour in the day. The next sheet had three lists. The first list consisted of tasks that had to be done everyday, and looked like this:

1. Prepare meals
2. Serve breakfast
6. Pick up clutter
7. Take kids to school
11. Job
12. Make beds

3. Serve lunch	8. Pick kids from school	13. Play with children
4. Serve dinner	9. Commute to work	14. Spend time with spouse
5. Do the dishes	10. Commute home	15. Sleep

The second list looked like this:

a. Laundry	e. School meeting	i. Doctor appointment
b. Phone calls	f. Grocergy store	j. Clean kitchen
c. Clean bathroon	g. Clean floors	k. Dust
d. Pay bills	h. Help a friend	l. Shopping (not for food)

The third list, labeled "disaster list" consisted of the following items:

Sick child	Major holiday	No car or bus
Broken appliance	House guests	Oversleep
Snow storm	Child's birthday	

The women are supposed to schedule in one day all fifteen tasks from the first list, fit in at least three items from the second list, and include at least one item from the "disaster list" into their imaginary daily schedules. Almost immediately Tami pipes up, her voice laden with amusement, "We don't need to worry about item 14, do we Akosia?" Akosia looks down to her sheet and bursts into raucous laughter. Item 14 on the first list: "Spend time with spouse." Soon we are all laughing at the suggestion that battered women in a shelter spend more time with their spouses. Kat gets all flustered at her faux pas and asks us to delete that item off the list. I put a neat line across item 14.

Soon I hear Sameera whisper to Zubeda in a panic, in Urdu, *"Arre! Kya karoon? Humein bacchein nahin hain!* What do we do? We don't have children!"* Kat asks them to pretend they have children just for today. Then Sameera begins giggling and talking more in Urdu, "I don't have kids, but I used to have in-laws in the house. Other than my husband, there were five other people in the house, and I did all the work." As she ends, her voice is a bit resentful. "Ooof oh!" exclaims Zubeda, exasperated at all these issues Sameera is raising. Just pretend they are not with you. This is, after all, America." As they begin filling out the sheet, they realize that prayers have not been included on the daily schedule. As Muslim women, they pray five times a day. This schedule did not accommodate their religious needs. Sameera writes in a neat cursive hand, "Clean up, get ready for prayers, and pray" in the 6:00 to 7:00 A.M. box.

Soon they realize they have no idea what time children go to school or what time school lets out. Are they part-time workers or full-time workers in this world of make-believe? Tami points out that without a partner, she will have to work full time and still won't be able to make ends meet. The two South Asian women, on the other hand, valiantly decide to be part-time workers and full-time mothers. Day care does not figure in their schema of the world.

The session ends at 8:00 P.M. Kat is sheepish because we were talking about time management, and she had gone overtime by almost an hour. Meanwhile, Akosia's 9-year-old daughter and Tami's three children are waiting for their mothers to return so they may have dinner and then go to bed. The women quickly rush out, except for Zubeda and Sameera. This is their first class with Kat, and they needed to fill in some paperwork. Both Zubeda and Sameera have undergraduate degrees in their countries of origin. While Zubeda complains how useless this education has been, Sameera interjects, "No. We can get jobs. I used to work outside in Pakistan."

Soon after, Sameera begins talking of her abuse. "The things he's done to me, I can't tell you. How can anyone treat their wife like that?" she asks, looking at our faces. "I could not stand it, and so I took sleeping pills. I was in the hospital for four days. He cried so much. I forgave him and went back. But that was not the end of it." Her husband tried other means to get rid of her. He kept all her jewelry and clothes and dropped her off at the airport with a one-way ticket to Pakistan. He promised her she would return in a couple of months. Perhaps seeing her family might be good for her health. Sameera believed him. When she was in Pakistan, he never returned any of her calls and never wrote to her. "How much I loved him. I wrote poetry to him almost everyday," Sameera said, smiling slightly. Then, with the help of her lawyer brother and a friend of theirs here in the United States, Sameera returned. She came to Apna Ghar directly.

Zubeda began her story, "Yesterday, as I was changing in the bathroom, he came in. I got so scared I wanted to scream. But no sound was emerging from my throat. He finally left." Fearing for her safety, she packed her bags and walked out of her house at 2:00 A.M. "There was no one on the roads, and it was cold. The DHS finally came and picked me up."

"Were you able to sleep?" I asked quietly.

"No. I sat in their lobby all night until 10:00 this morning when Laila [Apna Ghar worker] came to pick me up. But I don't know why, I'm not feeling sad. A woman should feel sad, right, when she leaves her home? Then why am I not feeling sad? I don't feel anything." I told her that was normal, but in two to three days she might get very depressed and cry a lot. Kat too added that because of Zubeda's very precarious situation, her body had probably pumped in too much adrenaline and in couple of days she might be overwhelmed with exhaustion.

"He never thought I would leave. But here I am. He is shocked" smiled Zubeda. "I have not changed my clothes and I haven't washed since last night. I am tired."

It was 8:45 P.M. We turned off the lights in the office. Zubeda, Sameera, and I walked toward the shelter house where I'd parked my car and left my Tippoo in the backyard. "Try make friends with a large network of women," I urged. "You shouldn't depend on just one person but instead have a whole community of friends who will care for you and be there for you in times of trouble." As we exited into the blustery evening, Sameera grabbed my hand and said earnestly, "You're a good person. I wish we could be friends for life." We held hands desperately, believing that we could truly be friends for life.

After dinner with my Chicago friends, I headed north to Madison. Tired, I pulled into a rest stop to nap so I wouldn't fall asleep at the wheel. Two hours later, still tired but nervous about being in an isolated place late in the night, I resumed driving. At 2:30 A.M. the next day I reached home. The dogs in the apartment building began barking and my Tippoo wagged his tail in response. Shortly I lay in my dog-hair-filled bed. As I fell asleep, I wondered at the possibilities for friendships and communities that last a lifetime.

This text I reproduce here, on the surface, talks solely about how to conduct the various tasks involved in everyday American living. At a deeper level, it also reveals gender/class realities and draws our attention to the ways in which American life is uniquely structured. While the lists of daily tasks—going to the grocery store, snow storm, taking children to school, picking up children from school, commuting to work, commuting home—may seem innocuous, these are phenomena that are uniquely American in many South Asian women's eyes. Most grocery stores are corner stores in large South Asian cities. Or, vegetable vendors sell their wares on the streets or in carts. Large shopping malls, with aisles and aisles of prepackaged foods are an American phenomenon for these immigrant women.

Upon reading the list of tasks to be accomplished in a single day, Sameera panicked, "What do we do? We don't have any children!" For a woman with no children, pretending to have children is ludicrous enough, but what is new to many of these women is wage labor outside the home. Quite a few South Asian women, like Zubeda, do not venture out of the house to engage in wage labor. Issues such as commuting to work may not arise for many of them. Yet, having said that, I recognize that many women of working class backgrounds have jobs outside the home—worsening economies in South Asian countries necessitate dual-earning families. Sameera herself worked outside her parental home in Pakistan. Many dual-earning families, however, rely on parents, grandparents, uncles, aunts—extended family—and neighbors to provide unpaid labor for childcare. Children often walk home from school or take the bus back with other neighborhood children; at home, women of the extended family or neighbor women help with childcare until their mother returns from work.

Sameera indicated the nature of South Asian families when she said that her husband's parents and brothers lived with them. Many South Asian shelter residents do not come from nuclear families as these parenting classes presume but from extended families. Hence, the tasks involved in everyday living are rather different for these women than for most other American women. Parenting classes, then, teach immigrant women the differences between South Asia and the United States and how to make an independent life here in the United States. Women are asked to take on double shifts, working in the formal economy, and then engaging in the task of reproducing home and family. The double shift is normalized.

Battered Women and Their Immigration Status

Prior to 1986, when an American citizen or legal permanent resident married a foreigner, the spouse was granted permanent residency fairly quickly. However, amid concerns of fraudulent marriages, the Congress passed the Immigration Marriage Fraud Amendments in 1986 that changed the procedures for obtaining citizenship through marriage. The married couple now has to wait for two years during which the foreigner spouse is considered a conditional resident. After the two-year period, the U.S. citizen or legal permanent resident has to petition for the conditional resident spouse.[38] If the marriage dissolves during the conditional residency period, noncitizen spouses can lose residency and become deportable illegal aliens. On the other hand, if the marriage lasts the two-year period, both husband and wife undergo personal interviews with the Immigration and Naturalization Service (INS). If convinced of the legitimacy of the marriage, the INS will confer permanent residency to the immigrant, dependent spouse.

Sameera and Zubeda talked about their immigration status. As a citizen of the United States, Zubeda was able to obtain permanent residency for her husband. Once all legal matters regarding immigration were settled, her husband began abusing her. Sameera's case was just the opposite; her husband, an American citizen, had married her in Pakistan. She was now a conditional resident but believed she needed to stay on in the marriage to prove to INS authorities hers was a genuine marital union and not just a green card sham marriage. Women conditional residents, as Sameera, are at risk for abuse because of their position as dependent immigrants. They are dependent on their permanent resident or citizen husbands for petitioning the INS to convert their status into permanent residency. As part of this the petition process, the women need to provide evidence that they entered their marriages in good faith (i.e., not for the sole purposes of immigration). Immigrant women, many who are conditional residents, are put in a particularly vulnerable position if and when domestic violence begins. For example, Michelle Anderson discusses the case of Sue, a Chinese woman who obtained conditional residency upon marrying an American citizen:

> Sue's husband repeatedly beat her. "You do exactly as I say, or I'll call Immigration," he warned, kicking her in the neck and face. "You need me."' Sue feared she would not live. "Her story is typical of the battered immigrant women we see," explains Beckie Masaki, executive director of San Francisco's Asian Women's Shelter. "The batterer uses his citizenship to control and humiliate his wife." Peggy Eng, founder of the New York Asian Women's Shelter, concurs, "Batterers invariably use the threat of deportation as a weapon in the abuse of their alien wives.'"[39]

To deal with precisely such dependency and potential abuse, the House Judiciary Committee on Immigration, Refugees and International Law held a hearing on domestic violence in marriages between American citizens and foreigners in 1989. Representative Louise M. Slaughter introduced a bill that passed in 1990, whereby, if the conditional resident could prove battery and extreme cruelty, she or he could file for a waiver during the two-year waiting period.[40] Yet, in situations of battery, the onus of proving abuse falls upon the immigrant woman.

For instance, Sameera thought there was no possible means for her to obtain residency in the United States other than through her husband. She had no inkling of the Violence Against Women Act, 1994 (VAWA) that allows her to petition for permanent residency independent of her abusive spouse.[41] In addition, she needed to prove abuse so that she may be deemed a legitimate candidate for citizenship under VAWA. She could prove violence if she provided evidence of abuse either through police records, orders of protection, hospital records, and testimonies of social workers or workers in shelters. Women like Sameera—who often have inadequate English language skills and few means of negotiating every day living in the United States, let alone an understanding of the American judicial system and immigration authorities—also have to prove that they entered into their marriages in good faith. Finally, they must prove that they cannot return back to their ostensibly "culturally backward" home country because of the severe social/economic/political sanctions they will necessarily face for walking out of a marriage.

Concluding Comments

Zubeda and Sameera saw similarities in their situations. Having left abusive marriages and also their community, on whom will they rely to make a life for themselves? A life devoid of community is inconceivable to them. I wax eloquent on the importance of large networks of friends who can provide support when things start to fall apart in our lives. I ask them not to depend on primordial community but to form new ones with people they meet in their everyday lives. Arriving from similar geographical locations but entering Apna Ghar for different purposes—she for escaping abuse and me for research purposes—Sameera hopes that she and I can form some community. She grabs my hand and smiles at me saying, "I like you. I wish we could be friends for life." I return her smile as I hold her hand tightly, truly believing at that moment we will always be in each other's lives.

But as I leave Chicago and drive back to Madison, I wonder at the possibilities for remaking meaningful community that transcends distances imposed by the ever-changing economies of late modernity. Where will Sameera be a year from now, I wonder. And where will I be located? Given the uncertainties of our geographical coordinates, our transience as immigrants, our lack of roots, what will it take to form communities in the late-twentieth-century United States?[42] Sameera and I no longer are present in each other's lives except as memories. We could perhaps not transcend our class locations that structured our choices and our own personal trajectories in this world. But what of the caseworkers, women who came from the similar class backgrounds? In the following chapter I write of the caseworkers at Apna Ghar.

Three

Workers at Apna Ghar

Introduction

Apna Ghar, to reiterate, understood that violence was a social phenomenon rather than an individual malady. As a result, they had two intervention strategies; first, they urged women to leave their abusers and become autonomous individuals. In the previous chapter, I focused on how Apna Ghar attempted to make immigrant battered women independent. Their second intervention, because they recognized the social origins of domestic violence, was addressing gender paradigms in South Asian American communities. As a result, they tried to politicize South Asian American women in an effort to build a larger social movement. A major way by which women got politicized was through their involvement at the shelter either as workers or as volunteers. In this chapter, I focus on these women who engaged in emotion labor at the shelter home for almost forty hours per week. Almost all of them were first- and second-generation Indians, except for one second-generation Pakistani and one White midwestern worker. Through participant observation and informal interviews, I illuminate the meanings these women derived from their work and their transformations through their engagement at Apna Ghar. Despite their desires, I show they were unable to make community with women having similar racial and class backgrounds.

Shelter Workers at Apna Ghar

The four older first-generation women—Arati, Tasleem, Nellie, and Parvati—worked at Apna Ghar for purely economic purposes. Arati and Tasleem were unmarried. Arati had earned a master's degree in education from Harvard in the late 1960s and then came to the University of Chicago, where she was employed for a couple of years. She returned to India in the mid-1970s to work as a school principal in the Central School System (a system of state run schools located in various Indian towns). As an Indian government employee, she was transferred from one town to another every three years. Under these conditions, she could not establish any community ties and felt lonely. In addition, she felt she was wasting her time in these small backwater Indian towns. She thought she deserved more in life. So she applied for permanent residency at the New Delhi U.S. Consulate and came to the United States for the second time, now in the early 1980s. She worked in Chicago at Truman College as an assistant director for adult education. She lived comfortably but began missing her extended Indian family. So she went back to India once again in the late 1980s. She bought a house in Delhi and started various businesses with the money she had earned in the United States. These businesses failed, and she lost her savings. She then returned to Chicago a third time, now in 1992 and as an older worker. She could not find suitable employment and lived in subsidized housing in the uptown area. For employment, she babysat for a University of Chicago professor. Arati soon heard of Apna Ghar and applied for a job as a shelter worker. Because she had been involved in socially relevant work in India previously, she felt especially qualified to perform similar tasks here in the United States. Arati began work at the shelter.

Now in her late sixties, she was dissatisfied with her job at Apna Ghar and looked for alternative employment. Arati felt burnt out and bore resentment toward the battered women at the shelter. She urged them to get their lives together and move on, just as she had. She got annoyed with the children; their noisy games and tearful arguments grated on her nerves. In our brief interactions as we relieved each other at shift changes, she often shook her head in exhaustion, exclaiming, "These people, I tell you! They try my patience so much. I just want to go home."

Unlike Arati, Tasleem was reluctant to share her life story with me. All I gathered was that she owned a house in suburban Chicago and was having difficulty making her mortgage payments. Tasleem had worked in Apna Ghar for the past four years and was also burnt out. She often forgot to perform little tasks around the shelter and was frequently reprimanded by the shelter supervisor and executive director for her laxity. Despite her emotional exhaustion, Tasleem cared immensely for the women residents at the shelter. The women's individual issues became her cause as she argued with her supervisors on their behalf, often getting into trouble herself. In addition, Tasleem concerned herself with maintaining the proper "ethnic" atmosphere at the shelter. She especially worried about the charity food items we received at Apna Ghar. She would interject in staff meetings, "Please, please one more thing. Please do not get those sand-wiches with egg and bread. The eggs have pork in them and we have Muslim clients. They eat pork without knowing, and it is against their religion. If some Muslim leaders hear about it, they will really make a huge hue and cry about it." At this point, other caseworkers would override her objections, saying we had women of all racial/religious backgrounds, and if the Muslim women did not want to eat the pork/egg sandwiches, others would. Moreover, some case-workers would point out that many Muslim women at the shelter had pulled out the pork from the eggs and microwaved the sandwich for dinner for them-selves and their children. In this manner, Tasleem's concerns were often silenced.

Nellie was the shelter supervisor. She had arrived into the United States just a few months earlier to join her second-generation Indian American husband. Nellie was originally from the western coastal state of Goa. She had worked for numerous years in Bombay as a social worker with children and women. Her employment at the shelter caused an uproar among shelter staff initially; her qualifications were not in question, but shelter staff balked at her religion. Nel-lie was Catholic. "This is a South Asian shelter," Arati had complained, "why do we have to hire someone in such a prominent position especially when she has a foreign [meaning non-Hindu] name?" Nellie however was hired and super-vised these very women who had earlier objected to her employment.

Another first-generation woman, Parvati, was a single mother and an abuse survivor herself. She was an Apna Ghar resident two years previously, and while there, she began searching for employment. Perpetually short of staff and impressed by Parvati's competence, Apna Ghar offered her a job as a shelter worker. Work at Apna Ghar had multiple meanings for Parvati. She felt she con-nected with the shelter's South Asian residents because she related to their experiences at a deeply personal level. She offered her life as an example to oth-ers who were in position similar to her situation a few years earlier. Parvati, how-ever, resented having to work with the African American shelter residents. She expressed they were troublemakers, creating a difficult work environment for her. Though she felt immense solidarity with South Asian abuse survivors, she was incapable of developing empathy for African American survivors and often expressed open hostility toward them in our conversations.

I was the fifth first-generation worker. I arrived at Apna Ghar as a volunteer because I wanted to be involved in politically relevant work as I conducted field research among Indian immigrants in Chicago. My earlier plans for my disser-tation had been to interview Indian American mothers and daughters—first-and second-generation immigrant women—to understand the centrality of gender in making home and community here in the United States. As I conducted my

interviews with Indian American mothers and daughters, I thought I would volunteer at Apna Ghar because I had naively perceived this shelter as a space
where I could practice my feminist politics as I aided battered women reconstitute their lives as survivors. Within two days of my volunteering at Apna
Ghar, a worker got fired. I was hired to replace her. I soon abandoned my
earlier research plans and narrowed my field site to Apna Ghar, because the
stories I gathered here provided far more compelling evidence on race/class/
gender practices than my interviews with middle-class Indian immigrants.

Most of us first-generation workers, with the exception of Parvati, had master's degrees. We occupied middle- to lower–middle-class positions. Nellie was
married, and being in a dual-income household, her economic status was reasonably secure. Tasleem, Arati, and Parvati's class positions, however, were not
much better off than many of the women who came to live at the shelter.
Tasleem and Arati were in their fifties and sixties respectively, and this job as
caseworkers was the best they could hope for as "unskilled," older workers in
the late-twentieth century American economy. Parvati was a single mother with
a ten-month-old daughter. She had previously worked as an assembly line
worker and then at the checkout counter of a large grocery store in Devon, the
South Asian business neighborhood in Chicago. Parvati had no marketable
labor skills, but as an abuse survivor herself, her work at Apna Ghar was invaluable. My class position, on the other hand, was in transition. My father is a surgeon in India, and growing up there, I derived numerous class privileges
through him. While I carried the symbolic capital of being raised in an upper-
middle-class family, my status as an international student in the United States
and lack of funding made my economic status during fieldwork tenuous.

In addition to the first-generation workers were the second-generation workers from various parts of the Midwest. They all had undergraduate degrees and
were planning to continue graduate studies. All these second-generation women
were in their early twenties and came from privileged class backgrounds with
parents employed as professionals. Vandana, like many other middle-class
second-generation Indian Americans, wanted to become a doctor.[1] She had just
graduated from a large midwestern university and worked at Apna Ghar while
she applied to various medical schools around the country. Other than being
involved in socially relevant matters, she felt this job would make her curricu-
lum vitae more impressive and make her application more competitive, thus
increasing her chances of admission into medical school.

Unlike Vandana, most other second-generation women at Apna Ghar
rejected their familial career expectations of them and instead sought careers
as social workers or counselors.[2] They saw themselves as being engaged in
socially useful work that was very gratifying to them. Sita, for example, had just

completed her undergraduate degree in a private midwestern university. She wanted to be involved in social work before she embarked on a professional master's degree in counseling psychology. With good grades and letters of recommendation from the executive director and the shelter supervisor, she was accepted with full funding in a Chicago school.

Asha, another second-generation Indian American, was an undergraduate in public health at another private midwestern university. In an interview, I asked her why she worked at Apna Ghar. She described that when she was a junior in high school she had gone through the forty-hour domestic violence training at Apna Ghar with an older woman she knew. "Trainings are pretty intense" Asha described. "Like four Saturdays in a row, from 9:00 in the morning to 6:00 at night. And I learnt a lot. So I think I continued. . . . I'd heard of a few cases in our community and I just wanted to help out."

"So how old were you when you began volunteering," I asked.

Asha replied, "I was sixteen. Yeah! I worked all through high school in Apna Ghar for two years. Then when I left I worked at another shelter in Charles Town [a smaller central Illinois town]. A Woman's Place. And you know, it was so funny, because I said, 'Yeah I have some shelter experience. I worked at Apna Ghar.' And that lady . . . wanted me in right away. Apna Ghar had a good rep. Maybe it still does. I was away for four years and then . . . they needed someone for this time."

I questioned Asha why she got involved in shelter work at such a young age. Did she see herself as a feminist, and did her political convictions motivate her? She disagreed emphatically, and then continued with a passionate voice, "I mean, a feminist is such a . . . potent word, isn't it? Its like, loaded. But like, I know my brother is a feminist. I don't know if he'd ever describe himself as that. I wouldn't say I was a feminist, and thus I wanted to work in Apna Ghar. It was just . . . I was aware of issues probably earlier than a lot of kids." Whatever her larger political passions, Asha was at Apna Ghar because she believed she could help battered South Asian immigrant women make changes in their lives. She said, "I feel that the shifts are crazy. Twelve hours is not a joke. It takes me a while to get to the city. But at the end of the day I feel like I did something. Its satisfying."

Another second-generation worker, Anita, described herself: "I'm 22 years old. I have a bachelor's degree in mathematics. I took a women's studies class and that made a big difference. And since then, it's been very important for me to do something about the status of women in society." Largely because she saw herself as a feminist, Anita worked at the shelter. She explained:

I guess being a feminist you're aware of a lot of issues. You look around and realize, wow, it's awful. It's up to us to change the world. We can't change it all, but making at least some people's lives better is important. There's also desire in me to feel needed. I guess I chose Apna Ghar because I knew about it through people I met. My mother volunteered here. I met you (laughs). I think it's a very good organization because it meets women's needs. I didn't necessarily want to work only with South Asian women, but I felt like they're looking for Indian staff here and I felt like I could get a job here even if I didn't have qualifications. I perhaps would not have been hired elsewhere.

"So, do you think you make a difference here?" I inquired.

Anita shook her head and replied, "I can't really say I've made a difference. I've worked here, maybe, a month. That's not a very long time. I don't think I personally have made a difference. One of the things I've done the most (laughter) is childcare. I still think its better to work here than in a corporation, where you don't care about anyone else but yourself. Its selfish." Anita knew that with her qualifications she could easily get a higher paying job. She graduated from a prestigious midwestern private university and yet received $7.00 per hour as wages. "My fourteen-year-old cousin makes $5.50 in his summer job, and I realize I'm not doing that much better you know," she said, shaking her head in disbelief. She wanted to live on her own, but could not afford to move out of her parents' home. Being engaged in socially and politically relevant work has its price, and Anita was willing to accept that. But she was often torn, "I mean, having a low-paying job means less pay. And you need to give up things like Starbucks Coffee" she chuckled. "Seriously, it's hard to give up luxuries. Then I ask myself—how important are these luxuries in the long run? There's other needs that working here meets. I feel I am doing relevant work here."

Anita's father objected to her working at Apna Ghar. He constantly nagged her to learn computer programming so that she could earn more money "instead of being a Mother Teresa." She laughed once again. I asked her whether working at Apna Ghar had changed her. "Yes," she replied, "I've learnt a lot. But the thing that's interesting is that Indian men react really strongly to it. My dad says that Apna Ghar destroys families. And I'm like, oh my god! What are you saying? Its not that he condones violence, but he does not know the reality and thinks we are just making it all up."

I asked Anita how she felt as a shelter worker. She replied, "Sometimes I feel pretty good. The kids come and hug me; women come and talk to me. And there's a feeling of connection. But at other times its just menial work. That is hard—is this all I'm supposed to do?" she often asked herself. "Like the other day, all I did was putting away food, and cleaning the fridge. I'm not against menial work, you know. But when people ask me—what do you do? And I'm like—I'm smart. What am I wasting my life for? I mean there are selfish reasons too. I want to do nonprofit work later. This is good experience. But how do I feel about doing these mundane tasks?" Anita was conflicted—work at Apna Ghar was turning out to be less than what she expected. Though this worried her, she still received some emotional gratification by working at Apna Ghar because she felt she can make a difference in women's lives.

Reena, our fifth shelter worker, majored in women's studies at a private midwestern university and wanted to be involved with Apna Ghar because she considered herself a feminist activist. She told herself she'd "be able to serve the best here, since I know more about South Asian families and how they work." However, she voiced that she was definitely not the feminist she was when she first started work. "Why?" I asked. "Oh, I don't know" replied Reena, but continued with much more emotion:

> I've been in feminist organizations in college, pretty much. And there's a definite spirit to it, maybe because we're so young, I don't know. But we were trying to start a Women's Center. So we put a tent in our commons and just sat there. You know, we questioned and changed things. Whereas here [Apna Ghar] it's just kind of like—we don't do much. I think you'd said this before. I thought a lot about what you'd said before, about how we don't empower the women? Did you say that? Its kind of true.

Reena added that power was an issue in the shelter. Often, working at the shelter just meant enforcing rules on battered women: "We don't want people to break the rules. Because then it does get kind of . . . it does get pretty annoying once somebody breaks the rules. And then everybody else asks—why do they get to break the rules? Or it creates a big mess somehow. But then it becomes a power issue, and the last thing these women need to face is somebody trying to get more power over them. I think it is just kind of hard to . . . to always understand what these women are going through." Reena wished she had been better prepared for the realities of working in the shelter, because it "was really hard to start out here not knowing anything about anything. I had the forty-hour training, yet I had no idea that they would react to me. It was hard at first to get used to this really paranoid behavior from them. From the clients. I wish I had been better prepared for that. And just about how things work around here as a house."

"So do you feel you are ineffective in Apna Ghar?" I asked Reena. She hesitated.

> My big goal was I thought . . . just to make these women feel good about themselves. And that takes a lot of time. I mean, hoping for results in just two months is really, really (slight laughter in voice) unrealistic. And I guess for me that is hard because you wish that you got a lot more rewards working

here because it's tough a lot of the time, and it's . . . I don't know. Its nice when
. . . it's really awesome when clients think you really helped them. Because
then you feel like, oh good! I'm actually doing this for someone else. Its actually working.

In addition to power issues between workers and abuse survivors, Reena
felt extremely disempowered by the way caseworkers treated each other or by
the way supervisors treated caseworkers. Often, staff meetings turned into sessions where people blamed each other for things that went wrong in the shelter. "There's major power/control issues going on at the staff meetings," she
noted. Instead of being supportive staff meetings further divided the staff.
The supervisor and director picked on individuals who got verbally flogged in
front of their co-workers. Such public humiliation worked as a disciplinary
tool, pushing workers to impose rules on battered women they thought to be
coercive and intrusive on their privacy. Reena felt she could not disagree with
her supervisors on any of the policies the shelter instituted. She monitored her
interactions with battered women to a far greater extent when the shelter
supervisor, Nellie, was at the shelter home. She felt powerless in her presence
and deferred major decisions to her. Reena explained: "When I'm on shift here
and she's [Nellie] here, I don't deal with the clients that much. I'm not sure
(hesitation in voice) . . . maybe it's just me . . . even if I say something she has
the final say on how to handle a situation."

Despite the many problems they voiced regarding the shelter, many second-
generation South Asian American women thought they were doing something
different compared with other South Asian youth. Even Sita, whose primary
motivation in working at Apna Ghar was to appear more competitive in her
counseling psychology program, knew she did not want the classic middle-
class South Asian American career route of computer engineering or medical
school. She instead chose counseling psychology as a vocation because she
wanted to intervene in the lives of South Asian families here in the United
States to facilitate the process of immigration. These young women clearly felt
a responsibility as *South Asian American women* and wanted to make a contri-
bution to the communities from which they originated.

Though Asha did not see herself as a feminist, she found immense satisfaction in trying to change gender relations in her community because she felt her
work contributed to women's empowerment. For Anita and Reena who defined
themselves as feminists, involvement in Apna Ghar gave them a sense of power
because they were no longer recipients of normative South Asian/American
gender ideologies; they felt they intervened in creating alternatives to existing
paradigms. Engagement with Apna Ghar gave them a sense of achievement, a

feeling of not being passive receivers but instead powerful agents in working toward a more equitable world. Anita persisted in working at Apna Ghar against paternal objection. She refused to accept her father's version of South Asian American family life. When he expressed skepticism regarding domestic violence, she disagreed with him, for work in Apna Ghar had revealed to her the realities of some immigrant women's everyday lives. Though she missed the advantages that accompany a better-paying job, her involvement in Apna Ghar made her feel part of a "caring community." She felt less selfish and got immense satisfaction in her engagement with what she perceived to be "real" social issues. She believed that if she wanted the world to be a better place, she had to take responsibility both as a woman and as a South Asian. She wanted to change the world, if not for all people, then at least for a few women.

Reena described herself as a feminist but perceived herself to be far less effective in Apna Ghar than in the feminist organization at her university. She had joined Apna Ghar with the hopes of bringing her feminist politics into her racial community—melding what she perceived to be her "nonracial" political part and her "racial" part—but she felt unable to do so. By working at Apna Ghar, she felt she was losing her political identity. Instead of empowering women, she observed that as a caseworker she imposed all kinds of strictures on battered women. She did not want, for example, to check up on the women's rooms to see if they were clean. She did not want to check on women and reprimand them for not feeding their children on time or not bathing them, but as a worker she had no choice but to obey work orders from the supervisor and executive director. She was uncomfortable with the power she exercised over the residents at Apna Ghar, because by doing so, she felt she contributed to their further disempowerment. To make matters worse, unlike at the university, she could not create any ties of solidarity with her South Asian co-workers at Apna Ghar. She felt alienated and isolated. Though she was part of a group of South Asian women working on issues of violence within their communities, she felt no solidarity with these women. Being involved in South Asian women's activism, then, disempowered her instead of rejuvenating her politics. She expressed acute disappointment in Apna Ghar's capacity to empower battered women. When work at the shelter disempowered even educated, middle-class feminists like her, how could it hope to empower battered, working-class women?

Apna Ghar wanted to politicize gender norms within South Asian American families but remained unable to do so because of the ways in which it operated. Rather than building community, as it initially desired, the shelter inadvertently shattered it. Volunteers and workers came to Apna Ghar so that they could meet others with similar politics and work together in changing gender paradigms within their communities. Yet, they paradoxically felt disempowered through their engagement with domestic violence intervention work. The reason is that though Apna Ghar is an ethnic shelter meant to provide alternative gender paradigms, care work at the shelter was commercialized, which was not conducive to it operating as a free space. This discrepancy in the initial objectives and subsequent disappointment occurred because the aspirations the women brought with them and the expectations the shelter had of its volunteers and workers to conduct themselves as professionals were antithetical to each other. As workers we were irredeemably transformed, but the professional ethos of the shelter did not allow any spaces to develop where we could share with each other how we'd been transformed and what these transformations meant for us as workers, and as South Asian American women. By closing off these spaces, Apna Ghar inadvertently closed off spaces where we could make community, and moreover, they unintentionally depoliticized domestic violence intervention work.

Channeling Stories of Violence, Providing Service to Clients

In her ethnography of a shelter she names South Coast, Loseke writes that clients were not allowed to talk about good times they had in the past with their abusive partners:

> It was written nowhere but agreed upon by all workers: women must remain focused on "why they were in this place." This was a rule about talk. Inside South Coast there were only three approved topics of conversation: How bad had life been with the partner, how good life would be without him, and how to achieve this better life. Of course, when clients talked among themselves they would cover a range of topics; they would talk positively about aspects of their past lives, and about their aspirations for reconciliation with their partners. But when a worker entered a room such talk would stop. At one time this disjuncture caused a real problem when clients petitioned workers to allow them to talk about "something other than our problems." Workers held firm. South Coast was a place for women to achieve independence; doing so required that they remain focused on why they were there, and what they must do to achieve the goal of independence.[3]

Apna Ghar, likewise, legislated the terms under which the abuse survivors could speak, and the formats, spaces, and timings in which they could narrate their lives. Quite often, immigrant women's survival narratives, told in broken English and with a liberal sprinkling of Hindi/Urdu, were channeled through individual sessions with White, middle-class counseling interns from Chicago universities who often did not understand the women's native tongues and had very little idea of their cultural backgrounds. In addition, survival narratives were to be raised in art classes, conversation classes, or group counseling. Attendance at these evening classes was mandatory. Every evening, right after work and picking up children from school, Apna Ghar residents had to be at the main office gearing up for some session or the other. They had no choice but to spend at least a couple of hours every evening talking about abuse, being coached on how to cope in the world, and how to raise children. They grew weary of these sessions and returned to the house from the main office, exhausted, but having to face hungry children who still needed to complete homework.

Residents frequently spoke with caseworkers at the shelter home. After dinner, with the children tucked in bed, the caseworker on duty and shelter residents might sit in the living room—as dirty laundry churned in the washer in the basement—and share life stories. These late night rap sessions began with much laughter and fun, followed by one inane joke after the other, and then turned into heart-rending exchanges where we shared life stories of pain and pleasure and compared notes on how to cope with various problems. Battered clients and caseworkers cried together, gave each other advice, and provided support for each other. Then once the residents went to bed, we workers stayed up and took notes on what had transpired. As caseworkers, part of our job was to listen to stories of violence and record these painful stories we had heard in the daily log. These emotionally charged moments that meant so much would now be written up in a suitable format so that we may pass on "information" to our co-workers.

While it was essential for all workers to know about the situations of each shelter resident, many workers found the clinical nature of reproducing these stories abhorrent. Because efficiency was imperative, we had no choice but to use sterile language to write about our interactions. The intensity of sharing, crying together, empathizing with the shelter residents was translated into barren data, indicating hours of "informal counseling." Using this sort of language made us feel like we were writing lies. In addition to retelling stories devoid of the context in which they were told, we were also supposed to record the length of these exchanges. When the executive director wrote up Apna Ghar's grants, we could account for extensive hours of informal counseling we provided to battered women. "2668 hours of counseling for women and children," proclaims the Apna Ghar informational brochure. I knew the endless hours I had spent with women at the shelter talking about our lives were now included in that cold figure, a number that conveyed nothing of the sharing, bonding, arguing, laughing, crying that went on in that three-story house almost every evening. The intense emotional bonding between caseworkers and residents was recast as a service relationship instead of a sharing relationship. Indeed, workers often hid such relationships because the shelter discouraged the friendships that sometimes developed between workers and residents because such conduct was "unprofessional."

Like our individual conversations, hotline calls too were recorded. Our first few inquiries on the hotline were to establish the race and age of the caller. Next we asked whether she had any children. How many? What age? If she sounded "foreign" we were to inquire and record her legal status—was she a citizen? If not, was she a permanent or conditional resident in the United States? If neither, was she here legally? To establish whether she was "truly" an abuse survivor we were to note whether she had filed a police report against the abuser. If not, then we had to urge her to get one because without a police report the shelter's residential facilities were unavailable for her. Amid information gathering the woman's story of abuse emerged in bits and pieces. The details of that story, however, remained unimportant for data gathering purposes. We were to get information that established the racial/age backgrounds of our clientele for statistical purposes, and we were instructed to gather information that allowed the shelter supervisor to make judgments on whether the caller was suitable for Apna Ghar residency.

An ideal client was usually in her mid-twenties to late-thirties. She did not have children. She was an American citizen, and spoke English reasonably well. She had also filed a police report against her abuser. If the woman spoke little or no English, was not a documented immigrant, or had too many children we often turned her down even though we had space in the shelter. Such women were perceived as problematic, because the shelter may not be successful in getting her onto welfare or establishing her as a fully independent being. Children, especially young ones who were not yet in school, were seen as a problem. Given the shrinking funds for childcare and the lack of availability of childcare services, Apna Ghar was unable to find childcare for these infants. As a result, the mother would not be able to get a job, and we could not eventually tout her as a "success." Hence, we had to screen her out as we "listened" to her stories over the hotline, and even though we had space, we declared we had no room in the shelter and gave her a list of alternatives she could call. "If, by chance, we have some space within the next week, the shelter supervisor will call you back," we informed her.[4] These hotline calls and conversations would all eventually be converted into hours of services provided so that we could show the state how well we worked when we applied for our next round of grants.

Caseworkers were frustrated with the conditions that structured how we listened to women's narratives and what we did to those narratives after hearing them. The conversion of these narratives into "data" and the circulation of these stories to tout Apna Ghar's "success" as a shelter caused discomfort. We often felt we were betraying the battered women for two reasons; first, the stories of battery and survival were often narrated at night, before we all went to sleep. These life stories were told in confidence, meant to remain within the group of shelter residents and the caseworker present at that time. However, we reproduced these stories in the daily logbook so that all workers would know the violence individual women had suffered in the past. In rewriting these stories, we felt we violated the women's trust by reproducing their pain on paper. We reduced the complexities of their lives to pat descriptions of violence for all to see.

This sort of reproduction of life stories felt like a lie because we called it "informal counseling." Calling the impromptu sessions of sharing life stories "informal counseling" identified them as a one-way process, whereby only battered women were "helped" because caseworkers "listened." Such a label ignored the reciprocity entailed in sharing these life stories wherein caseworkers too were affected. The stories we told each other changed our lives. These highly charged emotional exchanges were not informal counseling sessions, but instead were consciousness-raising sessions where the lives of both residents and workers were irredeemably altered. Listening to battered women's narratives, I came to realize, had two sides to it—the narrator who told us her life stories and we listeners who heard these stories. On one hand, the battered woman tried to make sense of her life and regain narrative control over her being. On the other hand, listening to the stories, workers were changed in ways we never thought possible when we began work at the shelter. Instead of changing "those unfortunate" women's lives, we emerged changed, sometimes feeling ineffective and antifeminist like Reena did at the end of her tenure in Apna Ghar. Our supervisors at the shelter did not recognize the transformations we underwent. Or if they did, they did not know what to do with these transformations for they asked us not to share our feelings, or how we felt we had personally changed with our co-workers. Such sharing was construed as making work more difficult for everyone else or being too emotionally needy.

Moreover, even as we were encouraged to gather as many stories as we possibly could, becoming friendly with shelter residents was strictly forbidden. We had to maintain rigid hierarchical relationships between worker and "client," and any breach of that relationship was instantly noted. Caseworkers were hauled into the office and reprimanded for being bad workers, breaking the hard efforts of other conscientious workers who had established order in the shelter. I reproduce my field notes where I breach work orders, and am reprimanded by my supervisor:

March 23rd, late 1990s.

I went in to Apna Ghar today at 6:30 A.M., with Tippoo on leash as usual. Sita, the previous worker, looked relaxed and she stayed up to 7:00 A.M., chatting. I made breakfast for Najma's children as she got her youngest child washed up and she herself got ready for her English classes. Nellie, the supervisor came in and I didn't hear her. She went straight to the office without letting me know she was in. Not even a hello. She shut the glass doors behind her and sat behind her officious desk, while the residents and I puttered around in the kitchen, involved in the mundane tasks of getting kids ready for school. I later walked into the office and was surprised to see her. Not as yet aware of any transgressions, I greeted her with enthusiasm, and she nodded back stiffly. Her eyes did not meet mine. She was clearly annoyed.

She tersely told me I was not supposed to cook for clients. Then she asked me whether I'd given my telephone number to Jyothi and Anil, two children in the shelter. When I answered in the affirmative, she said she did not want that to happen again because it breached professional ethics. I replied that I did not necessarily think these were good ethics—we got so much information from the women, so what was wrong in divulging parts of my life? We had their addresses. We even walked into their rooms to see if they kept it in order, so why the fuss about a telephone number? This was not the first time I'd done it, and probably would not be the last time, I replied. Nellie's lips tightened. She said that she too would love to give out her phone number but did not do so because it broke the workers' team spirit. Other workers would appear as ogres in comparison to me when they refused to give out numbers. And besides, it was in my own best interests not to give out my personal number, because the clients could bother me at odd hours.

Throughout the day Nellie sat protected behind her huge desk and glass doors. Each time she saw a resident go by upstairs to her own room, she might shout out from behind the desk, "Hey! I want to talk with you. Come here." Then the woman would walk in and be seated opposite Nellie. In the mornings, the eastern sun streamed through the window, lighting up the woman in the chair but keeping Nellie in the shadows. Thus illuminated, the woman might be asked about her public aid situation, job prospects, or questioned about why her children are unruly and why can't she keep them under control. I would remain seated on the maroon chairs along the edge of the room or beside the resident, not doing the reprimanding or being scolded myself, but feeling caught in between. I felt awful for having written in the logs about children running amok in the house or how frustrated I'd been when women had a disagreement about who'd do laundry later that evening. I'd feel guilt over having expressed my dissatisfaction in the logbook, looking for my co-workers' support on coping with the emotional labor of listening to survival stories. The logs served as a disciplinary tool used against the battered women, as Nellie went through the logs and every morning hauled the women in and barraged them with a battery of intrusive questions.

Yesterday, she asked me over the telephone from the main office, "Sharmila can you go and check Zina's and Najma's rooms?"

"Check them for what, Nellie?" I asked.

"Check to see if they are clean, or whether they smell of pee."

Both Najma and Zina's children have bed-wetting problems, and sometimes their rooms smell when the children have an accident. The mothers have to rush off for work or for an English class early in the mornings and haven't had time as yet to launder the sheets that lay in piles next to the bed.

"OK," I replied, but did not go upstairs to check the rooms as commanded.

I reproduce these field notes to not just show how I am reprimanded for breaking work rules, and possibly making the work process harder for others, but to also show the various ways in which residents and workers come under the scrutiny of the shelter supervisor and the executive director. Also, caseworkers monitored each other. What was their conduct with residents? What had they done in their shifts that weakened hierarchical boundaries between "clients" and service providers?

In addition to the very structured listening and information gathering, we were also asked to do other kinds of "unsolicited" listening—we were asked to monitor shelter residents' telephone calls. For example, Nellie, another social worker who had previously worked at Apna Ghar, and I were meeting socially. Nellie, the supervisor, told me not to reveal to any of the Indian clients which languages I knew. "Why?" I asked. Nellie replied, "These women are very clever. Sita (worker) told Jaya (resident) that she spoke only Kannada. Now Jaya speaks only Tamil on the telephone when she calls her family, and we can't follow what is said."

"But don't we step out of the room so they may have their conversations in private?" I asked.

"No, you should limit their calls to five minutes at the most. Listen to what they are saying and to whom they are speaking. Write this down in the log," directed Nellie.

At other times, we were warned abuse survivors could be manipulative. "Don't be taken in by every sob story. Use your head," we were told by our co-workers and supervisor. Some workers were considered too sympathetic by the supervisor, executive director, or co-workers. Our sympathy was construed as trying to become the shelter residents' "favorite" worker. For instance, in a staff meeting, Nancy, the White late-twenties counseling intern pointed out that there was no professionalism in the way caseworkers dealt with clients. Janet, the executive director agreed: "If need be, we should be willing to let them fall on their faces. They have to face the consequences for not following up." Also, if shelter residents left their children in the shelter unsupervised, we were asked to file a report of child neglect with Child and Family Services. Nancy added, "We could also give them a violation. Or do you not want to give them violations because you want them to like you?"

Caseworkers were not allowed to help Apna Ghar residents in any manner as they went about trying to negotiate everyday schedules that involved forty-hour work weeks, visits to courts and hospitals, attending endless "self-help" and counseling sessions at the main office, dropping children at school, picking them up in the evenings, cooking, and caring for children. Any help from caseworkers was seen to hinder the development of the residents' independence.

While we had assumed work at Apna Ghar to be about providing care and concern for women, most of the caseworkers' tasks entailed the endless monitoring of residents' activities so that the shelter may run smoothly—did Najma clean the bathrooms, has Sameera taken the trash out, has Zina fed her children healthy food, has Alushka cleaned the kitchen floor adequately, are all the dishes put away, has Lola returned before the curfew hour, how many counseling sessions has Jaya missed? In between, we fielded hotline calls, arranged for women's public aid, or if a woman was a "good client," we made sincere efforts at finding adequate housing for her. Caseworkers constantly checked on the residents—were they proceeding with job searches in a suitable manner? Were they making good efforts at trying to lead independent lives?

Emotion Labor at Apna Ghar

Donileen Loseke writes the following words of another shelter she calls Sun Coast. These words describing Sun Coast could just as well illustrate work at Apna Ghar: When clients broke rules, workers could become *rule enforcers*; when clients did not work out interpersonal troubles among themselves, workers could become *dispute mediators*; when clients did not do their share of communal housekeeping duties, workers could become *house cleaners*.[5]

Staff at Apna Ghar, in their concern for the smooth running of the shelter, were involved in actions antithetical to their motivations for first joining the shelter. We came to Apna Ghar thinking we could make a difference in women's lives but soon realized that social work had nothing much to do with transformation, forming community with other women espousing similar politics, or altering gender paradigms within our South Asian American families. On the

contrary, the tasks we engaged in—assigning chores to residents, checking to
see if chores have been done well, arbitrating fights between residents, disciplining unruly children, putting food away in the refrigerator—resulted in
disputes between workers and residents. Routine duties interfered with establishing supportive relationships. Instead of being "one big happy feminist family," to paraphrase Anita, workers found themselves imposing authority over
residents.

As employees, caseworkers were asked to maintain "an objective, detached,
scientifically rigorous base to establish professional identity."[6] The professional
relationship we were supposed to develop at work required the displacement of
personal motivations (to be caring persons) or personal political beliefs (feminist ethics of personal empowerment). We were asked instead to convert care
giving into an abstract problem solving process.

In Apna Ghar we performed emotional labor. Hochschild defines emotional
labor as work that "requires one to induce or suppress feeling in order to sustain the outward countenance that produces the proper state of mind in others."[7]
Amy Wharton further explains that emotional labor is "the effort involved in displaying organizationally sanctioned emotions by those whose jobs require interaction with clients or customers and for whom these interactions are an
important component of their work."[8] As emotional laborers, one of the most
important aspects of our work at Apna Ghar was the display of "organizationally
sanctioned emotions." We had to listen to stories of violence and survival with
a mind disengaged from the heart. That is, we had to listen to battered women's
stories and provide emotional support but keep our emotions, our empathy, and
our concern for the narrators to a minimum so that we may maintain a professional distance. Hochschild adds that "this kind of labor calls for a coordination
of mind and feeling, and it sometimes draws on a source of self that we honor
as deep and integral to our individuality."[9]

A disjuncture arose between the expectations and actual experiences of shelter workers. As shelter workers, we desired to enhance a conscious sense of
ourselves as caring persons, which guided not just our choice of work but also
the way we did our work in Apna Ghar.[10] We *wanted* to provide empathy to residents and help them reconstitute their lives, and we brought with us a complex
set of socially defined gender roles surrounding care giving. In addition, some
caseworkers defined themselves as feminists, wanting to actively put their
socialized gender roles of care giving into political use, contributing emotionally
to other women as they tried to change their lives. Some caseworkers actually
came with an almost missionary zeal of wanting to provide support for battered
women. We considered such emotional giving a fundamental part of our self and
integral to our individuality. We defined ourselves in relational terms, building

our self-identity as feminists, as South Asian Americans, and as women through caring and nurturing.

We were involved in the shelter because we wanted to make a difference in our South Asian American communities. Yet, we found ourselves engaged in tasks we did not expect to do. These tasks were often antithetical to our conceptualization of shelter work. The shelter supervisor and executive director dictated the terms on which and how our emotions could be displayed. Though changes in the women residents came through our caring, the shelter checked the ways in which we showed this caring. We were reined in from interacting with residents according to the immediate situations in which we found ourselves and instead acted according to scripts the shelter deemed professionally appropriate.

We were paid to listen to stories of pain and provide care and emotional support. Listening to stories of extreme violence, repeated by every woman who came in, everyday, in addition to the complexities of communal living and the disciplinary rules imposed on the workers themselves, emotionally exhausted us. Emotion labor requires workers to maintain a professional facade of calmness and being in control of their feelings to residents and to other workers alike. Very shortly, however, caseworkers could not maintain this facade of emotional control and soon fell apart.

Working in Apna Ghar compelled us to see our own mothers, aunts, grandmothers, and ourselves in the residents' stories. Asha said she was emotionally and physically exhausted. "The last two weeks I worked twelve-hour shifts every other day. . . . I think it's getting to me. . . . I don't remember being as affected when I was sixteen. Maybe it's because I didn't have regular contact with these women. But . . . I've been feeling really drained. And I'm thinking it's because it's the first month and maybe you'll get used to it. But I think I'm getting a little bit overly emotional when they start talking." There is a long silence as Asha and I looked at each other's faces. She continued: "I mean (long silence) yeah. I mean I think it really has affected me, because I (her voice chokes and she begins to cry) stop me, please. I'm trying to say is that . . . ah . . . I (silence) I felt a little pain, but I double or triple or quadruple that, and I can't just imagine what it would be like to experience that." Asha wiped her tears and continued with a stronger voice:

> Yeah. That's true. To realize how lucky you are in a way. But yeah—(silence) it's also a matter of ah . . . my aunt, actually. Well, I lived in India for just four months. I did an internship there this year from January and I returned on May 5th. And I got hired five days after. So I never really had the time to recuperate. And I lived with my aunt in India, because the hospital I worked at was near by. My aunt is basically like my second mother. She's my mom's sister.

I lived with her, my grandmother, and my aunt's husband. And . . . they were my family, right? My aunt was telling me throughout the stay, you know, that she's having problems with her husband, and there were some issues that were brought up. And then two weeks after I arrived, we all find out that my uncle married again. And he didn't tell my aunt.

There was a long silence, and Asha continued:

It's a long complicated story but ah . . . basically I never thought something like that would happen in OUR family I've never HEARD of it [bigamy] in my family. . . . So this happened and it has really, really affected me. So what happens is that during the days I think about these women here and at nights, I'm just haunted with the stories that my aunt was telling over the phone about my uncle. And I think I've been . . . it's really affected me. And I feel like, I don't know. I've never felt this sad before. When it hits home so hard then its unreal.

Asha now realized abuse does not happen in only "those" homes but also occurs in middle-class homes such as hers. The fact that domestic violence knows no class barriers was brought home especially starkly when she realized her mother's sister was in an abusive marriage. In all these years, Asha had never known these family secrets, and now, the inner workings of family were revealed. She felt surrounded by violence both at work and at home. Because of her aunt's emotional abuse, Asha empathized with Apna Ghar residents in ways she never had before, and her professional facade started to crack under emotional pressure.

Hence, we workers received the residents' stories in many ways. Some of us began with a professional demeanor and worked hard at maintaining a strong ethos of professionalism. Or sometimes we heard battered women's stories and adapted our actions accordingly, letting our feelings develop in response to what the battered woman was saying. Yet, at other times, we caseworkers imposed our own narratives onto battered women's realities. We inserted our visions of recovery and timelines for recovery, making battered women into objects needing intervention. Or at other times we fell apart, as did Asha, because we saw our own families in a different light.

Sympathy and Solidarity: How Does One Listen?

Bartky says that to develop political commitments that transcend differences, it is necessary for us to truly understand the standpoint of others. She says that first- and second-wave feminists have been accused of ethnocentrism because they worked from the standpoint of their privileged race and class locations and extrapolated from their particular experience to all others.[11] Bartky notes first and second wave feminists have done to disadvantaged feminists what androcentric political theory has done to women in general—by theorizing from their own standpoint they enforced invisibility on a majority of women.

To overcome the privileging of our own standpoint and develop empathy for others, Bartky says that we need to try to enter, through imagination, into their lives.[12] However, we need to be cautious in relying completely on imagination for developing empathy, because "when simply imagining [a woman's reality], I can escape from the demands her reality puts on me and instead construct her in my mind in such a way that I can possess her, making her into someone or something who never talks back."[13] We need to use our imagination to apprentice ourselves to the Other so that we may acquire knowledge that transforms our privileged self. Barthey asks us to develop "a knowing that brings into being new sympathies, new affects as well as new cognitions and new forms of intersubjectivity."[14]

These forms of intersubjectivity that lead to better understanding can be developed through what Scheler calls genuine "fellow feeling" or *sympathie*.[15] In understanding the Other's feelings, if I constantly asked myself the question, "What would I do if this were to happen to me?" I would be guilty of refocusing on my own ego than focusing on the Other. Sympathy does not entail the comparison of my feelings with the Other's feelings, because such a comparison limits my understanding of the Other only so far as their feelings correspond with mine. For, if all I felt in apprehending your suffering was in some important way merely a rehearsal of my own suffering, I would direct my attention away from you entirely and toward the amelioration of my own misery . . . egoistic rediscovery of myself in the Other gives me no appreciation of the Other's uniqueness as a personality.[16] If we constantly put ourselves in the Other's shoes, then we would be incapable of any enlargement of self, thus not allowing ourselves to grow morally, spiritually, and emotionally. Our explorations of intersubjectivity would be shortchanged "if fellow-feeling were a mere epiphenomenon, hovering over the Other but having its actual grounding in us. We will not be able to transcend" ourselves.[17]

To develop true sympathy, we need to maintain "the otherness of the Other."[18] While the maintenance of rigid ego boundaries might be viewed as excessively masculinist, Bartky thinks keeping ego boundaries intact is crucial because the "distance between persons can act against the temptation on the part of the one disadvantaged—if she finds profound commiseration and understanding in the one advantaged—to try to overleap and deny her oppressed condition in an act of emotional merger." Maintaining boundaries mitigates the dominant person's temptation to believe that "her oppressor's guilt can be overcome through heroic acts of ego-identification. . . . In short, the preservation of the otherness of the Other works against her re-colonization."[19]

How then does one develop true sympathy, or what Bartky terms fellow feelings, in a manner that does not recolonize the Other? Bartky asks that we use our intuition and imagination to develop genuine fellow feeling. For intuition to work substantial background information—linguistic competence, cultural understandings, and ordinary emotional capacities such as caring—is required. Once the proper background conditions are satisfied, Bartky says that she can leap out of her own experience into an intuitive understanding of the Other's emotional life. Imagination too is required so that we may visualize the conditions of the Other's existence. Bartky asks that we see with our mind's eye details of the reality in which the Other exists so that we may form the background conditions to move out of our own understanding into the emotional life of the Other. So to briefly summarize, listening and developing empathy necessitates a separation of self from the Other but also behooves us as listeners to have the background information and imagination to see the Other's realities so that we may understand their standpoints.

At Apna Ghar, because almost all workers were South Asian, that is, had the same cultural background as most of the shelter residents, one could presume we had the necessary background information and imagination to visualize battered women's lives. We understood the cultural context of her familial life, familial violence, her hesitancy in leaving her spouse, her concerns for her future as a woman of color who does not know English, her standing among conservative South Asian Americans who might ostracize her for walking out of her marriage, and the difficulties involved in raising children alone in what she perceives to be a hostile world. Yet—despite this cultural knowledge, and the best of intentions—many of us perceived ourselves to be inept at providing empathy. And, moreover, some first-generation workers like Arati resented working at Apna Ghar.

What explained our incapacities for providing true sympathy so that battered women could reconstitute their lives and emerge as survivors? Did this incapacity to listen come from the late modern conditions in which we live, where we do not have the time to listen, or where modes of communication are such that we are incapable of forming true empathetic ties with others? Or did the fault lie within us because, in spite of the cultural knowledge, we failed to comprehend the states and conditions of women with working class backgrounds? Or, were we so scared of the sacrifices demanded of us when we listened to stories of violence that we were apprehensive to even begin listening? Or, was the institutional structure of Apna Ghar such that we were unable to listen? Engaging in emotion labor at Apna Ghar and our incapacities to truly listen raised all of these questions.

Some shelter workers refused to exercise the imagination necessary to understand the everyday conditions in which the battered women existed. We had fixed narratives of what constituted abuse and the "proper" processes for emerging as a survivor. Any deviation from the norm we set was incomprehensible and unacceptable to us. Yet, at other times, the stories of abuse were so horrific and the pain so graphically described that we shut down. Listening to stories of battery and abuse everyday and the vastness of suffering became too much for many of us to bear. In trying to protect ourselves, we closed up. We had no more to give. We feared that we too may fall into an abyss of misery and never emerge out again.

At other times, like Asha, we inserted our own familial narratives of abuse as we listened to the residents narrate their stories. Bartky would find such insertions of our pains into the residents' narratives—imagining ourselves in their shoes—a problematic way to develop sympathy. Such a move on our part is an appropriation of the women's survival narratives, and our listening merely becomes a rehearsal of our own suffering. Instead of concentrating on their trauma, we focused on our own familial pain. Our attention was turned away from their distress to the alleviation of our own miseries. Nevertheless, how could we remain unaffected by the stories we heard at Apna Ghar? Inevitably these stories touched us and invoked within us memories of our own familial abuse. We caseworkers were fundamentally transformed. Our self grew in the presence of shelter residents, giving new meanings and contexts for feelings and interactions with others.

We sometimes wanted to share the transformation we underwent in the shelter with our co-workers, but we silenced ourselves because the supervisor and director construed such talking as complaining. In addition, we were urged by the counseling intern—"maintain professional distance between yourself and your clients, or else you will make their problems your own and you will burn out." But maintaining a professional distance was hard for us; the reasons we came to the shelter were not to maintain distance but instead to reconnect with other South Asian American women, change lives, and let ourselves be transformed. For many of us, shelter work was not a profession but was a political and personal passion.

Of all the reasons, the one factor that most affected our abilities to listen was the commercialization of care work. Our motivations for working at the shelter did not matter as much as the efficiency of the shelter. Shelter work rules partially imposed the way we listened to battered women's stories, leading to a feeling of alienation at work. Or, at other times hearing too many stories of battery emotionally exhausted us, and we shut our ears. Given the emotionally taxing nature of the work we performed, and the isolation and alienation we felt at work, we were burnt out. Burnout is variously described as "a state of fatigue or frustration brought about by devotion to a cause, way of life, or relationship that failed to produce the expected award." It is usually "a syndrome of emotional exhaustion and cynicism that frequently occurs among individuals who do 'people work' of some kind. A key aspect of the burnout syndrome is increased feelings of emotional exhaustion."[20]

Many of us came to the shelter to be involved in feminist projects within our own communities. Through this work, we hoped to meet like-minded individuals to solidify our commitment to social change through personal empowerment. Empowerment, however, involves the development of "a more positive self-concept and self-confidence, a more critical worldview, and the cultivation of individual and collective skills and resources for social and political action."[21] While Apna Ghar certainly endorsed such change, it was difficult to make this central to their everyday work. The workers at the shelter wanted to develop networks among persons with similar political passions, develop solidarity across class lines among South Asian American women, and raise the their own as well as their communities' consciousness on domestic violence.

Conversely, Apna Ghar wanted to build a stable organization that would serve as a resource for violence survivors. In addition, it sought to be the representative voice on violence issues for South Asian American communities. Apna Ghar institutionalized care work to ensure its survival as an organization, which led it to commercialize care work. This kind of commercialization forced us workers to listen in particular ways and ultimately to our alienation and anomie. Though Apna Ghar's and the workers' long-term goals of ending violence were identical, their ideas on how to get there were radically different.

Upon returning to our own homes after work, we workers sought emotional support from our loved ones and friends, trying to make sense of how listening to battered women's narratives had altered our lives in irrevocable ways. Over time, however, we stopped narrating these Apna Ghar stories to loved ones at home. Anita exclaimed that work in Apna Ghar was like entering a battleground, but she was unable to relate the stories of horror she heard at the shelter to any of her friends. The realities of everyday living at the shelter and the realities of her middle-class friends outside seemed so divergent that none of the stories she told made sense to them. After a while, she had nothing positive to report regarding her work. She felt she complained too much to her friends, and she began censoring herself. In addition, to build a detachment from the stories we heard, we stopped talking about Apna Ghar to our loved ones at home. Bringing up narratives of violence and misery constantly outside work hours made us feel we could never get away from violence. So we stopped repeating the Apna Ghar stories to anyone, anymore. We remained mute, hoping our lives outside work would rejuvenate us.

We tried to be strong and did our best to provide Apna Ghar residents the emotional support and understanding they needed, within the confines of the job. With time, however, we became ineffective caregivers, unable to provide an empathetic audience to the women who narrated their lives in an attempt to restructure their self. We workers at least had the option of quitting our jobs when we felt "compassion burn-out," but when we turned inward into our selves, the shelter residents bore the consequences. They had arrived at Apna Ghar seeking support, yet quite often, they were met with emotionally exhausted workers.

Concluding Comments

As Piven and Cloward have shown in their *Poor People's Movements* (1977), social movement organizations institutionalize themselves so that they may remain extant and carry on their social/political interventions. So they seek more resources in the form of "manpower" and try to raise funds from corporations, and central, state, and city governments. In addition, they attempt to streamline work and become more proficient through professionalizing services offered to "clients." These developments mute their politics to a far greater degree than they may be comfortable with, but they often continue to do so because they do not want to alienate these sources of support. Hence, Piven and Cloward posit that the more bureaucratic social movement organizations become, the greater are their chances of becoming co-opted to the detriment of their political efficacy.[22]

Working on South Asian domestic violence organizations in Canada, Agnew notes that though these organizations were begun as feminist organizations, the groups moved closer to conventional norms and values so that they may persist as social work agencies. She notes, "[T]he compromises that community-based groups make to survive are driven by political expediency and, in the long run, the character of the organization changes. Service providers in these groups become more circumspect in their criticism of state and society, hide their militancy, and address problems in non-confrontational ways. They become more moderate in articulating their feminism and in voicing their feelings."[23] She warns that feminist organizations can become co-opted and lose their political ideologies that distinguish them from state agencies. Provision of services to abuse survivors is important, but these services need to be contextualized in larger political frameworks of social transformation or they risk maintaining the status quo of race and gender inequalities and, in the long run, become band-aid measures in reducing violence against women.

Apna Ghar has survived since 1989 because it has managed to garner funds for its existence. Using state resources has, however, "meant working to some degree within the confines of bureaucratic structures, since the organization had to conform to state-defined specifications for the allocation of funds and the use of the shelter."[24] Statistics on hotline calls or shelter arrivals, rates of successful intervention, definitions of successful survivors, and so forth all affect the ways the shelter works. As a result, Apna Ghar has had to mute its politics and has lost some of its critical edge. Apna Ghar's dual-pronged approach to altering South Asian American gender paradigms by providing alternative routes to battered women and consciousness-raising among South Asian Americans has become watered down. In the previous chapter, I explained how institutionalization inadvertently led the shelter to subscribe to assimilation rhetoric. To make women's lives free of domestic violence and to make them autonomous, the shelter pushed women to leave their spouses, familial networks, and ethnic communities. Without consciously meaning to do so, the shelter exerted much energy on "de-ethnicizing" women. In this chapter, I explained how Apna Ghar's strategies of consciousness raising were unintentionally effaced because of its focus on professionalization. Through pushing its workers to conduct themselves as professionals—as workers in a corporation instead of activists in a feminist organization—the shelter was largely unable to meet its goal of politicizing South Asian American women and communities about domestic violence.

Four

The Indo American Center

"Integrating the Best of Both Cultures"

The Indo American Center can contribute greatly to help-
ing all immigrants maintain this balance of pride in being
Indians and appreciating all that India offer[s], but also
accepting wholeheartedly, the privileges and responsi-
bilities of American citizenship, developing loyalty, and
commitment to the adoptive country, and integrating the
best of both cultures.[1]

Introduction

The Indo American Center is located in the heart of Chicago's South Asian American business district in northwest Chicago. On California Avenue, within half a block of Devon Avenue, is the Indo American Center. The current premises of the Indo American Center had functioned as a Jewish Community Center up to 1992, when it was purchased and changed into the Indo American Center office.

I first became interested in the Indo American Center as a site for my research because I recognized it as a space where working-class, new immigrants were taught to become Americans by middle-class Indian immigrants. Here, I thought when I first began fieldwork, was an ideal space for me to examine Indian immigrants' perceptions of what it takes to fit into an American public world. Through my capacity as a part-time employee as a volunteer coordinator for different programs, I was able to examine the contents of various programs, as well as speak with middle-class volunteers on their motivations for working at the Center. As a participant observer, I was able to understand the practices that were deemed crucial for becoming American according to the Network of Indian Professionals (NetIP) volunteers and board members. The Center's citizenship classes, I thought, would be most interesting for my research purposes. In these classes, poorer new Indian immigrants studied hard so that they could pass the citizenship test instituted by the Immigration and Naturalization Services. Other than training these potential citizens on questions of who is the president, who is his wife, what is the national anthem, how many stars are there on the American flag, and so forth, the Center also held English classes. Command over English was perceived as central to becoming an American citizen. One volunteer said, "we want them [working-class immigrants] to learn English not just to pass the citizenship test, but they should be able to read notices, ask for directions at the bus stop, and interact with people outside the community."

If Apna Ghar, the shelter for battered women, would reveal to me the *private* disciplines of becoming American, the Indo American Center I thought, would show me how Indian immigrants grappled with race and *public* belonging in late-twentieth-century America. However, very quickly I realized that entry into American-hood was far more complex than just learning English and other "civic" facts. The Indo American Center not only trained working-class newcomers into citizenship, but also, it functioned as a cultural broker for the Indian American community in the Midwest. One of the organization's central tasks was to make the Indian immigrant more palatable to the larger American public. Such a task involved not only instructing new immigrants into becoming acceptable Americans but also working hard at representing Indians as having a traditional culture with contemporary inclinations, thus making them especially ideal for the American world. Indian immigrants' traditions ostensibly encouraged good values and superior work ethics, thereby making them suited for this nation. All that needed to be done was to reveal to the rest of the United States their unique cultural proclivities, and they would be deemed desirable additions into the national body.

Questions of cultural representation—the public-relations management for Indian immigrants—became far more interesting for my research. I had earlier started my fieldwork with the premise that Indian immigrants acted "White" in public and "became Indian" in private. Yet, what I observed at the Indo American Center was contrary to my expectations. Here were Indian immigrants caught up with definitions of ethnic culture not just for themselves but also for the wider American public. Instead of being restricted to the privacy of the home and family, Indian-ness was a whole set of carefully thought out, planned *public* rituals. This chapter addresses the Center's work.

The Work of the Indo American Center

Like the South Asian American business district on Devon during the weekends, the Center transformed into a public arena with tremendous energy, where working-class and middle-class Indian immigrants met, spoke, and fraternized with each other. Various young Indian American professionals arrived at the Center to volunteer their time with working-class immigrant children, helping them complete their school homework. In addition, the Center held computer classes for older, underprivileged adults. English classes and citizenship classes were conducted for new working-class immigrants who were filing for American citizenship. A clinic organized by Indian American doctors with the volunteer efforts of interns from various Chicago hospitals offered free medical examinations every Sunday. In yet another room, a young Indian American woman taught classical Indian dance to women who expressed an interest in (high) cultural pursuits. Amidst all this activity, the board of directors—equally energetic—would meet some Sundays to discuss the future direction the Indo American Center should take. They loudly and lengthily discussed matters such as the next set of projects they wanted to begin, how they could attract younger members into their ranks, and with which other ethnic organizations they should form coalitions.

The board members were all middle-class individuals, employed as executives in multinational companies, teachers or professors, or entrepreneurs running their own companies. Men and women composed the board, and though the men tended to speak a lot, their women colleagues were capable of making themselves heard and expressing opinions that were given serious consideration by the rest of the board. The Center was careful to not be associated with American electoral politics and avoided being linked to either the Democrats or the Republicans. They strove toward maintaining what they considered a "nonpolitical" image.

In addition, the Indo American Center was avowedly nonsectarian. Though some board members, employees, and volunteers were no doubt religious to varying degrees, in their involvement at the Center, they steered clear of any overt religious affiliations. The board had Hindu, Muslim, and Christian members, who collectively strove to maintain their Center as a secular organization, assisting anyone who originated from India, regardless of caste, creed, language, or regional origins. The Indo American Center visualized itself as a pan-Indic organization working toward the common good of the Indian immigrant community.

In a board meeting held on a typically noisy Sunday at the Center, board members Poonam and Susie presented the statistics regarding Indian Americans they had compiled from the 1990 Census. They identified that in the United States, overall, there are about 847,562 persons of Indian origins; 34 percent of these individuals were naturalized citizens. They estimated that by the late 1990s, the population was over a million persons. A majority of these persons (70 percent) were between the ages of eighteen and sixty-four years, and about 3 percent were sixty-five years and older. Forty-four percent of the Indian Americans were professionals, and another 33 percent were in technical/sales/administrative jobs, drawing a median family income of $44,696. However, 13,964 families, or 74,972 individuals, were below the poverty line.

The city of Chicago had 16,386 persons of Indian origins, and 41,606 Indian Americans lived in the suburbs (Cook County had a population of 39,225 Indian Americans; Du Page county had 14,172 persons; and other counties had 4,593 individuals). Of the Indian American residents in the Chicago area, 61 percent were foreign born. Individuals living in the city were more likely to not become American citizens compared with persons living in the suburbs. A majority of Indians in the Chicago area were between the ages of eighteen and sixty four years. There were about 1,000 persons over sixty-five years of age, though these figures had grown because 20 percent of the recent immigration from India comprised older persons. Most of these older adults lived in the suburbs. Thirty-two percent of the Indian American population in Chicago and its suburbs were professionals, 24 percent were involved in retail, and 27 percent had occupations relating to manufacturing. The median income of a family living in the Chicago metropolitan area was $44,000. However, this figure did not reveal that suburban family incomes were far higher, and if one looked at only the city, the median family income was just $28,600. Eighteen percent of those in the city lived below the poverty line, and 9 percent of them received public aid, though this number has risen since the 1990s. Indian families living in the city were far poorer than their suburban compatriots.

Based on this data, the board members decided that the Indo American Center primarily needed to focus on the poorer community members living in the city. Simultaneously, they needed to develop strategies to raise financial and volunteer support from suburban Indian Americans, who were better educated and wealthier. A large number of these suburbanites, however, did not even know of the Center's existence, and one of the board's goals was to increase the Center's visibility among these wealthier individuals. The problem was that the suburbanites—the bulk of the potential financial supporters—did not visit Devon very often where the Center was located. Satellite Indian grocery stores were opening up in suburbs and it was no longer necessary for people to drive into Devon, where parking facilities were horrendous. The Center struggled to come up with strategies that would increase suburban Indian Americans' interest in the Devon area, because only by coming here would they know of the Center's existence. The board members believed that middle-class South Asian Americans isolated themselves in the suburbs, making it harder to build a unitary community that interacted on a regular basis.

Much of the board meetings were dedicated to coming up with solutions for this dilemma. Individuals tossed around numerous suggestions, some of which were received with exasperation by the other members, while other propositions seemed more promising. Mr. Ahmed proposed that the Center needed to enhance Indian Americans' visibility; the IAC could get involved in developing this particular business district into an India Town, similar to Chinatown. The other members looked at him skeptically. Mr. Rao intervened with another proposal–perhaps they could work with the city and develop better parking facilities around Devon? Even before he could extrapolate further, Mrs. Rego forcefully interceded, "Excuse me, but the Center's goal is not commercial. We are not here to help the merchants on Devon improve their businesses. Let us not forget that we are a SERVICE organization!" With this, the board realized it was getting sidetracked. They could not make grand plans regarding Devon Avenue's "South Asian" future; they had to focus their energies on assisting Indian immigrants in more immediate ways.

The executive director recommended that instead of changing Devon, perhaps a better way to reach out to suburban Indian Americans would be to research this particular population segment. He suggested that the board develop a questionnaire to identify the following: Do suburbanites know where the Center is located? If yes, do they like the present location, or would they like to see satellites of the Indo American Center in the suburbs? Would they like the Center to develop different services such as cultural programs whereby suburban children would be taught Indian languages, Indian classical music, and Indian classical dance? In addition, he mildly admonished the rest of the board, "We should not look at these people [suburban Indian Americans] as only a potential source of money. Instead, we need to bring them together in spirit, behind the Center's mission and larger goals for the community."

Turning their attention to the statistics Poonam and Susie had compiled, board members noted the increase in the number of Indian American senior citizens. They wanted to have special programs to aid these individuals. Poonam added that while city seniors might come from poorer backgrounds, they were less isolated than suburbanites. Living in apartment buildings, close to Devon, city seniors were in closer proximity to other Indians as well as other seniors like them. On the other hand, suburban seniors were confined within homes, dependent on their working offspring to drive them around, and they felt a deep loneliness. Poonam questioned, "What are the obstacles to working with either sub-population of seniors? We need to decide on which subpopulation of seniors we should focus, in terms of information dissemination. Also, what about transportation needs of seniors in the suburbs? Will common programs for both city and suburban seniors work, or do we need different programs?"

The other members realized that they first had to figure out what seniors want in terms of programs, and the executive director noted that they should conduct a needs assessment survey before planning any further. "Once we plan the programs," Satish added, "we need to conduct aggressive marketing and information dissemination regarding the senior programs."

"Yes, but we need PR strategies not just for these programs, but also to increase an awareness of the Center," intervened Mrs. Nayar. She elaborated, "PR can increase the number of people who use our facilities, we can get more volunteers, and facilitate our efforts in increasing our funding base." The increased funding could be used for improving the present facilities, hire new staff, start up new programs, and perhaps begin satellite centers.

In addition, the board recognized that the number of working-class Indian Americans was growing, resulting in greater disparities between the haves and the have-nots among Indian Americans. The issue then, was the maintenance of a singular Indian American community despite class differences. The board members had invited the leaders of other Indian societies for a luncheon meeting so that they could develop a better understanding of "community" needs. In preparation for this meeting, various members took on different assignments; Mr. Ahmed and Mr. Singh offered to come up with one- to two-page proposals for senior programs. Poonam and Mr. Rao agreed to write a short proposal for suburban outreach plans. Satish volunteered to develop and coordinate a telephone survey regarding the Center's visibility. Susie and Mrs. Nayar decided to come up with a list of corporations and state/city agencies that might provide the Center with grants for its various programs.

And so, the board met at least once every month, discussing various issues regarding the Indian American "community" in Chicago that concerned them. The board members' commitment to the Center and its service-oriented goals were palpable; they volunteered a large part of their time and efforts to help make the Center a truly viable service organization. Mr. Shetty explained why he felt so strongly about the Center: "My values which I developed as a child growing up in India are the same I have now which are hard work, and charitable and voluntary work for humanity. We should strive to contribute significantly to society, which can bring happiness in our lives. The Center, I believe, is one vehicle that brings people to contribute to collective growth, while simultaneously giving them the opportunity for individual leadership." The Center's strength, he continued, was its capacity for "fostering, enhancing, and preserving a sense of community which is secular, involving people of Indian and South Asian descent. Building a community brings collective benefits to the community which are manifest in the various programs the Center runs." When asked what the Indo American Center's strengths were, he replied, "A nonconventional board with no sectarian attachments and the physical space we have in the South Asian business district."

Mrs. Rao thought the Center's strong points were its clearly articulated mission and the diversity of the board of directors in terms of gender, age, professions, religion, language, and geographical spread. Both Satish and Mrs. Nayar unhesitatingly said the Center's main asset was its volunteers. Mrs. Nayar added, "An institution is only as good as the people involved in it." Though the Indo American Center hired two full-time paid staff and two part-time employees, most of the services provided were through the efforts of volunteers, almost all of whom were first- and second-generation professional Indian Americans. The young volunteers, mostly in their twenties and early thirties, were predominantly members of the organization NetIP. NetIP had a cadre of dedicated volunteers who arrived at the Center once a week to tutor working-class Indian children and teach spoken English to older immigrants who wanted to pass the United States citizenship test.

Mrs. Nayar clarified the Indo American Center's role in facilitating Indians' absorption into the American national body:

> My dream for the Center is for it to have the resources to provide quality service as it works actively to help new immigrants get established and to promote the image and interests of our own community by networking with mainstream organizations. Janus-like, the Center should look both within the community and the outside, to the past to affirm its heritage and to the future to assure its place. This is what will make it unique. In the process it will have [an] impact as an institution that brings individuals together in a spirit of secularism and service and also facilitate cooperation among organizations. With the community, the Center should have working links with the regional and professional associations, service agencies, as well as with student associations at the different area universities. In the city, the Center should establish strong connections with the major cultural institutions, with the departments of the city that have a direct impact on the Center's surroundings (police, streets and sanitation, tourism, etc.) and with departments that have an impact on its programs. It should take full advantage of two significant trends in the society at large—the emphasis on community service and volunteerism (evident by the fact that many schools have now made this a graduation requirement) and the move forward toward multiculturalism. The Center can work to ensure that the South Asian community's needs and its contributions are kept in the picture.

The board members and the other volunteers perceived themselves as "well assimilated" into American society and firmly believed that the assimilation of the new 1990s working-class Indian immigrants was crucial for the well-being of the entire Indian American community.

Mrs. Shetty, a board member whom I quote at the beginning of this chapter, qualified the type of assimilation the Indo American Center promoted. She explained, "We need to maintain pride in Indian identity while desiring assimilation in mainstream America and becoming contributing members of American society." Mrs. Shetty continued:

> As an Indian I am proud of my country of birth and grateful to it for affording me opportunities for education that qualified me for further education and life in the United States. Yet, at the same time, I feel a deep sense of loyalty to the United States of America, which welcomed me as an immigrant and provided me with opportunities for further professional advancement. The Indo American Center can contribute greatly to helping all immigrants maintain this balance of pride in being Indians and appreciating all that India offered, but also accepting wholeheartedly, the privileges and responsibilities of American citizenship, developing loyalty, and commitment to the adoptive country and integrating the best of both cultures.

Assimilation in the perspective of the volunteers at the Indo American Center meant "integrating the best of both cultures." For these immigrants, Indian and American identities were not incompatible, but being Indian abetted them in becoming better Americans.

Therefore, I started to learn that far from being a service organization that solely helped immigrants with English language skills and children's math homework, the Center also held weekly Indian classical dance classes. Board members were keen on beginning Indian language classes for middle-class suburban children who were most prone to forgetting their ethnic roots. In addition, the Center conducted Ethnic Neighborhood Tours for the Chicago Tourism Board. On some summer weekends, busloads of tourists from various parts of the Midwest arrived at the Center, first to listen to a brief talk on Indian immigration and then proceed on a walking tour through the Devon South Asian neighborhood. Also, various Chicago schools invited the IAC to come into their campuses for a "show and tell" on India. Or, middle school and high school students visited the Center to learn about immigrants in their city. The Center had also received a Fulbright grant to help K–12 teachers in Chicago learn about India so that they may incorporate new material into their syllabi. It conducted a tour in India in the summer for teachers, followed by three day-long workshops at the Center's premises during the fall.

These types of activities served the dual purposes of defining and cementing Indian practices for both the outside world, as well as for the Indian immigrants themselves. The Center was perceived as a third space, neither fully private nor fully public, but an intermediary space that facilitated the creation of a unitary Indian community. As the representative of Indian Americans, the Center then interacted with American state institutions such as the city police and tourism departments and the Immigration and Naturalization Services. Volunteers at the Center recognized the importance of maintaining a good public persona for the Indian immigrant community to facilitate their integration into the American civic body. They voiced that the average American lacked an understanding of Indians and India, which hindered the new immigrants' acceptance to American society. So the Center pursued "public relations" work on behalf of all Indian Americans. The assimilation of Indians into mainstream America, they felt, could be furthered by "improving the average Americans' knowledge of the Indian American community."[2] In a national atmosphere of increasing backlash against immigrants, the Indo American Center felt pressured to present Indians as "good" immigrants who would fit into an American world painlessly.[3] Indeed, they were contributing members to this nation.

To summarize, the Indo American Center perceived its role in furthering the well-being of Indian Americans through three ways: (*a*) fostering a sense of community among Indian Americans that transcended class, religion, linguistic divisions; (*b*) helping Indian immigrants adjust to American life, first by training individuals in English, offering citizenship classes, and so forth; and (*c*) enabling mainstream America to recognize Indian immigrants' potential as good citizens so that less hostility would be directed toward them.

Reconstituting Culture, Constituting Ourselves

To achieve its goals, the Indo American Center was involved in cultural brokerage both for other Indians, as well as for the rest of America. In the first instance, the board members and the volunteers attempted to define a unified pan-Indic culture for the immigrants themselves so that they would see themselves as a singular community here in the United States. Through defining culture, board members and volunteers at the Center sought to determine the common bonds that held diverse Indian Americans as a community. In demarcating culture, however, they inadvertently marked cultural insiders and outsiders.

February 15th, late 1990s.

This Is Who We Are: Ethnic Neighborhood Tours

Yesterday the Ethnic Neighborhood Tours organized by the city of Chicago visited Devon Avenue. The tour began at the Indo American Center, and volunteers at the Center took the mostly midwestern older, White Amer-

icans on a walking tour of the neighborhood. This particular Saturday—
already teeming with people attending computer classes, child tutoring sessions, English and citizenship classes—got even busier. While Mrs. Nayar,
Anand and Anitha set up the large hall to receive the tourists, I was sent off
on the task of buying roses that would eventually get ripped up and used as
confetti on our guests. By the time I returned, they had set up an Indian flag
and an American flag on the dais, side by side. They had arranged tables
around the room with various Indian paraphernalia. "Exotic" spices in little
boxes were arranged in a row. Indian fabrics and clothes, men's kurtas and
women's salwaar kameezes, were exhibited. A silk sari was draped on one of
the tables. Photographs of Indian *rikshawallahs*, a child being bathed at the
local public tap, an aerial photograph of Bombay, and a woman cooking in her
home—scenes of "modern and traditional" India were juxtaposed in a hap-
hazard manner. Handmade dolls dressed in Indian clothes lay on the display
tables. On the "religions of India" table turbans, *kirpans* and *khalsas*, rosaries,
and an Islamic cap were arranged to represent the major Indian religions. Hinduism was represented by tiny images of gods and goddesses. There were no
symbols of Buddhism or Jainism. Parsi religious symbols were missing as
well.

Mrs. Nayar was dressed in a beautiful silk sari. Anitha wore a salwaar
kameez, and Anand wore a formal pair of trousers. I, on the other hand, was
dressed in khaki pants, a black sweater that had seen better days, and a purple bandanna around my head. Despite myself, I felt embarrassed at my singular lack of grace. Gawky in hiking boots, I felt thoroughly out of place. I
wished that I, too, had dressed up in my Indian clothes.

Older women who arrived at the Center for their English classes peeked
into the large hall. Standing at the door, but not entering, they loudly asked
us what we were doing. What was this special event at the Center, they
inquired. Children from the tutoring programs barged in, picking and examining the trinkets on display. Soon Mrs. Nayar directed me to make sure
these women and children would not disturb us. We needed to finish our
arrangements before the tourists arrived, and these women and children had
their own business to attend to at the Center. Ushering out the inquisitive children and women, I shut the door.

Very soon the tourists arrived. Almost all of them were older, White persons. A couple of young Asian American women stood amongst them. We
greeted them by placing red *tikkas* on their forehead. Some of them were
taken aback but awkwardly complied. Even as we were placing these dots on
their foreheads, Mrs. Nayar began sprinkling them with rose water. Then,
Anitha tossed rose petals on their heads. The poor tourists had no idea what

we would throw at them next, but relief was writ large on some faces as we led them to the main hall, to be seated in rows in front of the dais with the flags. In the dry warmth of the building, Mrs. Nayar began her pitch on Indian Americans. She stated that in the late '60s, there was a shortage of doctors and engineers in the United States [because of the Vietnam War, she said]. "Head hunters from the U.S. went to various parts of the Third World, recruiting skilled labor. And so we arrived thinking we were embarking on an adventure," she said, "thinking we'd stay for only maybe two years. But the two years have now become thirty, and we're still here." Mrs. Nayar's speech made immigrants sound like innocents stumbling accidentally into utopia. Alice-like, Indians had fallen into Wonderland.

Mrs. Nayar continued, "Beginning mid-1980s, merchants began to follow the Indian middleclass. Devon was a Jewish neighborhood, but shops were closing down, and storefronts looked bare. The merchants' arrival into Chicago revitalized this particular neighborhood." She added that these Indian merchants eventually brought over their family members into the United States, and they now lived around the Indian business district on Devon. These newcomers, as a group, were not as educated as the professionals, and had difficulties with the English language and faced hurdles in becoming legal citizens; so, Mrs. Nayar went on, the Center was opened in 1990 to primarily serve the needs of this newer immigrant population.

With this introductory spiel, our public went off with Anand and Anitha to see what was on display on Devon. Unfortunately, I could not go with them because I had to accompany Rajesh to get Indian foods for the tourists to taste when they returned. We walked down briskly to Annapurna's [local restaurant], and returned with *dhai vadas*, *pedas*, and *bhoondi*. Meanwhile Mrs. Nayar walked to the Georgian Jewish Bakery (Georgia of the former USSR) to buy "Jewish" food comprising bread and an eggplant dip strongly flavored with garlic. Our public returned. Was it cold, I asked an older White man. He grabbed my hands into his own and smiling warmly, replied, "Whew! Feel them, and tell me what you think!"

Even as the tourists helped themselves to the food, Susan Mathews, an eighth grader from the suburbs, originally from Kerala, walked onto the dais. She was dressed in a brilliant yellow sari, wrapped in the style of classical Indian dancers. Her hair was extended into a long braid with the aid of false hair. Strands of jasmine decorated her braid. Her eyes were heavily lined with black kohl. Rajesh started playing tape-recorded music, and Susan proceeded to give a ten-minute performance of *Bharat Natyam* [classical Indian dance]. Her dance depicted the elephant headed Indian god, Ganesha, riding his mouse chariot. Soon after, Rajesh explained the meanings of the various eye movements and hand gestures we had seen in Susan's performance. I noticed the chilled tourist standing in a corner and walked up to him. I asked him if he liked the food he had just tasted. "It takes getting used to but its good," he replied.

As the reader goes through my rather perfunctory descriptions of the neighborhood tours reproduced above, she may cynically interpret these tours as a means to increase city tourist revenues.[4] We can, however, also interpret these tours as serving another purpose; the state actually anticipates that mainstream Americans can learn something of value from visiting these ethnic enclaves. These Ethnic Neighborhood Tours are partially motivated by the recognition that for most of its history, Americans have either ignored or reached unsavory conclusions about newcomers. Ethnic Neighborhood Tours, then, stem from a multicultural agenda that promotes learning about cultures that are marginalized within the American national context. Those Americans who have perhaps never thought about the racial diversity of this nation are forced to acknowledge the different kinds of peoples who compose the real face of America. The nation is not just Black and White; there also exist darker and lighter shades of brown. Only by learning about these others can there even be a possibility of national dialogue between established citizens (Black, White, or otherwise), and new arrivals.

Recognition of the different kinds of peoples, such as Indian immigrants, however, may not mean much if mainstream Americans are unable to understand where and how these newcomers fit into the national body. The limitation with Ethnic Neighborhood Tours is that it does not attempt to go beyond simply exhibiting cultural "Others." The tour effectively ghettoizes South Asians into this enclave in northwestern Chicago, presenting them as existing only here and not working as doctors in small American towns, computer programmers on temporary work permits laboring in companies located in periurban sprawls, motel owners along highways close to dying American towns, and cab drivers traversing Chicago and New York. The sole purpose of Ethnic Neighborhood Tours is to reveal interesting ethnic enclaves within the city, whereby new immigrants are presented not as one of "us," but as cultural Others. The Tours present immigrants as the "exotics at home."[5]

Yet, we cannot help but observe that the immigrants themselves are complicit in the whole process. We see them performing and narrating "Indian-ness" in particular ways. They have control over a public space where they can talk about themselves to captive audiences willing to listen to what they say. Indian immigrants become the authors of themselves, writing their racial identities into being. Mrs. Nayar's brief talk to the tourists illustrates beautifully the ways by which immigrants interject their own narratives; instead of displaying Indians as solely "Other," Mrs. Nayar valiantly attempts to insert her community as an integral part of the national body. She speaks of Indian immigrants as doctors, engineers, other professionals, and grocery store owners taking part in the nation's economy and lifeworld.

However, these immigrants' interpretive acts need to be contextualized. These tours may allow them to become active agents, presenting themselves in ways they think appropriate, but these perceptions of appropriateness arise for them because they clearly have a sense of what is expected of them. They sense their audiences' expectations and deliver lines that more or less meet these beliefs. The tourists have not come here to listen to political speeches or race talk but have come to gaze at the difference extant within their nation's borders. Instead of focusing on what Mrs. Nayar says, paying attention to her omissions are far more instructive on not just how Indian immigrants at the Center present themselves but also on how the audiences want to perceive them.

For instance, Mrs. Nayar completely ignores the early-twentieth-century South Asian immigrants from the erstwhile British India who arrived as sojourners, to earn a living on the Californian agricultural fields and timber stands of the Pacific Northwest. She does not reveal how, when they decided to stay on, they were not allowed to bring in their families or how they were denied citizenship because they did not meet the White prerequisites to naturalized citizenship. All Mrs. Nayar focuses on is the post-1965 immigration of skilled professionals from India.[6] There is no word of racism. Not a hint of the alienation these middle-class immigrants feel in American suburbia. No words on the anxieties of growing old in a culture where they feel they will never belong. These topics come up only in the company of other Indians, and the public face presented to the tourists is a cheerful, content one. Also disappeared from Mrs. Nayar's talk are the newer working-class immigrants, employed as cab drivers, housemaids, restaurant cooks, and waiters. Though she brings in the merchants, admittedly of different class origins than the professionals, she does so only under the pretext of them improving a dying urban economy. Like all other Indian immigrants, these individuals do not deplete the nation through any sort of dependence but contribute to the American economy by rebuilding a declining business district abandoned by established Americans. Indians, then, are new but exemplary citizens.

Even as we cast a critical eye on Mrs. Nayar's speech, we need to recognize it as a part of a repertoire of strategies by which Indians attempt to make the most of the space given to them in the city. They combat existing negative stereotypes regarding newcomers like them in what they perceive to be the most effective ways. Interventions such as Mrs. Nayar's are politically astute moves on immigrants' parts whereby they legitimate their inclusion into the body politic, not as rights seekers, but as nation builders. They insert themselves back into the picture as contributing members to the American nation.

The public presentation of the racial self does not come naturally but requires a self-reflexivity on the part of the immigrants. The self presented to the tourists emerges through conscious and deliberative intent. Indian immigrants at the Center contemplate, discuss, and argue about the content of their cultural heritage, what elements are central or peripheral, essential or marginal to their Indian-ness. And once these ostensibly essential elements are defined, they figure out which symbols are the most effective means to signify these Indian cultural elements. Therefore, the presentation of self is not a simple, unmeditative process but is made possible through intellectual labor. In addition, public presentation takes extensive backstage preparations that involve the physical work of gathering artifacts; arranging these artifacts in particular groupings; and crucially, draping out bodies with appropriate clothes so that they may appear authentically ethnic on the stage they have set.

Though the women—Mrs. Nayar, Anitha, and Susan—wear jeans, skirts, trousers, and other "mainstream American" clothes everyday, they dress up for the tourists in Indian clothes. They present themselves to scrutiny, converting themselves into ethnic objects. They serve themselves up as cultural props, fetishizing Indian clothes, and inviting the tourists' gaze on their ethnicized bodies. These ethnic outfits are not impositions, however; Mrs. Nayar, Anitha, and Susan choose to wear these clothes themselves. The Ethnic Tours present an opportunity to inhabit a "different skin"—the hide they presume that best represents their origins—from the ones they live in everyday. They derive a certain pleasure in pulling out their silks and cottons from the dark recesses of their closets and donning an Indian facade for the presentation of a racial self not just for others but also for themselves. Wearing these clothes gratifies them because they delineate Indian-ness to themselves, to other Indian immigrants, and to mainstream Americans. Through their clothes they claim authenticity, feeling themselves to be "stabilized, justified in [their] splendor."[7]

I start to feel illegitimate in this whole display of the Indian self—more like an interloper than someone who belongs—because I am not in the appropriate garments that exhibit my Indian origins. I feel I do not have the legitimate right to speak out or explain any practice, trinket, item, and so forth on display because in my jeans, old sweater, and hiking boots I am not part of the ethnic display. Do I feel inauthentic because I am a woman but am not clothed in racially signifying clothes? The men, after all, are not dressed in any ethnic garb. Do the men too, I wonder, feel a similar sense of unauthenticity as I do?

The stage is set for the tourists. We place tikkas on their foreheads, sprinkle them with rose water, and toss rose petals at them. There are displays of saris, kurtas, handmade dolls, religious artifacts such as kirpans, spices in little boxes, photographs, and so forth. In addition, there is Indian music to which Susan performs an Indian dance, while guests taste Indian foods. Hence, the prepared stage is intended to provide a full sensory experience of Indian heritage and ethnicity, which involve touch, taste, sound, and sight. Yet, because of the way they are displayed, these objects and performances have a frozen, museum-like quality about them instead of conveying a sense of a constantly changing, dynamic culture. The ethnic objects become objects of wonder, whereby they "stop the viewer in his or her tracks, to convey an arresting sense of uniqueness, to evoke an exalted attention."[8] These items and practices "are severed from their ritual sites," enhancing their objectification as cultural "curios."[9] They are unable to reach beyond their setting on those tables into the larger world from which they come forth.[10] By encapsulating Indian-ness in this static manner, decontextualized from the homes, kitchens, streets, temples, mosques, and so forth, the artifacts become objects of artifice. These objects of artifice tell us nothing of the significance of the kirpan to the Sikhs, the ways in which the spices on display get used in everyday meals, or the times/occasions on which pedas and dahi vadas are eaten. They fail to live up to their task because they are dislocated fragments sitting inert on those tables as objects of curiosity.[11]

Perhaps it is impossible to overcome the dull, inert museum effect when one displays objects neatly arranged on tables, serving as unique, cultural markers. Perhaps we should think of these displays as simply encouraging a particular way of seeing, so that we may tell and instruct persons about our racial selves. Yet, in this telling, the Center assumes the role of a cultural emissary, canonizing the practices of the Hindu majority as "high culture," and thus leading the tourists to develop a particular understanding of what is India and who are Indian Americans. The interpretive focus is on Brahmanic Hindu culture, excluding other castes and religions from the Indian nation. Placing tikkas on people's heads and the Bharat Natyam dance performance about Ganesha—are Hindu rituals and texts.

Uma Narayan notes that for a large part of western history, the East has been depicted as culturally weak and amoral. Western reformers and early feminists often construed Third World women as victims and positioned themselves as intrepid individuals on a mission to rescue the oppressed Third World masses. Today instead, we see "cultural emissaries" who are "missionaries with the mission of rescuing westerners from their negative stereotypes and attitudes towards Third World cultures and contexts."[12] Emissaries present their cultures in positive ways to undo the negative stereotypes attached to their cultures. However, offering only positive images of their cultures as an ameliorative measure against western stereotypes limits Third World individuals to valorize their "home" cultures. In addition, only the "high" culture of a region is presented as truly representative. Third World cultures—as Western cultures—are premised on exclusions of minorities. Narayan cautions those of us engaged in the task of representing our cultures to also call attention to institutions and practices that oppress minorities within our sending societies.

In the process of defining an Indian heritage out of which to build an Indian American racial identity, the cultural brokers at the Center excise individuals and practices they deem marginal. In authoring the racial self, they silence working-class individuals, Indian Muslims, and Indian Christians. They also cast popular culture so heavily informed by Bollywood as inauthentic expressions of Indian-ness. In the process of representing themselves, only one particular class of people gets to narrate the community into being. The working-class women and children, who mostly live around the Devon area and who come to the Center every weekend, are not allowed to be active participants in the Ethnic Neighborhood Tours. When these individuals barge into the large hall, inserting themselves into this "stage" being prepared for the tourists, they are asked to leave. Their presence disrupts Mrs. Nayar, Anitha, and Anand as they go about getting the room ready for the tourists. Their working-class comportment is an intrusion; their puzzlement and open questioning over why these cultural artifacts are presented in this manner, their lack of English skills that hinder their capacity to communicate effectively with tourists, their gauche appearance in saris made of synthetic fibers, their plastic sandals, their mismatched winter jackets from the Goodwill store a few blocks away all do not cohere into a presentable racial facade for the tourists.

Mrs. Nayar, Anitha, and Anand run "through [their] performance, checking for offending expressions when no audience is present to be affronted by them; . . . poor members of the team, who are expressively inept, [are] . . . dropped from the performance."[13] Excluding these working-class women and children and relegating them to the "backstage" is understood and explained in terms of efficiency, for these individuals "take up time" with their questions. Though these working-class individuals who mostly live around Devon too are being represented, they are not allowed to participate in the narration of Indian-ness. The tourists on the walking tour gaze at their kith and kin at work behind various store counters, displaying saris or selling Indian sweets, but the working-class immigrants remain voiceless for much of the tour.

The following day, Mrs. Nayar and Poonam were pleased with Susan's Bharat Natyam rendition. They amusedly reminisced of the time they had asked two young Indian American girls to perform an Indian dance for visiting school students. The two girls climbed the dais wearing salwaar kameezes, the ubiquitous long blouse and loose pants worn by South Asian women. They turned on their music system and out blared the latest Bollywood song. They began to gyrate their hips, flash their eyes coyly, and shake their *dupattas* (long scarves) over their heads in blatant imitation of the dances they had seen in Hindi films. Mrs. Nayar and Poonam were horrified by the girls' dance, for they felt this was not "true" Indian culture. Contradicting the Center's perspective, the two young girls' rendition of Indian dance shattered any notion of a monolithic, singular Indian culture, upsetting an otherwise carefully set-up stage. Mrs. Nayar and Poonam lost control as the racial script they had prepared slipped out of their hands and was taken over by the two young girls' performance of Indian-ness. What this indicates is that the realities presented by racial performances are frail realities, easily shattered by disagreements, contestations, and minor mishaps. Ever since this incident, Mrs. Nayar and Poonam were very careful about whom they invited to perform Indian dances at the Center. Perceived as inadequate members of the performance team, the young girls were never again asked to perform their Indian "filmi" dance. There was a certain level of bureaucratization and sense of "quality" control so that a homogenous ethnic performance was rendered at every neighborhood tour.[14]

In accordance with their understanding of Indian authenticity, only Bharat Natyam was taught on the Center premises on weekends. The early twenties, extremely talented dance teacher, Anjana, complained of her students, "These girls learn dance here [in the U.S.] for four to five months and think they know it all. It takes years of training and practice to be good. All they want to do is perform a couple of hip-shaking, chest heaving dances you see in Hindi films. That's not Indian dance," she ended indignantly. Anjana, like many other Indian Americans, recognized Bharat Natyam as an ageless tradition, representative of true India.

Contrary to this perception, however, Bharat Natyam has more recent origins tied squarely to the nationalist movements that arose in nineteenth- and twentieth-century India. Questions of authentic Indian culture, Hinduism, women's place in the home and society, and so forth all appeared during colonialism, in a search for an alternative Indian identity that was diametrically opposed to western, imperial Britishness. Prior to 1932, Bharat Natyam was known as *sadir*, and practiced by women temple dancers. Sadir was a reviled art form associated with debauchery, and the anti-*nautch* (anti-dance) movement launched by British and Indian social reformers in the late 1800s sought to halt temple dancing and rescue young girls from the clutches of the temples. By the 1920s, however, in the process of formulating indigenous traditions separate from the West, Indian "classical" dances were revived by the Indian intellectual elite. Sadir's links with temple dancers were erased, and it came to be canonized as Bharat Natyam through the interpretation of a second century text, *Natyashastra*, and an eleventh-century reinterpretation of the original *Natyashastra*.[15] One of the dance's earliest proponents was Rukmini Devi Arundale, an upper-class Brahmin woman who began a dance school. She invited Brahmin male teachers to "teach in her institution and [thus] formulated Bharat Natyam as the legacy of a male Brahmanical tradition."[16] By 1953, the newly independent Indian state established various national cultural academies such as the Sangeet Natak Akademi (music, theater and dance), the Lalit Kala Akademi (art), and the Sahitya Akademi (literature), which consolidated the claims that Bharat Natyam is an authentic classical Indian art form.[17]

In the United States, young Indian immigrant girls are often taught classical dances such as Bharat Natyam.[18] These classical dances are one of the ways through which immigrant communities construct their identity as both Indian and Hindu. Dance classes are held either in community halls, individual homes, or temples. In her ethnography of Indian Americans, Aparna Rayaprol writes that Bharat Natyam was taught at the Sri Venkateshwara temple, Pittsburgh, Pennsylvania, since 1977. At the time of her research, sixty girls attended dance rehearsals at the temple. Mothers drove their daughters "to rehearsals, help[ed] them learn their acts, [made] their costumes, and set the stage. Women travel[ed] long distances to the temple every week to train their children for the programmes."[19] Rayaprol notes that mothers and daughters play a critical role in the reproduction of Indian culture here in the United States—"learning classical Indian dance is considered as much a feminine trait as learning ballet in the West."[20] If boys expressed interest in dance, they were actively discouraged. Instead, they were directed toward sports such as tennis or soccer.[21] Bharat Natyam, as an authentic dance tradition, is taught to young Indian American girls as an initiation into an *ur* culture.

Authors such as Sunita Sunder Mukhi and Shamita Das DasGupta note, however, that Bollywood song/dance sequences have far wider circulation than classical dances both in India and here. These commercialized popular cultural forms—perceived as Western influenced and overtly erotic offer a powerful alternative to the Brahaminic renditions of Indian culture.[22] Hindi film videos, cassettes, and CDs of film music are accessible in places like Chicago's Devon Ave., and immigrants' filmi interpretations of Indian culture seep into their dances at religious holidays, parades, and other occasions. For example, at the 1994 India Day Parade in New York City celebrating India's independence, despite the cultural committee's requests for classical and folk dance renditions, most participants performed "filmi" dances. Six of the nine dances approved for the parade were Bollywood-inspired dance performances.[23]

Classical dances, as the Indo American Center dance instructor Anjana indicates, require long hours of arduous practice under the tutelage of an expert dancer. These dances require years of training and money in the form of dance class fees, dance debuts, and so forth. On the contrary, Hindi film dances are different; immigrant youth need not wait to be driven to dance classes over weekends or follow rigorous training under the eagle eyes of a guru. Instead, films can be played and replayed over the VCR, and the actors' steps mastered within a few hours. These popular dances are far more accessible to immigrant youth, allowing them to be "the author, as well as authority of [their] dance, talent, and expression of Indianness."[24]

A concluding note on the Ethnic Neighborhood Tours; one needs to note that the ethnic tours are a performance that present an idealized view of South Asian immigrants. To this extent, when immigrants present themselves, their "performance will tend to incorporate and exemplify the officially accredited values" of the larger society."[25] The elements that make up the rituals might be presented as quaint, but the *values* that guide their everyday immigrant lives are presented as being the same as American values. These Neighborhood Tours attract tourists because they present exotica in hermetically sealed packages that do not threaten any sense of American-ness. Indian-ness is contained geographically because it is present only in these neighborhoods or is practiced in private homes. Exotica is also contained culturally because rituals are all superficial. Contrarily, values such as strong families, the ethic of hard work, the spirit of adventure and enterprise—things that really matter for incorporation into the national body—are presented as extant in immigrant communities as well. To this extent, the Tour is a performance that "highlights the common official values of the society in which it occurs, we may look upon it . . . as a ceremony— as an expressive rejuvenation and reaffirmation of the moral values" of the larger imagined American community.[26]

January 24th, late 1990s.

Hinduism and Its Multiple Spokespersons: What Is It, Anyway?

Yesterday Philomena, the Goan Christian volunteer coordinator whom I was replacing at the Center, and I headed down to the Indo American Center at 8:00 A.M. We were going to take part in the Workshop Seminar for K–12 educators, titled "Religions of India." Diane, an older White woman married to an Indian professor at a Chicago university and an extremely active Center person, introduced the speakers. It was her grant-writing skills that had brought in the Fulbright Grant to the Indo American Center, and she meticulously planned the training workshops for teachers. She wore a cotton, hand-printed, vegetable-dyed salwaar kameez and introduced herself as an Indian by marriage—"in India the bride always goes to the husband's family and loses all connection and rights to her natal family. So I guess I'm Indian by marriage."

Professor Latimer, a sociologist at the University of Illinois, Chicago, and Steve Smith, graduate student in South Asian Studies at the University of Chicago, were the featured speakers on Indian religion. In the audience, along with the teachers, were Mrs. Nayar, Poonam, Aruna Agarwal (from Chinmaya Mission, a Hindu religious organization), Philomena, and I. After introductions, Professor Latimer began the workshop with his lecture titled "Preserving And Adapting Traditions: South Asian Immigrant Religious Institutions." He presented facts and figures on how many Indian Muslims, Hindus, and Christians live in the larger Chicago area and proceeded to show us maps of where mosques/temples/churches are located. The location of one of the temples was wrong, and much discussion ensued within the audience over the precise whereabouts of this particular temple. Next, Steve Smith lectured on "Religious Practices in Nepal, Katmandu Valley." He began with a short video of a religious procession in Katmandu to convey a visual image of his topic. Acutely conscious of the rising right-wing Hindutva movements in India, he focused on practices of Hinduism rather than the doctrinaire. He mentioned that in Hinduism there was no single religious text or a single god. He described Hinduism as an umbrella category that covered all practices not included in other religions.

At this, some members of the audience began to move restlessly in their seats. Poonam leaned over to whisper to Diane. Diane nodded her head and interrupted Steve, "Excuse me, but we have a real, live Hindu in this audience who wants to add something," and Poonam began to loudly object to Steve's definition of Hinduism. She did not think her religion was an odd collection of things "left over" that did not quite fit in anywhere. Such a portrayal of Hinduism, she thought, misrepresented the complexity of the oldest religion in the world. At this point, I jumped in, taking Steve's side, "What we understand as Hinduism today arises in the early to mid-1800s." Mrs. Nayar interrupted, "I don't know about that," she said, shaking her head. Diane then broke into what might have developed into a long drawn verbal battle on colonialism, culture, and religion in India. "My mother-in-law performs these rituals every morning along with her prayers. Its all so beautiful to watch," she exclaimed. The tremendous confusion that ensued from Steve's incomplete talk confused the teachers. Leave these arguments behind, they begged, "Just give us facts regarding Hinduism so we can teach our fourth graders."

Professor Latimer's lecture, in acknowledgment of India's religious diversity, addressed Hindus, Christians, and Muslims. The second lecture, however, focused specifically on Hindu practices in neighboring Nepal. The special attention to Hinduism is because close to 80 percent of Indians are Hindus, and also, it is professedly indigenous to the Indian subcontinent. Upon entering the room, I had assumed the two White men from elite academic institutions were invited to add an aura of intellectual authority to the workshop proceedings. I soon realized, however, that even though these men were posited as experts, "real live" Hindus in the audience interceded constantly, correcting geographical errors or challenging what they perceived to be misrepresentations of their religion. By declaring Mrs. Nayar, Poonam, Aruna Agarwal, and me authentic Hindus, Diane positioned us insiders, a social location which eventually "work[ed] to intimidate and silence mainstream members of the audience [and Steve Smith in this case], causing them to refrain from articulating questions or comments that reflect their own critical understanding."[27] The weight of our experience as Hindus—asserted as our fundamental identity for this particular workshop— implicitly set us as having a proprietary relationship with Hinduism. We were the privileged providers of real knowledge about "our" religion. Nevertheless, much to the frustration of the teachers, the "authentic insiders" themselves end up having disagreements about their religion.

Though the teachers were confused regarding Hinduism, the ensuing debate conveyed more about this particular religion than they realized. The heated discussions that arose among Hinduism's many spokespersons revealed that Hindus made sense of their nonmonotheist religion in multiple ways. Hinduism does not have just one single authoritative religious testament but has been recast by numerous Sanskrit scriptural texts transmitted orally and through written treatises over centuries. Actual religious practices differ vastly among Hindus around the world. To describe Hinduism as a collection of "leftover" rituals, at some level, attests to its diversity of scriptural texts and heterogeneous ceremonial practices arising from the appropriation of local customs/belief systems. Hinduism's heterogeneity defies any attempts at coming up with a singular definition.

Steve Smith's characterization of Hinduism as not having a single text and as having contradictory practices marks this polytheistic religion as an undefined entity, still in the process of being made. Its nebulously defined boundaries and practices can therefore be subject to all kinds of claims and counterclaims. Such a characterization of vagueness renders Hinduism a vulnerable space, a location into which Indian Americans cannot safely retreat, for here too their truth assertions can be contested. As a rebuttal to Steve Smith, Poonam and Mrs. Nayar assert their religion as the oldest in the world. This claim is questionable because Hinduism in its present form originates with nineteenth-century modernism, regenerated largely through Bengali and Maharashtrian

Brahmin dialogues with British colonialism.[28] The equation of Indian tradition with Hinduism, specifically Brahminism, is a modern phenomenon that arose from the ways in which nineteenth-century nascent nationalists reformulated traditions and archaic texts to fashion a new, "imagined" national community, in complete contrast to their British colonizers.[29]

In addition, some members in the audience maintained Hinduism as indigenous to India, in contrast to Islam and Christianity. Such a postulation, by inference, casts the latter two religions as foreign and, therefore, illegitimate Indian cultural/religious expressions. Hinduism's authenticity claims and its consequent equation with an unadulterated, pure Indian culture is utilized by the Indian ultra-right to delegitimize the profound influences Islam and Christianity have had on Indian societies. Any such influences are seen to degrade an *ur*-culture, and cultural nationalists have sought to wipe them out to resurrect a new national culture along Brahmanic Hindu lines.[30] Right-wing movements in India have held onto the notion of an *ur*-culture throughout the late 1980s and 1990s, contributing to the current strength of Hindu fundamentalism in India. And though the Center is avowedly secular and unconditionally antifundamentalist, its particular renditions of Hinduism and Indian culture, contrary to its intentions, pushes it into the very political corners it so fiercely shuns. The identification of "some cultural expressions or artifacts as authentic, genuine, trustworthy, or legitimate simultaneously implies that other manifestations are fake, spurious, and even illegitimate."[31] They hold onto the fallacy of cultural purity instead of the constantly altering, hybrid nature of Indian-ness, thereby excising persons they do not mean to exclude. Their consumption and reproduction of Indian-ness—driven by the need to prove their worthiness—leads them to unintentionally reproduce the very structures of exclusions they strive so hard to overcome at their Center.

February 7ᵗʰ, late 1990s.

Can Indians Be Christians?

A short, dark South Indian in his late 50s, Rajesh's managerial capability was the glue that held the Indo American Center's everyday operations together. His expertise was called upon for various matters, ranging from soothing irate employees, to disciplining rambunctious children at the Child Tutoring Program, to even cleaning out clogged bathrooms. Without him, the Center unraveled. Looking up from the fax he was sending off, Rajesh informed me that we were going to have visitors later that day. The Christian Youth Service was visiting the Center to learn about us and decide if they wanted to volunteer with us. "They will come here by the busload, Sharmila," emphasized Rajesh, "so please get that conference room ready." As I aligned tables and straightened chairs for our guests, Mrs. Nayar came in, casually attired in blue jeans and her long, purple winter jacket. She had a plastic bag in her hands. "I need to change," she exclaimed, as she rushed off to the room where we store our various paraphernalia we use to represent India.

Soon, the Christian Youth Service people arrived at the Center. The five young men and boys and two women, all ranging from twenty-two to fifteen years of age, arranged themselves awkwardly into the bright orange plastic chairs. After a few clumsy introductory words on both our parts, Diane and I began to describe the Center's various projects. Mrs. Nayar poked her head through the door to do a quick appraisal of the guests before she walked in, and I noticed her kohl-lined eyes open wider. Absolute surprise was writ large on her face. Her eyebrows drew in as she quickly composed her face into a smile and walked into the conference room. She was clad in a beautiful Bangalore silk sari. On her forehead was a large, black *bindhi*. She sat next to Diane and I overheard her whisper embarrassedly, "These are Indians! Somehow I thought they would be Americans, so I quickly changed into all of this, you know."

Though the Indo American Center board has prominent Christian and Muslim members, slippages such as Mrs. Nayar's are extremely common among South Asian Americans and others. I wonder too, among you readers, how many of you thought the Christian volunteers were not of South Asian origins. Only Hindus get equated with India, and Christians especially, are erased. Christianity is seen as a purely western phenomenon, and Mrs. Nayar assumed that the Christian Youth Services was a White American organization. Mrs. Nayar was thoroughly embarrassed by her mistake for multiple reasons. First, she did not mean to exclude Christians from the "Indian community," and her unintentional exclusion embarrasses her. Second, because she thought they were White, Mrs. Nayar changed from blue jeans to a sari, that is, from her "American" into her authentic "Indian" persona. She wanted to be an authentic ethnic for the visiting youth. Her chagrin arises from the fact that the Indian American Christians, accustomed to role switching themselves, saw through Mrs. Nayar's faux pas.

People underplay those activities and facts that are incompatible with an idealized version they want to present of themselves and their racial communities. Individuals cultivate "the impression that the routine they are presently performing is their only routine or at least their most essential one . . . the audience, in their turn, often assumes that the character projected before them is all there is to the individual who acts out the projection before them."[32] However, contrary to Mrs. Nayar's performance, our ethnic identity is not necessarily the "most essential" identity at ALL times.

There is no way by which Mrs. Nayar, representing the Indo American Center, can tactfully back out of her error. We are all collectively caught in the act of performing Indian-ness, mutually embarrassing each other. The very act of changing her clothes to present herself as Indian—something we all do to emphasize our authenticity to "outsiders"—inadvertently casts the Christian youth as outsiders to the Indian immigrant community. Both she and the Christian youth recognize the meaning of this oversight, and there seemed no way to recuperate this awkward social moment inscribed with so much significance.

"If We Don't Respect Our Culture, Will Others Respect Us?" *Disputes in Displaying Culture*

February 27th, late 1990s.

Today forty-two fifteen-year-olds from an Evanston school trooped into the Center at 12:00 noon; they were here for a field trip. Once the children sat in their chairs, Diane introduced me as living in Bangalore, India. I interrupted, "Ah, Diane, my parents live there but I live here in Chicago." Diane flushed at my correction; I stood by her side in blue corduroy jeans, a cotton shirt, a scarf around my neck, and hiking boots on my feet. I had been in the United States since 1989. Diane, a self-defined "Indian by marriage" was dressed in a cotton salwaar kameez complete with a dupatta. Around her neck was an Indian silver chain. Lekha Mehta was supposed to join us, but she had not as yet arrived.

We were to teach the school children how to drape a sari. Two schoolgirls volunteered; Diane draped the sari on one, and I worked on the other girl. Her fellow classmates applauded when they saw her draped out in a sari. I went over to Diane to help her with the pleats, and as I worked on them, she said effusively, "Now watch Sharmila's fingers. Even the act of draping a sari is an art form!"

The children had sat in the room for close to two hours, and now they were ready to go explore Devon. They were hungry, and they wanted to buy henna to paint their hands. I passed around bindhis, and many walked out the door with colorful dots stuck on their foreheads. After they left Diane, Lekha, and I sat on chairs and spoke. Lekha began by apologizing for her tardiness. Apparently her daughter at Rush Medical School had just finished an exam. She wanted to speak with her, but the daughter had called at 11:45 A.M., thus delaying her. Lekha then proceeded to talk of her extended family in India.

Suddenly she stopped and self-consciously interrupted herself mid-sentence, "I'm so sorry I'm going on like this, but when I talk about India I get so emotional. I can't help it. I love it so much. My husband is a very good man, and one couldn't ask for anyone better, but the kids love India and know so much about our culture only because of me! Even here they try remember what India is. Not like these other kids nowadays—there's this club called Karma Club . . ."

I jumped in, "Oh yes, I've been there!"

Lekha then said, "Well, I won't go any further. Tell me what you thought about it."

Occupying three floors in a prime downtown location, Karma Club's interiors were done up in rich velvets in reds, violets, blues, and greens. All over the walls hung images of Indian gods. The proprietors of the Club were three first-generation Indian men in their early thirties. A large idol of Nataraja (an avatar of the Hindu god Shiva) surrounded by lamps that were lit hung by the bar. This image, used as décor, had raised an uproar.

At this point, Lekha interrupted me to say that she did not like decontextualized displays of religious idols. Lekha added that her daughter and her Indian American friends used to frequent the Karma Club, but one day they were tremendously offended. Their waiter came up to them dressed as Ganesha [another Hindu god], replete with an elephant head. He moved his head vigorously from side to side and made clumsy dance movements—very clown-like—with his over-sized Ganesha body. The whole effect was supposed to arouse laughter among patrons, but instead it only offended them. They complained to the proprietors who remained unsympathetic. The daughter then went back to her Indian American friends at Rush Medical College, and they organized a silent protest, replete with placards, in front of Karma Club. Lekha was so proud of her daughter. "Is it not interesting," she remarked, "that my daughter who's been raised here has so much more respect and understanding of her heritage than these boys raised in India? Children raised here are much better Indians because they know Hinduism better than these children raised in India." Lekha concluded, "If we don't learn to appreciate and respect our own culture, then how will others respect us? If we want to be respected then we must respect ourselves."

I title this subsection "Disputes In Displaying Culture" because the cultural conflicts are apparent not just in Lekha's story but also in the way Diane and I want to be perceived by the school children. Like Mrs. Nayar who always wore a sari when the Center had visitors, Diane too wore her Indian clothes when she presented India to an audience. Through their clothing these women literally embodied Indian culture. Perceiving me—dressed in jeans and hiking boots—as too inauthentic, Diane attempts to give me a modicum of Indian genuineness by stating I live in Bangalore. Instead, I correct her and state I may come from Bangalore, but now I live in Chicago. After having lived in the Midwest for one-third of my life, this too has become home, as is India. By openly disagreeing with Diane, I partially want to complicate the fifteen-year-olds' understandings of Indian-ness and American-ness, but more strongly, I wish for her to recognize me as a valid resident here in the United States. Diane is embarrassed because she realizes that her introduction inadvertently casts me as an outsider to this nation, and this is not her intention.

Immigrants, especially post-1965 immigrants, have homes in their sending countries such as Vietnam, Ghana, and India, as well as the receiving nation, the United States. Instead of being bounded by loyalties to just one or the other, these individuals negotiate culture/family/national communities both here and there. Mrs. Nayar, Poonam, the Christian Youth Service people, Diane, and I are not products of a single nation-state but instead straddle, albeit uneasily perhaps, both the East and the West. Yet, this quest for authenticity and the establishment of the legitimate Indian voice forecloses the possibility—indeed the very reality—of our lives in the late twentieth century, where a growing number of us cannot be confined to the geographical and cultural boundaries of any one single nation-state.

The establishment of legitimate Indian-ness is crucial for the diaspora precisely because they have moved out of India. It is not just the issue of making community here in the United States, Indians in India and new immigrants constantly question these transnational individuals' claim to being Indian. For instance, a derogatory term used to describe second-generation Indian Americans is "American Born Confused Desi," which acronyms to ABCD.[33] It is precisely within this context that Lekha claims her second-generation immigrant daughter knows Hinduism better and, therefore, more authentically Indian than the three first-generation proprietors of Karma Club who were raised in India.[34] The three owners of the Karma Club never played any Hindi movie song remixes that are popular among Indian American youth, or even desi music such as *Bhangra* hip-hop and Asian funk from Britain or Chutney from the Caribbean. They only played "White" music; yet, they decorated the place with Indian paraphernalia. The second-generation Ms. Mehta was appalled that "her culture" was not only being commodified and displayed in a decontextualized manner, but worse, Hindu gods were made into objects of amusement, invoking laughter from the public at large. This construed disrespect for Hinduism could only mean that the three entrepreneurs had no respect for their Hindu and, therefore, Indian origins.[35] If one has no pride in their origins, asked Lekha Mehta, then how can anyone else respect them? By fashioning Hindu gods into objects that invoke laughter, these three men were seen to contribute to the closing of America to all Indians.

"We Need More Indian Voices": Educating K–12 Teachers

March 14ᵗʰ, late 1990s.

Today was the second Fulbright workshop, titled "Women In India." I too spoke at this workshop. First the teachers presented their lesson units. I had to attend to other work at the Center and missed all lesson plans except Madhu's, a second-generation Indian American teacher employed in the Chicago school system. When I entered the room I saw she had written neatly on the blackboard: *Pre-industrial India Industrial Brazil Post-industrial U.S.A*

She divided the audience into three unequally sized groups. The largest was India, the second largest Brazil, and the smallest group represented the United States. The groups were asked specific questions on education levels, development of infrastructure, and population figures for these countries. Which countries have birth control, she asked, and then proceeded to answer the question herself—Brazil did not because of religion. Indians also did not have access to birth control because of lack of education. The United States was the only one of the three where birth control was freely available to all women.

Next Madhu brought out a bag of candy. She poured down a whole heap of candy on the table by the United States group. She then handed less candy to the Brazilian group. Lastly, she gave one dry cracker to the "India" group, which had the largest number of people. The point she wanted to illuminate with this economics lesson plan, she said, was the paucity of resources and the unequal distribution of income across nations. The reason for unequal distribution was because Third World countries such as India were overpopulated. If women had access to better birth control, they would have fewer children and fewer people depleting the nation's resources.

Edith Janson, an anthropologist at a community college in the Chicago suburbs, went on next. She had slides from rural India, taken during her trip over thirteen years ago. She began her lecture by saying, "We were really lucky. The village headman let people know we were there, and we even got to open their cupboards and photograph their belongings." I wondered silently if Edith would allow someone to walk into her home so that they may take photographs of her closet, her home, her privacy as representative of "authentic" Americana? In quiet whispers, I shared my concerns with the teacher sitting next to me. She agreed, but whispered that these slides were valuable archival material. Edith proudly declared that she had stayed at this Indian village for ten days. "I lasted it out when others did not," said with pride in her voice. "Their toilet plumbing is different. It is a ceramic hole in the ground. And I could manage fine. Now compared to Thailand a few years earlier, where I went outside and had to use a stick to keep away the pigs, this was a luxury," she ended.

My presentation was scheduled to go on last. Each speaker had been assigned forty-five minutes, but because people went overtime, I had less than twenty minutes to talk about feminisms in India. I spoke about the early 1990s anti-alcohol agitation in Andhra Pradesh, interspersed with clippings from the documentary *When Women Unite.* Later a couple of teachers came up to me and said they enjoyed my presentation. They asked for copies of the articles I used. One teacher added—"what the workshop really needs is more Indian voices like Madhu's and yours."

Madhu's lesson plan was well received because its interactive nature would engage school children and compel them to think analytically. The substantive issues she raised, however, were problematic. First, she overlooked the fact that birth control (barrier methods such as condoms and IUDs and hormonal methods such as the pill) and abortion are easily accessible in India. The Indian state maintains a network of 20,847 primary health centers and 1,300,000 subcenters all over the country, focusing chiefly on reproductive issues. The problem has never been access to birth control; the predicament for many Indian women has been the state's goal of population control. The sorts of health services available to women are heavily biased in favor of permanent sterilization, with financial incentives for persons who undergo these procedures. These centers may stress the voluntary nature of their birth control projects, but the programs are organized around achieving a set number of sterilizations within a period of time.[36] Madhu ignored the ferocity with which population control programs were implemented in the mid-1970s that resulted in widespread, serious health repercussions for working-class women in general, and Muslim working-class women in particular. Second, the lesson plan blamed women and their bodies as dangerously fertile. Madhu failed to understand that high birth rates are not the cause for poor economies. Instead, high birth rates are a dependent variable; impoverished couples opt for large families as a means of social/economic security in the face of an uncertain future. Moreover, Indian women's fecundity is not a causal factor in the India's global economic standing. India's economy is affected by a whole host of factors such as economic liberalization programs, technological innovations in industry, transnational corporation (TNC) investments, agricultural performance, global markets, state investment in human capital, and global/internal financial markets.

Edith Janson, who took the stage next, began to show her slides of a village in India taken in the early 1980s. Her slides harked back to an India seemingly untouched by modernity, and, therefore, the source of an *ur*-tradition. There is no understanding in her slides of the ways in which men migrate out of these impoverished villages in search of employment, the ways in which these men participate in unions, or that these women work on larger landlords' properties as wage laborers. These individuals too are incorporated into global economies, and their everyday lives are fundamentally affected by structural adjustment, economic development policies, and international trade agreements. Diane is irritated because Edith's lecture is not specifically about women. At the end of the workshop, I heard her exchanging words with Edith. Both their bodies were tense. Their faces looked unhappy.

I, the other "Indian voice" along with Madhu, spoke of one of the strongest women's movements of the 1990s in rural India. Tired of the trope of the oppressed Indian woman and the presumption that feminism is a "western," urban phenomenon, I spoke of rural women's struggles against the sales of country-made liquor in their villages. I hoped to destabilize any presumptions the teachers might have of Indian women as submissive, or that only "westernized" Indian women occupy public spaces. A couple of teachers, in appreciation of the information they received, came up to Madhu and me after our talk and told us, "What the workshop really needs is more Indian voices." I am uncomfortable with this statement; I pointed out my knowledge does not come by virtue of my being Indian, but I spoke of this anti-alcohol movement only because I had read articles, watched a documentary film, and developed an analysis of this particular social movement in conversation with others.[37]

"Yeha aakar hum sub gadhe hothe hain": Immigration and the Loss of Self

March 8th, late 1990s.

The board met today to discuss the Center's long-term plans. Mohan, the janitor, came in to help me clean the room after the meeting. He also worked at the airport as a janitor. This gig at IAC was his second job. As we engaged in idle chitchat, it came up that my brother was a surgeon in India. Mohan then said in Hindi, "Don't ask him to come here. He will be happier there." Why, I asked. He replied, *"Yeha aakar hum sub gadhe hothe hain"* (we all come here and become donkeys or foolish asses, or literally, beasts of burden). In Gujarat, prior to coming here, Mohan had a shop—"just like the Patel Brothers here on Devon, *didi*. I used to make Rs. 1,500 every day in cash! I had plenty to be happy with. Then my sister, who lives in Los Angeles, called me here." Thinking he could make more money, he arrived at Los Angeles. He did not speak English and found it hard to make ends meet. Mohan worked two part-time jobs without any benefits and barely slept five to six hours per day. His wife worked one part-time job. With all the expenses involved in a four-member household, they barely managed to save $200 per month. He thought this country is such that even a doctor could fall into bad times.

"*Didi*" he said in Hindi, "I'm scared. I'm growing older and I don't have enough money. What will I do when my children want a college education? The other day my friend's son wanted $50 from his father. But my friend had only $25 with him and couldn't give him more. Then the son turned around and said to his father—'then fuck you!'" These last three words are the only English words Mohan used in our conversation. Mohan worried that American culture makes Indian children bad. Mohan concluded that Indian culture was best, and I should never ask my brother to come settle in the United States, like his sister asked him.

Mohan explained that in this country even a mother does not breast-feed her child, and this is one reason why children turn bad. Mohan continued, "In this country people do not help each other. In India if someone falls down, others rush to the person's aid. (At this point Mohan held my upper arm like I had fallen and he was helping me up). Even if someone comes to help, the person who has been helped can turn around and sue his helpers. So you see," Mohan explained, "no one wants to help. Even a mother will not breast-feed her child. If a mother breast-fed her children, then the children would get some of her intelligence and compassion. But because she does not, the children grow up warped. This makes the entire American culture bad. Its not just White women, Indian women too become selfish in America."

I tried to rationalize with Mohan that whether it was in India or here, mothers often did not breast-feed because they had no choice. They had to be at work to earn a living so they could make ends meet and ultimately raise their children. Women did the best they could, given their circumstances. Mohan reluctantly agreed, nodding his head in an unconvinced manner. He instead picked on the theme of overwork in my spiel, and he added that the worst part of American culture was how hard people had to work here. Mohan said people in India think money in America grows on trees but instead, "it all rests on your back" (at this point Mohan bent over low and pointed to his lower back). "This is where all the money is, *didi*," he repeated once again, pointing to his back. He straightened out and said that even though one worked hard, it was not enough. His example was just one of many. He'd asked his wife and kids to join him eighteen months ago. "I thought, *chalo*, let them too see America. So I asked them to come join me here."

Mohan had been in the United States for four years and his immediate family for eighteen months. His two children did well in school, but English was a problem. "They are good children so far, but one has to wait and see," he said. We finished up the last bit of cleaning and left. I climbed into my car and headed home, to rest up, write field notes, walk the dog at Pratt Beach, and then begin my twelve-hour night shift at Apna Ghar. Mohan stayed on to clean the rest of the Center and then head over to O'Hare later in the evening for his daily night shift.

Mohan felt that he was losing his old, familiar "self" upon immigrating to the United States. His class location, his old networks of kith and kin, his expressions of parental love, children's respect for parents, and so forth were all dissipating around him. Taken for granted ways of behavior, social protocols, and familial expectations did not hold true anymore. In Mohan's eyes, the United States was a nation where fathers are overworked, mothers selfishly refuse to breast feed their babies, and sons scream expletives at fathers, with no regard for the pain they cause their parents.

When Mohan first began to talk about American motherhood, I presumed he meant to tell me that American culture was such that even "primordial" ties as the ones between mother and child were fragile. Even the mother-child relationship, a universal icon for understanding relationships of absolute dependence and nurturance, were rendered feeble in the United States. Mohan very quickly dispeled these ideas, however. For him, American culture was fundamentally embodied in woman's roles as both biological and cultural reproducers. Though he acknowledged that the economy affects our lives—whether we are doctors or day laborers—the central causal factor behind alienation in this nation is that mothers do not breast feed their children. In Mohan's eyes, the mother-child relationship is not an intrinsic part of American womanhood and, therefore, American mothers did not impart any values of caring to their children. When something as basic to "human nature" as mothering itself was missing, how then could we expect a citizenry that was any different? The selfishness of American women was transmitted to their children and eventually resulted in an American society that was individualistic and where everyone acted as an atomized self-interested actor.

My discomfort at this line of reasoning was apparent in my speech and mannerisms, and Mohan abandoned his analysis of American culture. He instead returned to the theme of work I had introduced in our conversation. He spoke about how hard he worked. The loss of self that Mohan felt is furthered by his endless workday, toiling as a janitor first at the Center and then at the airport. Mohan felt he is not a human being anymore, but described himself as turning into beast of burden, working day and night. For him, coming to America resulted in a loss of an old self and converted him into a low-end worker who sees no meaning in his work. He felt acute alienation in his new life as an American.

The juxtaposition of events seemed bizarre to me; earlier in the day, board members had sat on these chairs—eating bagels and cream cheese, with coffee and orange juice, complete with a fruit platter—discussing what the Indo American Center's role should be in the future. Community service. Helping people integrate into American society. I write about all of this at the beginning of this chapter. Approximately two hours later, I helped Mohan—the very kind of person the Center wants to help—clean the room. The only assistance he needed to "integrate" into the United States was a well-paying job with benefits, and what the Center provided for new immigrants were only stopgap measures. Thousands like Mohan slipped between the cracks of English as a Second Language training, citizenship classes, and computer coaching. Even if he took these classes, there was little hope for a better living, given the changed economy. The Mohans of immigrant communities stood in the margins, seeking to make a home in this late modern world. But all that is solid constantly melts into air, and they find themselves clutching at last straws to hold onto a life of dignity and meaning. They have willingly, yet unwittingly, participated in their conversion from human beings into beasts of burden.

Five

The Politics of Cultural Authenticity

. . . why can't I be "Indian" without having to be "authentically Indian"? What is the difference and how does it matter? In the diasporean context in the United States, ethnicity is often forced to take on the discourse of authenticity just to protect and maintain its space and history. . . . Why should "black" be authentic when "white" is hardly even seen as a color, let alone pressured to demonstrate its authenticity? . . . When we say "authenticate," we also have to ask "authenticate for whom and for what purpose?" Who and by what authority is checking our credentials? Is "authenticity" a home we build for ourselves or a ghetto we inhabit to satisfy the dominant world?
—R. Radhakrishnan, Diasporic Mediations:
   Between Home and Location

Introduction

A recurring theme throughout the various fieldwork vignettes I present in the previous chapter, so far not fully addressed, is that of authenticity. The first vignette regarding Neighborhood Tours is all about presenting a genuine Indian face to the tourists. In such a presentation, contestations arise over "true" Indian dance, the valid Indian immigration story, and the best immigrants—middle-class professionals dressed in Indian silks—to tell this story. Ethnic authenticity is not about telling it like it is, but instead it is a process of choosing narratives that best represent the ways in which you want to be seen. The second episode is a description of conflicts over what is Hinduism and who are its appropriate spokespersons. The third event I describe is an inadvertent casting out of Christian Indian Americans from the bounds of community because they are not Hindu and, therefore, inauthentic Indians. The fourth episode is replete with Diane's and my claims and counterclaims to Indian and American belonging. In addition, Lekha says Indian Americans are more authentic than Indians raised in India. We are all jostling for a place at the table, for our voices to be validated as genuinely belonging so that we too may vested with legitimate personhood. The fifth vignette is a description of a workshop for the teachers where Edith Janson shows her slides of "authentic" rural India. In addition, Madhu and I are seen as providing the "truest" version on India because of our racial origins. My conversations with Mohan focus on the collapse of his prior easy, comfortable self. "We come here and we become donkeys," he says, to depict the loss of authenticity and his personal quest for a life of sincerity and dignity.[1]

While I have discussed the wellspring of Indian authenticity—the nation of India and Hinduism in particular—what is at stake in claiming authenticity? Do claims to an Indian authenticity provide a platform from which to speak confidently?[2] And if so, why do claims to authenticity legitimate one to speak with authority? How do authenticity claims affect the contents of one's speech?

Defining Authenticity

Authenticity is defined as something that has fidelity to actuality, compatible with a certain source or origin, in accordance with tradition, or something that exists in sincerity without feigning or hypocrisy. Authenticity indicates authority that is not usually open to challenge. It endows an object or practice with acceptability because the object conforms to standards of fact and reality and is not contradicted by evidence. It is trustworthy, credible, and convincing. Authentic can also mean something that is vested with due formalities and legally attested, that is, something properly qualified. It suggests something that is not imaginary or specious; it is real, genuine, and original. The origins of an authentic object/practice cannot be questioned. It is seen to indisputably proceed from a given source that is avowed. Lastly, authenticity is defined as being marked by conformity to widespread or long-continued tradition. A thing is authentic when it accurately and satisfyingly reproduces the essential features of a portrait, or in our case, the essential features of a culture. Synonyms of authentic include genuine, veritable, and bona fide. Genuine emphasizes the real as contrasted with a fraudulent, deceptive appearance. Genuine may also describe emotions or mental states honestly experienced and not falsely simulated. Veritable indicates a true existence or actual identity. Bona fide suggests good faith and lack of intent to deceive.

Authenticity and Modernity

The quest for authenticity among people, then, is the search for a true self-identity. It is all about discovering the fountainhead of a genuine self and then transforming into a "real being" in a world of hypocrisy. Berman, Bellah et al. and Di Leonardo identify the search for authenticity as arising from the angst we feel about the loss of self in the rapid currents of modernity that sweep us away.[3] Some persons identify this angst as intensely antimodern because it arises as an unease with modernity and seeks a turning back to origins. They see the pursuits of authenticity as cravings "for experiences of unmediated genuineness [that] seek to cut through what Rousseau called 'the wound of reflection,' a reaction to modernization's demythologization, detraditionalization, and disenchantment."[4]

However, when one reads Herder's German authentic arising from the volk and Sartre's existential authenticity, or Marshall Berman and Ken Plummer's descriptions of the modern authentic self, it is apparent that the ways in which we recover our lost selves is through processes that invoke sentiments that accompany modernity. Sartre's existentialist version of authenticity is based on the "assumption that every human self possesses an essential core, a kind of psychological DNA, which it tries to assert *through* its interaction with others."[5] Being in society helps us realize who we are, but this social belonging imposes a certain level of civility upon us, which curbs the natural tendencies of our self. Sartre was convinced that "public, civilized behavior was contaminated by hypocrisy and inauthenticity" and becoming "civilized had only undermined his own inner sense of self."[6] Only those cast outside the bounds of civilized society—Black Africans, homosexuals, Jews, and other marginalized groups—the paradigmatic Others to Sartre's French culture, had a greater chance at achieving authenticity. He held that "members of marginal groups were oases of potential authenticity in a desert of bad faith. He believed he could rescue himself only if he could fully identify or transform himself into a symbolic outsider like them."[7]

Herder, on the other hand, recognized that only some societies generated the symbolic material out of which authentic selves arose. He criticized "urban manners, artifice in language, behavior, and art," because these spurious elements allegedly suppressed the German authentic present in the pastoral way of life.[8] Contrary to urban life, rural society held the promise of a true, uniquely German state of being, and so he singled out "folk poetry as a locus of folkness, inspiring contemporaries and an entire social and literary movement to absorb and imitate the authentic aesthetic of the folk . . . the verbal art of the peasantry became a means for humanity at large to get in touch with its authenticity."[9] The German authentic based on an idealized rural *volk* became the basis for German fascist nationalism.

Marshall Berman states that the quest for authenticity is people's deepest responses to modernity. Authenticity is "bound up with the radical rejection of things as they are," because modern societies are often perceived as constraining structures that strangle individuality.[10] These stifled individuals strive for a new society in which their authentic selves may flower into existence. Berman writes:

> Our society is filled with people who are ardently yearning and consciously striving for authenticity; moral philosophers who are exploring the idea of "self-realization"; psychiatrists and their patients who are working to develop and strengthen "ego-identity"; artists and writers who gave the word "authenticity" the cultural force it has today—some consciously influenced by existentialism, others ignorant of it, but all bent on creating works and living lives in which their deepest, truest selves will somehow be expressed; young people, hip or straight, seeing to "get themselves together," determined above all to "do their own thing"; countless anonymous men and women all over who are fighting, desperately and against all odds, simply to preserve, to feel, to be themselves.[11]

Authenticity arises in transformative politics too, propelling individuals into social movements by asking them to understand themselves in terms of "difference." People are urged to think of their action as "contributing to the construction of an authentic communal identity—their own—as well as contributing to the secure expressive space for that identity within the public arena."[12] Ken Plummer examines sexual stories that people tell—coming out stories, rape survivor stories, recovery tales—to illuminate the various means by which people undergo a process of self-discovery, uncover their true selves, and become a part of larger "authenticating" communities. He sees these personal narratives as late modernist stories through which individuals tell their lives into being. A starting point for these personal narratives is the suffering of impending danger or a squelched desire society imposes on individuals. The stories then generally move to the various paths by which an "authentic self" struggles against social threats and impositions and emerges out into the open. The emergence of this authentic sexual self through storytelling, Plummer says, leads individuals to participate in larger social movements, eventually building up sexual communities that nurture authentic selves. Examples of such communities are the gay and lesbian communities that arose from the 1970s onward.[13]

Ethnic Authenticity

Hence, the quest for authenticity—an emotion structured uniquely by modernity—arise in diverse realms, from GLBT liberation movements seeking to establish an unfettered authentic sexual self to right-wing nationalisms that are based on notions of a singular culture and an authentic constituency. Immigrants at the Indo American Center too seek authenticity to cope with the processes of spatial displacement through a nostalgic return to their origins, a return to times when things were ostensibly all right with the world.

Park and Miller observe of eastern and southern European immigrants in early-twentieth-century Chicago—"in Europe, the question of personality was not the subject of much reflection, because everything was habitual, but here the realization of the incongruities between himself and American life makes the *question of personality* acute."[14] They note that the process of immigration resulted in an acute self-reflexivity among immigrants; though persons who immigrate are no doubt changing in their home countries, they are not as self-conscious of these changes as they are when they arrive as immigrants into a new national context. Immigration entails such an explosive upheaval in social and personal life that life in the sending country, though changing all the time, seems stagnant in comparison. Moving to a new nation—into a new cultural context—is a sudden, radical transformation. Immigrants have to create completely new selves over a short period of time, which is done in far more self-conscious ways than ever before. Immigration means that everyday ways of doing things are not taken for granted anymore but require careful deliberation. The manner in which they structure their days, occupy public space, walk down the street, the way they look at people or avert their eyes, the modes through which they interact with neighbors, or shop in markets are all reassessed and worked out to fit into a new context. Older, established methods of doing things give way to the new, as they become Americans. Also, in many cases, immigrants to the United States move into a culture that is far more fiercely focused on the individual and the actualization of the self than the country they left.

Like these other immigrants that came before them, South Asian immigrants too have to produce themselves anew in very short periods of time. In this multicultural era, however, where we recognize or even *expect* difference, the tasks that lie ahead of these new non-White immigrants are different from the ones their (now White) predecessors faced. While their European predecessors had to give up ethnicity in order to become White, South Asian immi-

grants are "minoritized" upon their arrival into the United States. Their naturalization into American citizenship makes them minorities, and instead of
being plain Indian, they are now racialized as non-White Americans.[15] They
seek authenticity as racialized Americans, and differ in two crucial ways from
the other moderns described by Herder, Sartre, Berman, or Plummer:

1. In the first instance, Indian immigrants do not search for an existential
   authenticity but seek to become authentic *Indians*. "Doing their own thing"
   is not an atomized, individualistic thing. Instead, its all about "doing their
   own *Indian* thing."
2. Being authentic Indians is not a means by which they claim belonging to
   India; being authentic ethnics is about staking a space out for themselves
   in the United States. The pursuit for the authentic among Indians is to find
   their *ethnic American selves*.

A large majority of the Indian immigrants in the United States are Hindus,
and the question of being Indian arises differently for them in their sending
country, India, where there they are the norm. It is not as if their normative
identities are a natural pregiven essence, but many Hindus conceptualize their
identities in ahistorical ways that puts the onus of unnaturalness and nonbe-
longing on Muslim or Christian Indians. Many equate being Indian with being
Hindu, both intentionally and unintentionally writing out others from what they
perceive to be their nation. Hence, Muslims and Christians have to explain
their existence in India.[16]

Indian immigrants' lives in the United States as racial minorities entail a
whole slew of anxieties that are fundamentally different from the ones they may
have in India. Immigration entails a change; their movement across continents
and oceans into a new space also moves them from being the cultural norm to
occupying the racial margins. Questions of who they are, can they fit in, and
what they become by fitting in all create chaos in self-identity. The thirst is not
just for self-knowledge, but self-knowledge as Indians in the racial cartographies
of America. Just as a fish that swims in water does not think of the water itself,
in India they do not actively think about how their Indian-ness is fashioned. Only
by being out of the cultural tides in which they swim, their unself-conscious
ways of being are altered into self-conscious practices, carefully thought out,
debated, and practiced with a ceremonial carefulness. For example, many families go to temples far more frequently than they may have when growing up in
India, or parents worry their children are losing their culture and send them to
Hindu culture summer camps, which are uniquely American phenomena. R.
Radhakrishnan points out that the issue is not "'being Indian' in some natural

self-evident way . . . but cultivating 'Indian-ness' self-consciously."[17] They can never be plain "Indian," but instead have to be "authentically Indian."

So why seek an authentic ethnic self? As immigrants, they are cast out of both there and here, cultural exiles in both India and the United States. Their absence from India makes no difference because life there goes on without them—Hindi films hit the silver screen with brand new painted faces, fresh political parties blossom into being, while old ones mutate into new forms, Bombay turns into Mumbai, its *bastis* ruled by the fascist Shiv Sena, dams get built rendering a few thousands more homeless, baby cousins grow up and get married, new nieces and nephews are born, grandaunts pass on. The immigrants' presence here in the United States too seems just as inconsequential—they discover that contrary to their naiveté, racism does exist and they are now at the receiving end. They can work twenty years in a company and be downsized the next day, just another statistic in a cost-efficient world. During cigarette breaks at work and social gatherings, conversations revolve around 1970s TV shows or early 1980s cultural icons that make no sense to them, reminding them they still are outsiders. They can be doctors, computer programmers, cab drivers, or live-in maids, pay their taxes, and vote predominantly Democratic, but they remain largely invisible as noncontributing members in a culture that so aggressively seeks uniqueness that it can only be mass produced.

Immigration entails a loss of self-confidence that they are active, alive actors in the world. The return to Indian tradition, then, is partly a search for their selves as they existed in India prior to their marginalization. Part of their feeling is that by turning back, through rediscovering, and reliving the way they were, their crises in self-identities, the questions of racial belonging, the way they organize their lives, their workplace relationships, the ways in which they raise their children, everything will be all right. The pursuit for Indian authenticity is a means by which to bring order in their fragmented lives. As immigrants, they appear to be still journeying, in transit, between here and there, amid then and now. They have yet to arrive.[18] Indian Americans are endlessly creative in narrating their origins so that they can make sense of their locations. But there is no return to origins for we as individuals, as well as India itself, have moved on. In Rushdie's *Satanic Verses*, the Bombayite Changez Chamchawala admonishes his London resident son Saladin Chamcha: "O my son. You must stop carrying me around like a parrot on your shoulder. What am I? Finished. I'm not your Old Man of the Sea. Face it, mister. I don't explain you anymore."[19] Likewise, Indian Americans need to acknowledge that they cannot carry India on their shoulders like a parrot, for it alone does not explain them anymore.

Moreover, the pursuit for authenticity pushes Indian immigrants into defining a singular Indian culture. There is only one version of culture that can be true, genuine, actual, whereas the rest are spurious. Asserting Bharat Natyam as the only legitimate Indian dance, and not the flashy hip gyrations in simulation of Hindi film song sequences; the easy ways in which Hindu = Indian and, therefore, the inadvertent casting out of Indian Christians; the aversion to publicly admitting Hinduism's many versions all indicate the anxiety that the immigrants felt in proclaiming the crassness, the inanity, the hybridity that make for vibrant, lived cultures in India. The sublime and the virtuous are the only elements worthy of representation. The issue of authentic representations of Indian-ness flattens out the complex, and often contradictory, juxtapositions of various elements in Indian culture(s). If this cultural space is conceded as being inherently contradictory, where the virtuous and the vulgar cohabit happily, where high art breathes beside tackiness all the time, where Coke-stands exist alongside stone carved twelfth-century temples, where women politicians have a strong public presence even as female foeticide is on the rise, then it becomes difficult to defend this cultural space as sacred and out of bounds for opposing claims. The positing of an unviolated, singular culture gives immigrants an incontestable space from which to launch ethnic identities in a White world. If this cultural space is admitted to being inherently conflicted and unstable, then what are the grounds for positing a stable racial identity?

The thirst for authenticity remains unquenched because it tantalizes Indian Americans with promises of access to full citizenship and personhood. Authentic personhood provides a platform from which to speak and act. Immigrants can never be bona fide Americans because they will always be upstarts, but at least, they can be genuine Indians in a White, White world. Put simply, authentic ethnicity gives immigrants too the power to become legitimate. The end game, then, is to become real, live Indians, like the ones they make in India but are now here in America. So immigrants at the Center discuss, dispute, and display what they perceive to be genuine Indian-ness willingly. Their performance are not the acts of wily, calculating individuals, bent on deceiving others; it is instead a sincere effort at becoming real once again, like they felt they were in India. Yet, in the process of their search for self-knowledge, they are rendered into a "new medium, the medium of ideas, in which [their culture] loses its old dimensions and its old place. [The immigrants'] animal habits are transmuted by consciences into loyalties and duties, and [they] become 'persons' or masks."[20]

All said and done, whether Indian-ness is a mask or not, it remains a cultural space *they believe* is uncolonized by the American world outside, for here they author themselves into being. This is precisely why, at the Indo American Center, I witness "real live" Hindus battle over the meanings of Hinduism with academic experts Steve Smith and Professor Latimer. The contests are not just about the "truth" regarding Hinduism, but are also challenges to the two White men's right to interpret Indian-ness. Their ability to explain Hinduism is questioned, and as non-Indians, the two men can only cede ground to those who claim authenticity. Poonam and Mrs. Nayar protest loudly, reclaiming their religion as the oldest one in existence, rather than a modern tradition redefined within a mid-twentieth-century Indian nation. Claims to Hinduism's ancient roots establish it as a set of practices followed from times immemorial, by literally millions of people, therefore setting it apart as something that cannot be questioned. Hinduism's claims to antiquity imparts to it an almost natural aura, a given, a fact that cannot be changed. In other words, its antiquity gives it authenticity. Belonging to this apparently ancient tradition gives its members a genuineness that cannot be disputed. We observe that in the United States, immigrants such as Indians are cornered into making the ethnic authentic just to give themselves a coherent communal/personal history and to protect and maintain their identities.[21]

Yet, even as authenticity is a home, a safe space from which Indian immigrants launch their selves, it also becomes a ghetto into which they are herded by a White dominated world. Largely because they are unable to speak and be heard in the mainstream as solely Americans, they are driven into this racial space that legitimates them. Their singularly defined culture is the sole launchpad from which Indian immigrants can thrust themselves as full citizens into the public sphere of American nationhood. This process of ethnicization of Indian immigrants is, paradoxically, both their marginalization and empowerment simultaneously. Authentic ethnicity, says Radhakrishnan, poses one question for us—"when we say 'authenticate,' we also have to ask 'authenticate for whom and for what purpose?' Who and by what authority is checking our credentials?"[22] Whiteness does not have to be authenticated by anyone. Indeed, whiteness is a pregiven, even natural thing.

What Does Ethnic Authenticity Have to Do with Whiteness?

So what do negotiations of authenticity among Indian Americans have to do with whiteness? Though none of the persons who appear in this book speak of whiteness, I raise it as an issue because whiteness is the foundation on which American-ness is based. It is a set of racial beliefs, discourses, and acts that has the power to validate or nullify some modes of expressions, allow certain public debates to happen, and deem entire groups of people noncitizens or immoral additions to the polity based on their religion, geographical origins, or phenotypic characteristics. Whiteness is the underlying, yet invisible principle that guides the ways in which immigrants think and formulate their lives. When I first began field work in Chicago, I would ask first- and second-generation immigrants what "becoming Indian" meant to them, and they would usually reply with a slew of answers—eating Indian foods, wearing saris and salwaars, speaking native languages, Hindi music, Bhangra parties, and the celebration of ethnic holidays. I then followed with a question on what practices entailed "becoming White" in public. I would meet silence. Some ventured carefully—"you know, becoming American." What does that really mean, I'd persist. After looking a bit unsure, they would shrug their shoulders and say that becoming White meant conformity, and they would revert back to talking about "Indian-ness."

I soon realized that Indian-ness could be explained through minute details of consumptive behavior, such as foods, music, or clothing. Yet, whiteness remained unexamined. They acknowledged the power of whiteness in their lives but were unable to lay out in words what it really is. Whiteness has a palpable presence in our everyday lives, structuring our feelings, thoughts, and actions, yet we are unable to give it shape or form. So when our White colleagues, students, friends, lovers tell us there is no such thing as a White American culture, or if there is, it is all-inclusive in these multicultural times, and concomitantly, the quest for authenticity is universal, we get tongue-tied.

Ruth Frankenberg elucidates that whiteness is "a set of locations that are historically, socially, politically, and culturally produced" that are "intrinsically linked to unfolding relations of domination."[23] The power in whiteness is so efficient because it works as an everyday politics, a habitus if you will. A polity's social practices are not random; instead, social practices are tempered along definitive paths through our habitus, which is an interlocked system of durable, transposable dispositions, a set of practical hypotheses that unconsciously structure our beliefs and our everyday actions. The habitus is a collective property of an ethnic group, a class, or in this case, of a nation of people. Bourdieu notes that habitus is a product of history, but it also simultaneously

> produces all individual and collective practices . . . in accordance with schemes generated by history. It ensures the active presence of past experiences, which deposited in each organism in the form of schemes of perception, thought and action, tend to guarantee the "correctness" of practices and their constancy over time, more reliably than all formal rules and explicit norms.[24]

The habitus of a people is collectively orchestrated and is by no means the product of a single person's actions. The social perceptions and actions of a person more or less correspond to the practices of other members in the same group without any deliberation or conscious planning on anyone's part. Persons have a mastery over a common code because of the "harmonization of agents' experience and the continuous reinforcement that each one of them receives from the expression . . . of similar or identical experiences."[25] A particular habitus is reasonably homogenous within a group, which causes practices to be mutually intelligible and are, therefore, taken for granted.

Whiteness is a racial habitus. It is so commonplace, so ordinary, and so self-explanatory that it does not warrant investigation. It *fails to create the conditions under which it can recognize itself,* thus positing itself as lacking, empty, vacant of all identifying markers. In contrast, any deviations from whiteness are marked, categorized, and explained so that their existence may be comprehended.[26] The public sphere is structured by whiteness, but whiteness remains unexamined and therefore without form for a vast majority of Americans, White or otherwise. For a formless identity, however, whiteness has a great deal of power because it serves as a point of reference for measuring others. Their racial privilege allows Whites to produce knowledge about Others or ask Others to produce knowledge that emphasizes their difference.

Patricia Williams remarks that in the United States, Whites have been historically, and also in the present, marked as the cultural norm, while African Americans are marked as the Other.[27] In law schools where she taught she was struck

> by the general absence of reference to White people in exams written by people who do specify race when they are referring to non-Whites. Yet we all know that there are white gangs (e.g., skinheads, the White Aryan Resistance) as well as black, Asian and Chicano gangs. None of these exams, or any I could find, present gratuitous "white people" problems. "White" is used only to distinguish from blacks and other nonwhites. The absence of "white" thus signals that "everyone" is white. "Blacks" therefore become distant, different, "othered." In order to deal with such a problem on an exam, moreover, students are required to take the perspective of "everybody"; for black students this requires their taking a stance in which they objectify themselves with reference to the interrogatories.[28]

Ian Haney Lopez terms this phenomenon of not marking whiteness as "transparency." The logic of transparency, Lopez says, is that "the race of non-whites is readily apparent and regularly noted, while the race of Whites is consistently overlooked and scarcely mentioned."[29] Whites "experience difficulty in accurately perceiving their relational position in society exactly because they constitute the norm." Transparency arises from the fact that whiteness exists at the epicenter of race talk, yet remains blind to its centrality. He writes that "whites very rarely find themselves burdened by race in a manner that draws on this aspect of identity to view; their whiteness therefore remains unexamined, shrouded in background shadows." Many whites, however, become aware of their racial identity "when they find themselves in the company of large numbers of non-Whites, and then it does so in the form of a supposed vulnerability to non-White violence, rendering whiteness in the eyes of many Whites not a privileged status, but a victimized one."[30]

In addition to being recognized only as a besieged racial identity, Lopez notes:

> [W]hiteness exists as a linchpin for the systems of racial meaning in the United States. Whiteness is the norm around which other races are constructed; its existence depends on mythologies and material inequalities that sustain the current racial system. The maintenance of whiteness necessitates the conceptual existence of Blacks, Latinos, Native Americans, and other races as tropes of inferiority against which whiteness can be measured and valued.[31]

Whiteness is known only in superior opposition to non-Whites, and is almost always defined in terms of superordinate attributes. Lopez says whites are described "as innocent, industrious, temperate, judicious, and so on, in a series of racial accolades. . . ."[32] In contrast, Blacks are construed as "lazy, ignorant, lascivious, and criminal; . . . For each negative characteristic ascribed to people of color, an equal but opposite characteristic is attributed to Whites."[33]

By focusing only on whiteness, I have been charged with ignoring how racial hierarchies in the United States are fundamentally structured along Black-White lines. However whiteness, especially in the ways Lopez and Williams describe it, is a relational term.[34] By invoking whiteness, they are also simultaneously referring to how it develops, not solely but to a large degree, historically in dialogue with blackness. It would not exist if it were not located within a racial hierarchy, so strongly drawn along Black-White lines. Whiteness as a racial habitus structures civic debates, the making of public space, and the cultures of citizenship in the United States, and has the power to set the political and cultural context within which African Americans, as well as other racialized communities, struggle to gain voice and legitimacy. When immigrants deal with whiteness as a set of racial practices, they are entirely cognizant of the fact that blackness too is a silent referent to how they formulate their racial identities. But blackness is so overladen with negative connotations in mainstream America that new non-White immigrants distance themselves from being identified as such. Newcomers recognize that being hailed as Black automatically deems them illegitimate additions to the polity, and they know it is socially and economically expedient for them to dissociate themselves from Black Americans. Hence, immigrants strive to structure their lives, communities, and politics in accordance with the terms set by a White habitus. Noel Ignatiev has brilliantly shown us how Irish immigrants, historically deemed non-White became White over time.[35] Like other immigrants, Indian immigrants too attempt to reproduce themselves as "model minorities," as worthy additions into the American polity.

Multiculturalism and Authenticity

As I discussed in the previous section, whiteness has the power to exnominate itself, remain unexamined, and there is no question of White authenticity. Yet, its been pointed out that White ethnics, too, such as Italian Americans and Irish Americans speak of difference and make claims to authentic ethnic culture. The search for authentic ethnicity is not unique to non-Whites alone, and as Berman and Bellah et al. indicate—discussed in greater detail in the following chapter—the search for a more meaningful life has led White Americans to also seek their ethnic roots to fill their lives with more meaning in attempts to come to terms with the fragmentation and alienation they feel in late modern American society.[36] Some sociologists have noted that what the first generation of immigrants long to forget, the third generation seeks to remember. The pursuit of genuine ethnic culture—as "Grandma cooked up"—is more important for the third generation than for the immigrants themselves. So the question is, is the quest for ethnic authenticity common to *all* or unique to racialized Others?

The quest for authenticity, especially under multiculturalism, among people of color is qualitatively different because non-Whites have to explain their existence to a White world.[37] In explaining themselves, Indian Americans at the Center are compelled to authenticate their existence. It is difficult to determine whether the quest for authenticity comes from Indian Americans as a self-affirming act, and if that is indeed so, then we need to ask why they feel a compulsion to affirm their selves. Authenticity for these Indian immigrants arises through repeated, implicit comparisons between their racialized selves and whiteness. Every attempt by the mainstream to marginalize them through denigration of their home cultures is countered with invocations of their personal worthiness, because they are bona fide members of a superior culture whose premises cannot be questioned. Their ostensibly ancient, revered culture is the source of authenticity in a world of bad faith. In this sense, appeals to an authentic culture are "admissions of vulnerability, filtering the self's longings"[38] into achieving American subjecthood. However, as American subjects Indian immigrants can never be plain "Indian" but are compelled to be authentically Indian, which legitimates their existence; their voices; and ultimately, their slotted space in the multicultural, imagined American community.

Repeatedly, especially in my Asian American Studies classes, students attempt to refute the existence of whiteness by claiming we live in an era of multiculturalism. They say "ethnic"—never racial—diversity is celebrated, and difference is the norm rather than the exception today. But the problem with multiculturalism is that it dictates the topics on which persons of color can legitimately converse, how they can speak on these matters, and what matters are off-limits. An example I offer is of Kalpana Prakash, whose artwork is the cover of this book. A White colleague critiquing her work remarked how startled he was by the fact that though Prakash was an Indian immigrant, she did not draw on themes from her own cultural heritage. Why don't dancing many-limbed gods, multieyed goddesses sitting astride tigers, blue-skinned Krishnas show up in her art, he questioned. He could not comprehend what he took to be "western" symbols of detritus and urban decay that appear in her paintings. But the point is that Prakash examines the ways we make meaning in our everyday racialized lives through the ravages of time, and there is no obvious reason for exotic gods to inhabit her canvases. Conversely, the apparently western symbols of rusting objects, shattered glass, and industrial wreckage too are part of her cultural repertoire on which she draws to symbolize her childhood in industrial Bangalore, her immigrant displacement, her dealings with racial/gender hierarchies, and her own individual resilience.[39]

Multiculturalism is distinguished as something that allows diversity, even encourages individuals to celebrate their difference. But yet, multiculturalism is a politics that exists within the domain of whiteness. This whiteness no doubt works differently at present than it did in the 1960s and 1970s, yet persons of color still have to depend on the largesse of whites to permit us to speak. And when we do so, we are allowed to articulate on matters that are most relevant to our colored difference. As we see, Prakash is asked to put on her Indian accent so that she may be interpreted properly. She is comprehensible to her critic only if she speaks in ways assigned to her. Or for example, political philosopher Uma Narayan points out that she is just as qualified to speak on Roe vs. Wade, or women's rights to reproductive choice, but is invariably slotted to speak on the condition of Indian women, or sex-selective abortion in India.[40] Multicultural politics validates us when we speak on issues that ostensibly relate to only us in our specific differences. At the pulpit of multiculturalism, we become talking heads who open our mouths only to let silence emerge.

The advantage, if one can characterize it as such, is that multiculturalism gives us our corner of social space where we are the sole arbiters of the truth of matters we raise. Such developments, however, privilege ethnic authenticity. As a real Indian, an authentic ethnic, any of my words regarding "my culture" carry more weight than when spoken by someone who is not Indian or appears less authentically Indian. Multicultural politics propels us to establish authenticity because it renders us more easily translatable. When we can be translated with lesser effort we gain greater acceptance in mainstream America. So we see Indian immigrants at the Center adorn clothes, claim to be better Hindus than the ones in India, or assert birth in India to give their words greater truth value. We strategically ethnicize ourselves to even greater extents so that we may be heard and allowed our space in public. We learn that our ethnic roots allow us to become American.

Six

Becoming American
*The Racialized Content of
American Citizenship*

The Making of Imagined Communities

The conferring of citizenship through the Immigration and Naturalization Services, while crucial, is not solely what I mean by becoming American.
Instead, my descriptions of becoming American refer to the processes by which
one becomes incorporated into the national imaginary, one grows into American-
ness or develops a national subjectivity. National subjectivity and the making of
an imagined national community in the United States are qualitatively different
from many other nations, because the issue of national belonging here entails
a self-conscious replacement of older selves with a new American identity. It is
not as if other nations other do not have newly forged identities, for questions
of belonging and nationalisms are *the* politics of the twentieth century. For
example, we see Indian nationalist movements against British colonialism and
the eventual rise of Hindu fundamentalism in India from the 1980s onward that
defines a new national self in religiously exclusive terms, with virulent hate
speech, physical violence, and pogroms directed against Muslims in India. Or
we see German nationalism, with its extreme manifestations in the Final Solution. Questions of German belonging have historically been based on having
German blood; hence those who were, for example, formerly of the Soviet
Republics but could prove German ethnicity could become citizens, whereas
Turkish guest workers or their German-born children, until the mid-1990s,
could not receive German citizenship.

Constituted by immigrants, the United States is among the few nation-states
where a national identity has been forged constantly, self-consciously, by a large
group of people throughout the twentieth century. The issues of membership

in the imagined national community are consistently in the forefront, as immigrants (especially those classified as non-White) arrive into this nation. The older, established citizenry ponders over whether the new arrivals will change the American national character, while on the other hand, immigrants try to work out ways in which to belong to this nation. This is also true of European nations, but unlike the United States, they do not conceive of themselves as nations of immigrants. The making of the imagined American community is under constant scrutiny by both the established citizenry and newly incorporating immigrants. Hence, so-called American values are continually hailed, either by the established citizenry about how newcomers can never be Americans, by new immigrants clamoring that indeed they are better Americans than most, or by social movements attempting to reveal the myth of American values. National identity in the United States is a curious thing; it is cast as being open to anyone who avers to become an American; simultaneously, entire groups of people are under suspicion for being un-American right from the start. Asian Americans, for example, have been forever foreigners, and since September 11, 2001, Arab Americans by the very fact of their geographical origins or religious beliefs are deemed a threat to the idea of America.

Though other nations, notably the European ones that have seen massive migrations from their former colonies, have similar kinds of nationalist anxieties, I hold onto an American exceptionalism regarding nationalism because becoming American entails a self-reflexivity and self-alteration that is qualitatively different from that which happens in Britain, Germany, or other such nations. In India, for example, becoming an Indian is tied to finding an *ur*-self scriptured in the ostensibly ancient texts of Hinduism; German-ness is based on blood. Contrarily, becoming American is premised on achieving a modern, abstract individualism, consciously leaving behind the past to make oneself anew. As an immigrant, one needs to leave behind the old country and aver in the new one, leave primordial family and community and make oneself an abstract citizen who will participate in civil society on the basis of secular abstractness rather than ethnic/racial or religious particularism. While most nations work on a sense of a past tradition to invent a national community[1]—German nationalism fashioned on a notion of the volk, British on idealized "Englishness," Indian on Hinduism—the United States, as a nation constituted by immigrants, *claims* not to have a singular *ur*-tradition that serves as a foundation for constructing a national identity. The imagined American national community, it is commonly believed, does not have a distinct religious or cultural tradition to fall back on.[2] Yet, the only Catholic president we have had so far is John F. Kennedy, and the 2000 presidential candidate Al Gore's vice-presidential choice, Lieberman, raised concerns among various Americans who worried

Lieberman would not be able to keep his Jewish faith out of what they took to be secular American politics.

Though realities constantly tell us something else, American national identity is perceived to be cast upon ideals thought to be uniquely secular, uniquely modern, and therefore uniquely American. Americanism is based on civic nationalism.[3] Anyone, it is commonly perceived, can become an American as long as they have faith in the doctrine of progress, hold an individualistic understanding of the self, and believe that society is a contractual entity out of which emerges a sense of rational justice. Hence, it is believed, one is not born an American but becomes one through the adoption of certain so-called modern, secular cultures of citizenship. And how does one achieve these values? Through assimilation.

The late nineteenth and early twentieth centuries' massive urbanization, rural-urban migrations, incorporation of southern/eastern European immigrants, all raised questions of belonging in acute ways and heightened nationalist anxieties across the United States.[4] Factory owners, public schools, and social workers deliberated over the evolving nature of the American imagined community and focused their reformatory energies on immigrants who were initiated into American-ness through Americanization programs. The first bout of "American-ness" anxiety, Gleason points out, arose between 1830 and 1860 when Catholic immigrants, mainly Irish, arrived into an America made up of predominantly Protestants. Though *Americanization* came into usage as early as 1850 during a period of heightened nativism, the term gained prominence from the 1890s to the 1920s, when southern/eastern Europeans began arriving into this nation. Anxieties about the "inherent nature" of these immigrants and their lack of potential for Americanization reached a fevered pitch by World War I.[5] Americanization programs initiated immigrants into a civic nationalism that was drawn starkly along racial lines.

However, the civil rights movements, second wave feminism, and the economic crises of the 1970s rang the death knell to the overt whiteness of American-hood. The rise of White ethnic movements, post-1965 immigrations, transnational capital, and the globalization of American culture—not just American influences on cultures around the world, but also, transformations of the American mainstream itself—heralded the rise of multicultural politics. By the 1960s, Americanization had fallen into disuse, but the term *assimilation* was revived to describe the successes or failures of post-1965 (mainly non-White) immigrants in the United States. Assimilation theories posited by Alejandro Portes, Min Zhou, and Margaret Gibson proposed that selective retention of ethnic culture among new immigrants led them into becoming good Americans. In this era of multiculturalism, it seems as if the maintenance of difference

makes the United States a coherent nation. Yet, an interrogation of these assimilation theories reveals that the cultural differences described are not really differences but are characteristics consistent with moral American-ness. By the
end of the twentieth century, the nature of the American state and the cultural
contents of citizenship were fundamentally altered, and whiteness in these contemporary times is less decipherable. It is within this context of a racialized state
and citizenship that I locate Apna Ghar and the Indo American Center, both of
which train South Asian immigrants into becoming American.

American National Identity in the Early Twentieth Century

Rogers Smith notes that the United States is driven at one level by liberal democratic principles, yet these liberal principles are often sacrificed at the
altar of nation building. Even as European immigrants were incorporated into
the national body, Blacks, Asian Americans, and Latinos continued to be
excluded from the national social contract.[6] W.E.B. DuBois pointed out that in
direct contradiction to the egalitarian ideals espoused, "there were half a million
slaves in the confines of the United States when the Declaration of Independence declared 'that all men are created equal; that they are endowed by their
Creator with certain unalienable rights; that among these are life, liberty, and
the pursuit of happiness.'"[7] In addition to various exclusion acts that barred
Asians from immigrating, citizenship by naturalization was limited to only persons classed as "White" until 1952. Hence, Indians, Japanese, and Chinese
immigrants fought legal battles to be classified as White so that they too could
obtain American citizenship.[8]

American citizenship, which has historically meant sacrifice, was accessible to mainly European immigrants. Early twentieth-century European immigrants were mandated to give up the cultural, linguistic, and religious
particularities of their sending nations. Becoming American for these immigrants was a high modernist transformation, whereby the fabric of older cultures had to be rent asunder to give birth to a new American with abstract,
secular ideals of individuality and noncommunitarian belonging. "True" Americans professed civic nationalism. So how was one to develop an American
nationality? The answer, historically, was Americanization. Becoming American was not just "the mere adoption of American citizenship, but the actual
raising of the immigrant to the American economic, social and moral standard
of life." An immigrant Americanized "only when his mind and will" had "been
united with the mind and will of the American so that the two act and think
together."[9] Americanizing newcomers made democracy possible because it
fostered general intelligibility among people. Americanization entailed altering people's attitudes "in accord with the fundamental American principles of

government and conduct, . . . and [their] industrial, civic, and home practice and mode of living conform with American standards."[10] Hence, both the public and private lives of immigrants had to correspond to American principles for them to become American.

Altering the Public Lives of Immigrants

The ideal of a shared public sphere was central to American civic nationalism and literacy became a focus so that through "reading the printed page," people from diverse national backgrounds could share common thoughts. From the mid-late nineteenth century onward, print capitalism had taken off, and newspapers and the printer's office had become a key element in American communications and community intellectual life.[11] Schools were seen as a tremendous force of Americanization because children of different European origins mingled there, which broke "the habits of any one of the foreign nationalities."[12] By teaching the English language and American history, a new national solidarity was built among immigrant children. The American educational system "was transformed into a machine for political socialization by such devices as the worship of the American flag, which as a daily ritual in the country's schools, spread from the 1880s onward."[13] In addition, public schools were perceived to work on the personalities of children because schools were the "first and chief trainer of the immigrant child's mind to fit it for originality and inventiveness," which "enlarge[d] the child's capacity."[14]

Moreover, adopting American national identity entailed the development of a particular kind of work culture. In the beginning of the twentieth century, immigrants were hurled into an unfamiliar universe, where assembly line production in large factories was fast becoming the norm. Companies hired social workers to train their labor force because Americanization forged immigrants into disciplined industrial workers.[15] For example, the Ford Motor Company employed 12,880 men, of whom 9,109 were foreign born. Poles, Russians, Romanians, Italians, Sicilians, and Austro-Hungarians made up a majority of these workers.[16] In December 1913, between 800 and 900 Greek and Russian Orthodox Christian workers, 6 percent of the work force, failed to show up at work, massively disrupting the assembly line. These workers followed the Julian calendar and celebrated Christmas thirteen days earlier than the rest of the Ford workforce. A month later, the Company dismissed these men because as a Ford official stated, "if these men are to make their home in America they should observe American holidays . . . it causes too much confusion in the plant . . . when nearly a thousand men fail to appear to work."[17] Hence, Ford held compulsory Americanization classes for its workers.

Trade unions were also important sites of Americanization because here, it was believed, people did not see themselves as Italians, Jews, or Poles anymore; instead their identities as workers became crucial. Primordial group identities gave way to secular identities that arose from processes wrought by industrialization. The union was believed to teach "the immigrant self-government. . . . The union [gave] the immigrant a sense of common cause, which leads to a sense of public, not merely private, interest." Unions "develop[ed] foresight in the immigrant."[18]

Altering Immigrant Homes

Simultaneously, social workers were concerned with the private sphere of the immigrant home. Morris Knowles writes, "Americanization is more a psychological process than a physical one."[19] Since space and place play on people's psyche because their surroundings affect their mental states, immigrant homes too had to be altered so that their occupants could easily assimilate. The prime purveyor of immigrant homes were immigrant women who strived as wives and mothers, to keep the "old culture" and, therefore, ostensibly hindered the success of immigrant families' assimilation and subsequent social/economic mobility. Hence, Helen Varick Boswell, prominent member of the General Federation of Women's Clubs, wrote that the immigrant woman, "far from being an aid in Americanizing her family, becomes a reactionary force. Sadly or obstinately as it may be, but always ignorantly, she combats every bit of Americanism that her husband and children try to force into the Southern European home."[20] She urged social workers to "reach the immigrant woman. It is the only way to produce American homes," for the work of "Americanizing immigrant mothers and immigrant homes [was] in the highest sense a work of citizenship, a part of a *national* patriotic ideal."[21]

Cities such as Chicago, Cleveland, Pittsburgh, Worcester, Fall River, Cambridge, Stamford, and Springfield, Illinois, hired visiting housekeepers to check on immigrant homes and teach women the art of American living.[22] And though some social workers recognized that deplorable economic conditions had to do with the living conditions of immigrant families, they complained they had great difficulties working with immigrant women because they were "stubborn, indifferent, inert, obstinate, lazy, difficult but responsible, easy but shiftless, and not performing what they undertake."[23] Social workers held unyielding ideas about how these homes needed to be changed. In the words of one social worker, "old standards must be changed if we are sincere in our desire to attain a higher form of civilization. The strangers from across the water must be taught to discard un-American habits and conventions, to accept new ideals."[24]

Speaking of social workers in New York City, Elizabeth Ewen notes that most of them were middle-class women from older immigrant Protestant families. Their fathers were well-off professionals, and a majority of these women were from the northeast or midwestern cities. They were all well educated—90 percent had gone to college and more than 50 percent had attended graduate school either here or in Europe. Most were unmarried, younger women with a median age of twenty-five years. Notions of Americanization for these social workers were based on their standpoints as White, middle-class women. They invaded immigrant homes, focusing their reformatory zeal on immigrant women, with "firm scientific ideas about proper infant care, family life, parent-child relationships, diet, and hygiene."[25] Becoming American meant the adoption of a particular set of household practices prevalent in their White, middle-class families. The social workers sought to change the patterns of the everyday lives of new immigrants, with the hope that by becoming American culturally, they could progress economically and achieve social mobility. However, Horace Kallen notes that what worried many Americans about immigrants was "not really inequality; what trouble[d] them is *difference*."[26]

By 1915, the U.S. Chamber of Commerce had established an Immigration Committee. By 1916, The General Federation of Women's Clubs became involved in Americanization. The YMCA expanded its Americanization programs. Samuel Gompers, president of the anti-immigrant American Federation of Labor, also endorsed Americanization.[27] Statements such as the following made by President Woodrow Wilson in his 1915 address to newly naturalized Americans in Philadelphia were not extraordinary. He says "You cannot dedicate yourself to America unless you become in every respect and with every purpose of your will thorough Americans. You can not become thorough Americans if you think of yourselves in groups. A man who thinks of himself as belonging to a particular national group in America has not yet become an American, and the man who goes among you to trade upon your nationality is no worthy son to live under the Stars and Stripes."[28]

Anxieties about Americanization

Randolph Bourne, while commenting on the ethnocentric contents of Americanization, observed that despite all these programs, immigrants retained their diverse nationalistic feelings. He writes just prior to World War I:

> [I]f freedom means a democratic cooperation in determining the ideals and purposes and industrial and social institutions of a country, then the immigrant has not been free, and the Anglo-Saxon element is guilty of just what every dominant race is guilty of in every European country: the imposition of its own culture upon the minority peoples. The fact that this imposition has

been so mild and, indeed semi-conscious does not alter its quality. And the war has brought just the degree to which that purpose of "Americanizing," that is, "Anglo-Saxonizing," the immigrant has failed.[29]

Americanization as a form of social control of immigrants became especially acute with the breakout of war in Europe. One of the most influential persons in propagating Americanization was Frances Kellor who was considered an authority on the subject.[30] She saw Americanization "as the science of nation-building,"[31] and noted—"we are on the way to supplementing scientific management with citizenship management. Some of us believe that in this new spirit lies the hope of the nation."[32] By World War I, Americanizing immigrants became a national concern, and the first National Conference on Immigration and Americanization was held in Philadelphia, January 19 to 20, 1916. Philanthropies, businesses, civic, and educational organizations were brought together to discuss Americanization as it affects them all; that Americanization was recognized as a national movement, requiring national standards; and that one and all, organizations governmental and private, of all kinds and all creeds, and of varying methods of work, pledged themselves to co-operate in carrying out Americanization as a national work.[33]

Americanization, however, was not uniformly embraced; it had both its liberal as well as reactionary critics, the latter turning especially virulent by the early 1920s, just prior to the passage of the National Origins Act of 1924, which halted almost all immigration into the United States. A series of articles in the *New Republic* between 1919 and 1921 described Americanization as the cultural tyranny of the middle classes. One article stated—"with his characteristic blend of hard sense and sentimentalism, the new patrician sailed forth among the imported plebs to urge it to adopt his grammar and his bathtubs, his soap, and his patriotism. . . . Americanization . . . became a thing to frighten children with."[34] In milder terms, but no less critical, John Dewey and his students called for cultural pluralism. Isaac Berkson, former student of John Dewey, and the supervisor of schools of the Bureau of Jewish Education, said that

> the splendid loyalty that immigrants have shown toward America and their heartfelt reverence for the new Promised Land are the result of no "Americanization" program, but of living under institutions which by their very nature permitted economic advance, educational opportunities, and individual freedom in a degree unknown to them in the lands of their birth. It is the excellence of American tradition working indirectly and spontaneously which Americanizes, not the direct application of strict methods.[35]

The *Sunday Evening Post*, too, attacked Americanization from a conservative angle in an article titled "Americanski," on May 14, 1921:

> In spite of the evidence on every side, sentimentalists still picture Uncle Sam as a clever chef who can take a handful of foreign scraps, a sprig of Americanism and a clove of democracy, and skillfully blend the mess into something fine and desirable. . . . Race character is as fixed a fact as race color. . . . We are fatuously strengthening the levee here and there with a few sandbags of Americanization, while we complacently watch the whole river rush through a mile-wide crevasse. . . . The trouble with our Americanization program is that a large part of our recent immigrants can never become Americans. They will always be Americanski—near Americans with un-American ideas and ideals.[36]

American public schools, extolled by some as bastions of Americanization, were also denigrated. In his 1908 *Race or Mongrel*, Alfred Shultz wrote:

> The opinion is advanced that the public schools change the children of all races into Americans. Put a Scandinavian, a German, and a Magyar boy at one end, and they will come out Americans at the other end. Which is like saying, let a pointer, a setter, and a pug enter one end of a tunnel, and they will come out three greyhounds at the other end.[37]

Hence, southern and eastern Europeans—who eventually entered the realm of whiteness—were seen by most native-born Americans as racial Others and beyond assimilation. Anti-immigrant sentiments reached such a fevered pitch that in response, the U.S. Congress established in 1921 a temporary quota system designed "to confine immigration as much as possible to western and northern European stock." Finally, the National Origins Act of 1924 was passed that more or less blocked the entry of immigrants for the next few decades.

Post-1924 Questions on Assimilation

The Celts, Slavs, and Irish, often targets of anti-immigrant sentiments and who existed earlier as separate racial categories, dissolved by the end of the 1920s and entered the portals of the White race.[38] For instance, in 1920 Lathrop Stoddard wrote that the United States "originally settled almost exclusively by the Nordics, was toward the close of the nineteenth century invaded by hordes of immigrant Alpines, Mediterraneans, not to mention Asiatic elements such like Levantines and Jews" who compromised the integrity of the American nation.[39] But within the decade—with the passage of the National Origins Act of 1924—Stoddard was singing a different tune. He amended that these White

Others belonged to the greater family of Europeans and assimilated easily in comparison to non-Europeans. Stoddard noted "[W]hat is thus true of European immigrants, most of whom belong to some branch of the White racial group, most emphatically does not apply to non-White immigrants like the Chinese, Japanese or Mexicans; neither does it apply to the large resident negro [sic] element which has been a tragic anomaly from our earliest times. Here, ethnic differences are so great that assimilation in the racial sense is impossible."[40] The absorption of White Others, those "inferior Europeans," into whiteness was consolidated by the 1930s. They now stood as a more or less singular White race in contrast to those non-Whites, namely Blacks, Mexican Americans, and Asian immigrants.

However, there was a brief period of anxiety regarding newly incorporated Whites during World War II. The rise of organized anti-Semitism in the United States, "the noisy antics of the German-American Bund, and the pro-Fascist orientation of much of the Italian-American press" raised concerns once again about the "commitment of hyphenated Americans to so-called American principles."[41] Despite the threats these long distance nationalists posed in their overt manifestation of Euro-patriotism, as members of White America, German and Italian Americans did not inspire fear as did Japanese Americans on the West Coast who were incarcerated in internment camps. Slavs, Poles, Italians, Germans—all European immigrants—had now crossed over the threshold into the dominion of whiteness, and as such, posed no danger to the fiber of the American nation.

There is very little written on assimilation programs between the 1920s and 1960s. Part of the reason is because of restrictions on immigration; Gleason says that in 1924 "racialist nativism brought about a reversal of America's century-old tradition of almost completely unrestricted immigration,"[42] and the passage of the national origins quota law ended a century of massive overseas immigration. Concomitantly, the anxiety regarding immigrants' perceived threat to American national identity abated. Immigration restrictions between 1924 and 1965 purportedly gave the United States a forty-year period to assimilate European newcomers into whiteness.[43]

The Roles of Immigrant Organizations in Americanization

The targets of Americanization, the European immigrants, expressed ambivalence at assimilation. Park and Miller note that immigrants brought with them "habits, customs, and traditions, including language, dress, social ritual, sentimental ideals and interests, and a sense of moral worth." It was in connection with these that immigrants maintained a social standing in their sending nations.[44] In the United States, however, "the very signs of personality (dress, language, etc.), which in the old country were signs of self-respect, were regarded with contempt and made the occasion of humiliation."[45] Immigrants mourned the loss of their old selves. In addition, incorporation into early-twentieth-century America, new immigrants felt, was antithetical to the social principles underlying immigrant communities. The newcomers felt that "the older ways [lay] in the practice of bread-giving, not bread-winning; yet, the social basis of American culture lay in winning, taking, making it in a world where money is a reward for good behavior and hard work. . . . To be American meant to equate independence and freedom with upward mobility, with leaving the community behind in order to become a successful individual."[46]

Contrary to these commonly expressed sentiments, immigrants organized numerous self-help groups. For example, in early 1900s, the Italians of Chicago had 110 mutual-aid societies to help a population of 150,000 individuals.[47] Most of these immigrant societies were established for the primary purpose of mutual insurance. The immigrants' precarious economic situations made them rely on each other for financial support.[48] Breckenridge quotes an appeal sent out by a Russian society in 1912, "while we are in this country we are doing the lowest kind of work, and many accidents happen to us; if we do not belong to an organization we are without help. . . . The purpose of our brotherhood is to help our brethren in a strange country."[49] Each member in the mutual benefit society paid a small sum of about 25 cents per month. Out of the funds raised, sick benefits of $3 to $5 per week were given to families when wage earners fell ill. Or in the event of the death of a member, other members paid an amount of 50 cents to $1 each to the bereaved family to help meet funeral costs.[50]

Eventually, as the various societies' members became more economically stable, they undertook educational and social projects. The local lodge became "a center for discussion of problems of concern to the local community or the national group, and often the field in which the education program planned by the national society [was] carried out."[51] Though "the national educational and welfare movements carried on by the 'American people' . . . ignored the organization and leadership in the foreign-born community," for these societies did not receive any aid from federal, state, or local agencies, these immigrant organizations inaugurated various projects for their coethnics.[52] The National Croatian Society, comprising 50,000 members in 1915, served all Croatians, other Slavs, and persons in Chicago who could speak the Croatian language, except Jews and women "living in concubinage." The purpose of the Society was to

> help people of the Croatian race residing in America, in cases of distress, sickness, and death, to educate and instruct them in the English language and in other studies to fit them for the duties of life and citizenship with our

English-speaking people, to teach them and impress upon them the importance and duty of being naturalized under the laws of the United States, and
of educating their children in the public schools of the country; these purposes [are] to be carried out through the organization and establishment of
a supreme assembly and subordinate assemblies of Croatian people with
schools and teachers.[53]

Many of these organizations focused their energies on newly immigrated
women. The Ukrainian Women's Alliance, started in Chicago in 1917, stressed
immigrant women's responsibilities in the private sphere of the home, as well
as their public responsibilities as citizens in America by speaking of women's
place in government and the importance of the suffrage movement.[54] Sophonisba Breckinridge described how the Lithuanian Women's Alliance, organized
in 1915 in Chicago, helped new immigrants assimilate. Only Lithuanian Catholic
women "who are in good standing in the Church" were admitted so that they
could get assistance in adjusting "to the new circumstances of life in America."[55]
The Alliance held weekly classes in English and housekeeping. It also published
a monthly magazine titled *Women's Field* that exhorted women to learn English
and shoulder the responsibilities of American citizenship. In addition, "one
page each month [was] devoted to questions of general hygiene and the care
of children [which was] edited by a Lithuanian woman physician."[56] Attempts
were made by the Alliance to inculcate among new immigrants an interest in
proper cooking and wise spending. In housekeeping lessons, "washing, scrub-
bing, washing windows, and even dishwashing and the setting of the table
[were] taught."[57]

The purpose of these organizations was not to keep their members "ethnic";
they worked hard to Americanize their immigrant brethren. While these organizations were commonly perceived as an indication of immigrants' self-
imposed isolation from the rest and as instruments in abetting ethnic
particularities, they actually worked in the opposite direction. Ethnic organizations aided immigrants in becoming American. These associations, Park
and Miller observed, "are signs, not of the perpetuation of immigrant groups
here, but of their assimilation."[58]

To summarize, early-twentieth-century European immigrants were exhorted
to adopt secular notions of liberty, individuality, and republicanism and take on
a particular kind of consumer and work ethos, which was all premised on giving up ethnic particularities and replacing it with ways of cooking, diet, raising
children, and family relations peculiar to native-born middle-class Protestant
families. Italians, Croatians, Russian Jews, or Polish immigrants metamorphosed into "White" people who could be included in the imagined national

community. However, Americanization should not be seen as simply the exchange of one national identity with another, but it was centrally an "initiation of people into an emerging industrial and consumer society."[59] The Lithuanian women immigrants in Chicago, whom Breckinridge speaks of earlier, were eager to read English so that they too could participate in the world outside, and they "may know what is in the attractive-looking magazines they see on the news stands."[60] These women wanted to participate in a consumer culture so attractively advertised in mass produced magazines at newsstands. Becoming American also meant being initiated into the ethos of modern capitalism as industrial workers and consumers.

The Rise of White Ethnicity: American-Ness in the Post-1960s Era

For decades, success and upward mobility in America was based on the concept of individual achievement, unfettered by family or community ties. But by the late 1970s, economic success alone seemed to have lesser and lesser value (and one might add, lesser achievable by a larger number of Americans), and individuals who left behind family and community to succeed economically now yearned to reconnect with others and be grounded in community so they may regain meaning in their lives. The conflicts of modernity first set in motion with massive urbanization at the turn of the century, Bellah et al. observe, had "become half-hearted. There was a time, when, under the battle cry of 'freedom,' separation and individuation were embraced as the key to a marvelous future of unlimited possibility," but by the 1980s, "there [was] a note of uncertainty, not a desire to turn back to the past, but an anxiety about where we seem[ed] to be headed. In this view, modernity seem[ed] to be a period of enormously rapid change, a transition from something relatively fixed toward something not yet clear."[61]

To exemplify these turnings to the past to make sense of the present, Bellah et al. write of Angelo Donatello. Donatello was a successful Italian American businessman who became a community leader in a Boston suburb. He described his trajectory into politics: "One of the important things that got me into politics was that I was a confused individual. I came from a real old fashioned Italian family in East Boston. We spoke both languages at home, but I was more Americanized than my brothers or sisters, so to speak. We were forgetting our heritage—that meant becoming more free, more liberal, being able to express myself differently."[62]

However, a change came over Donatello around the early 1970s when he attended a meeting of a chapter of Sons of Italy. He was catapulted into political involvement by the unexpected appearance of prejudice when his organization was denied permission to buy a piece of land to build the Sons of Italy Hall. Bellah et al. say of Donatello—"remembering his heritage involved accepting his origins, including painful memories of prejudice and discrimination that his earlier efforts at 'Americanization' had attempted to deny."[63] His personal experience with prejudice helped Donatello see there was more to life than escaping his past, and as he became more involved with the community he once tried to forget, his life became richer and more meaningful. Bellah et al. comment that "while leaving behind 'Americanization' he became American." By the 1970s communities of memory—a community defining itself by a memory of the past—in this case, Italian Americans and the Sons of Italy give Angelo Donatello "a qualitative meaning to the living of life, to time and spaces, to persons and groups."[64]

Since the 1970s, there has been a resurgence of ethnic rememberings and the concomitant rise in White ethnic identity. An ever-growing number of hyphenated Americans emerged, as third-generation Americans sought to discover their ethnic roots their parents so desperately attempted to forget.[65] By the late 1970s, White ethnics such as "Irish Americans, Italian Americans, and Slavic Americans pressured the state to change the census form by adding a question that would allow them to identify potential members." In response, the Census Bureau added the ancestry question in the 1980 census. Eighty-three percent of Americans gave some ethnic response on the 1980 census.[66]

Unlike Bellah et al. who deem the rise of (White) ethnicity as a benign form of politics that serves as a security blanket to keep away the cold uncertainty of late modernist living, Micaela di Leonardo identifies the rise of White ethnic groups as a reactionary response of Whites to the changing cultural/economic politics of the 1960s and 1970s.[67] White ethnicity emerged at the intersections of other social movements, namely the "Civil Rights and Black Power movements, the antiwar movement, the student/youth movement, and the revived feminist movement."[68] Mimicking Black nationalists' celebrations of Black cultural perseverance in the face of White oppression, White ethnic cultures were similarly pronounced as having valiantly endured Anglo Saxon repression. White ethnic communities were proclaimed endangered but idealized as historically continuous and stable institutions.[69]

Mary Waters too explains that the celebration of White ethnicity is a reaction against the political challenges to American race hierarchies the Civil Rights movements precipitated. As a result of their particular understandings of American history, many Whites are unable to comprehend that not all ethnicities are equal, "all are not symbolic, costless, and voluntary."[70] She notes that White ethnics engage in symbolic ethnicity; they eat foods and celebrate holidays such as

St. Patrick's Day, but such symbolism does not interfere with their choice of marriage partners or chances for economic upward mobility. White people maintain an ethnic identity but are unable to say what this identity means to them and why they choose one particular ethnicity from a range of possibilities. They understand ethnicity as a biological given, but in reality, White ethnics "have a lot more choice and room for maneuver than they themselves think they do."[71]

White people's experiences with their own ethnicities—the ease with which they can slip in and out of being ethnic—creates a lack of understanding on their part regarding the experiences of those classified as non-White. Many cannot understand why Blacks or Latinos speak of discrimination. Waters says that some White ethnics posit that their own ancestors did not complain but instead persevered in the face of anti-Irish sentiments, anti-Polish discrimination, or anti-Semitism without asking for any intervention by the state. They question why minorities cannot be more like them.[72] In summary, White ethnics perceive that (*a*) all ethnicities are equal, all discriminations are the same, and discrimination against non-White ethnics will one day disappear as it did against the Irish, Polish, or Italians; or (*b*) non-Whites should accept that they just do not have the intrinsic make-up or cultural wherewithal to succeed as the White ethnics.

Central to the idealized version of White ethnicity was the ethnic woman in her ethnic home. Di Leonardo writes:

> The cumberedness that Chicago school social scientists saw southeastern European immigrants as inevitably losing in the gesellschaft of modernizing urban America was rediscovered in the 1970s as a surviving feature of White ethnic selfhood. Scholarship, journalism, and grassroots expressions celebrated White ethnics for their family loyalties and neighborhood ties. In fact, advertising in this period began to exploit "cute" White ethnic imagery—the pizza-baking grandmother, the extended family at the laden dinner table—in order to invest in frozen and canned foods with the cachet of gemeinschaft.[73]

Whereas earlier the ethnic woman was the target of virulent Americanization programs, she was now the celebrated progenitor of ethnicity. The White ethnic woman in the White ethnic home was praised for her devotion to home and family. Di Leonardo urges us to place such imagery in a context of rising feminist activism, because the White ethnic woman whose focus was hearth and home was directly contrasted to 1970s feminist activists, who were perceived to be "anti-family" noisy public agents who demanded equal rights.

This reappearance of tradition was a not retreat from modernity but was a way by which to give meaning and reconstitute the world around us. The rise of uncertainty about American-ness and the modernist, individuated subject occur at precisely a time when the established social order was being challenged in the 1960s and 1970s. And subsequently, the economic tremors of the early 1970s that shattered one American urban economy after another lay the tombstone to the concept of the individuated, modernist American. Ethnicity raised its "traditional" head once again, this time not to the xenophobia witnessed in the early 1920s, but to the laudatory noises of mainstream America. The very notion of ethnic particularity in the United States helped one negotiate an increasingly fragmenting and economically collapsing world, because it allowed one to nostalgically identify an ideal past that provided a stable basis for facing an uncertain future.

The earlier modernism, so suspicious of tradition, gave way in the 1970s to a peculiar kind of modernity that looked to the past in order to make sense of the present. Marshall Berman observes that the stalled economic growth and urban economic recession meant that "the moderns of the 1970s couldn't afford to annihilate the past and present in order to create a new world ex nihilo; they had to learn to come to terms with the world they had, and work from there."[74] Whereas earlier modernisms "found themselves by forgetting," the modernism of the 1970s found itself by remembering the past; "the modernism of the 1970s was a modernism with ghosts." The global recessions of the 1970s revealed to American citizenry that they were not immune from world processes, but instead their geographical and historical connected-ness still had relevance to the way their lives were at present. Berman posits that the "new departures of the 1970s lay in attempts to recover past modes of life that were buried but not dead. This project itself was new, and took on an urgency in a decade when the dynamism of the modern economy and technology seemed to collapse."[75] The central theme of the 1970s modernism

> was the rehabilitation of ethnic memory and history as a vital part of personal identity. . . . Modernists today no longer insist, as the modernists of yesterday often did, that we must cease to be Jewish, Black, or Italian or anything, in order to be modern. If whole societies can be said to learn anything, the modern societies of the 1970s seemed to have learned that ethnic identity—not only one's own but everyone's—was essential to the depth and fullness of self that modern life opens up and promises to all.[76]

By the 1970s, popular and media perceptions of ethnicity had changed. The emptying of ethnic particularities, so central to conceptions of becoming American, had now given way to the celebration of White ethnicity. The fertile fields of White ethnic neighborhoods allegedly nurtured a crop of moral Americans in contrast to barren Black urban wastelands. A good American was not Black or an unhyphenated unencumbered White American but an ethnic White.

To summarize, in the early twentieth century, European immigrants were compelled to become Americans by deleting their ethnic particularities. The immigrant woman was especially the target for Americanization, because through her, one could reform the entire immigrant family. Subsequently, in the 1970s, in a complete reversal, we celebrated White ethnicity. Ethnic White culture is extolled because it compelled people into a spirit of volunteerism, fostering a sense of community and belonging-ness that had was purported lost in the preceding high modernist traditions of the United States. The resurgence of White ethnicity made people better Americans. In this context, the ethnic woman was championed for her supposed dedication to her home, tirelessly working with a smile on her face, to foster a family with good American values.

Altered Whiteness in the 1980s

The Reagan-Bush era from the 1980s on heralded a whole new form of White culture that parallels the radically altered income distributions among White families. We entered the portals of a new Gilded Age, an age of excess where $2.5 to $6 million houses, replete with swimming pools, tennis courts, three-hole golf courses, and pony barns are routinely advertised.[77] And by the 1990s, unprecedented, unadulterated, and undisguised greed enveloped corporate culture. While free-market aficionados tie executive performance to financial remunerations, Krugman says wages are determined by social norms: "[W]hat happened during the 1930s and 1940s was that new norms of equality were established, largely through the political process. What happened in the 1980s and 1990s was that those norms unraveled, replaced by an ethos of 'anything goes.' And a result was an explosion of income at the top of the scale."[78]

Over the past three decades, the average American's salary has increased only modestly; adjusting for inflation, salaries rose from "$32,522 in 1970 to $35,864 in 1999." In contrast, over the same period "the average annual compensation of the top 100 CEOs went from $1.3 million—39 times the pay of the ordinary worker—to $37.5 million, more than 1000 times the pay of ordinary workers." Income disparity has grown. A Congressional Budget Office study found that between 1979 and 1997 the after-tax incomes of the top one percent of the families rose by 157 percent compared with the 10 percent gain seen by families near the middle of the income distribution.[79]

The Great Society established earlier had been systematically dismantled. This egalitarian American society in the 1930s and 1940s had mostly worked for

White persons, for during this era, inequalities in pay and compromised quality of life were rampant for non-Whites. However, the social contract among White Americans consolidated in the middle of the century was shattered along class lines by the 1980s.

Micaela di Leonardo perceives a change in White ideology in the 1980s, when wealthy Anglo-Saxon whiteness took back the center stage, and "a new halo was constructed over the image—embodied by Nancy Reagan—of the elegant, dignified, adorned, and (publicly at least) devoted wife and mother, the curator of the proper WASP bourgeois home and children."[80] Popular culture witnessed the rise of television shows and movies that were condescending toward White ethnicities. Films on Italian Americans such as *Godfather, Moonstruck, Married to the Mob, Working Girl*, and *True Love* "represented working-class and better-off Italian-Americans as philistines, tasteless boobs, Guidos, and Big Hair girls, the kind of people who would have mashed potatoes dyed blue to match the bridesmaids' dresses." White ethnicity came to represent the coarse, chaotic "enactment of others' life dramas for our condescending amusement—minstrelsy."[81]

Though crass, White ethnics were not depicted as depraved, for how could they be given that we had a nation ostensibly held under siege by undocumented workers from across the borders, post-1965 non-White immigrants with their alien ways and Black welfare mothers? Proposition 187, Clinton's welfare reform, backlash against non-White immigration—evinced by print productions such as Lind's *The Next American Nation*, Brimelow's *Alienation*, and Brigg's *Mass Immigration and the National Interest*—only revealed the tip of the consolidation of White citizens in American politics. In popular media accounts, ethnic Whites were not ideal, but at least they were partially perfect Americans engrossed in their vulgar working class lives. These ethnics did not have the refined inclination for multimillion dollar homes, Beluga watches, and Mikimoto pearls, but like the Jewish Fran on mid-1990s television, they were a loveable, affable people who laughed loudly, wore flashy clothes in bawdy colors, and generally exhibited bad taste. In other words, they had no "class," but at least they remained worthy Whites.

1990s Whiteness

Whiteness metamorphosed again in the 1990s into what I term whiteness of a different shade. We are witnessing the dismantling of monolithic whiteness to make way for an accommodating whiteness, where patterns of consumption reveal a proclivity for traveling the globe even as you sit comfortably in your Vanilla suburbs. Japanese motif tattoos are rampant. Saris are draped as window dressings. And ethnic *chicas* are chic. The globalization of capital by the

1990s and its endless search for exotic products that can be converted into consumables has at present led to a particular kind of post-Fordist White culture in the United States, whereby we witness the diversification of cultural products consumed and used as class-identity markers. Origins matter no more, for once these goods enter the global market, especially zeroing in on Western urban zones, they remain only that—exotic goods with no originary locale that are mixed and matched into an attractive, market-able pastiche. The penchant for Thai dinners, Ethiopian coffee for breakfast, so-called World Music often produced by persons of color living in the metropole itself—are all an essential part of what's hip and cool among White, middle-class urbanites in their twenties and thirties. Peppering one's lifestyle with exotica provides an individual with social capital. Third World-ist ethnic chic is in, but Third World people in the United States are not.

Theories on Assimilation

As in the early 1920s, by the mid-1980s American nativism had raised its paranoid head once again, this time in reaction to the post-1965 predominantly Asian and Latino/a immigrants. These new immigrants were perceived to be only taking from instead of giving to the United States, their nation of adoption. Anti-immigrant organizations such as the Federation for American Immigration Reform (FAIR), American Immigration Control Foundation (AICF), the National Association for the Advancement of White People (NAAWP), Californians for Population Stabilization, and the Sierra Club all have growing membership rosters as Americans worry about the integrity of the imagined national community.[82] Alongside, we experienced the scary effects of anti-immigrant rhetoric in the widespread support for the Californian Proposition 187 that invited "whites to express openly and in public the racial resentments, prejudices, and paranoid fantasies that they previously entertained in private."[83] The distribution of rights was once again brought up as an issue, marking Mexican immigrants as unworthy additions to the national body. Citizenship rights were used by political elites to delineate both the nation and whiteness. Lipsitz notes that Proposition 187 served to "insulate white voters and property owners from the ill effects of neoconservative economic policies. Blaming [California's] fiscal woes on immigrants rather than taking responsibility for the ruinous effects of a decade and a half of irresponsible tax cuts for the wealthy coupled with disinvestment in education and infrastructure enabled the state's political leaders and wealthy citizens to divert attention away from their own failures."[84]

Partially, because the kind of immigrant we saw in the post-1965 era was ostensibly beyond assimilation, Americanization had fallen into disuse in popular discourse. These immigrants who arrived from Latin American and Asian countries threatened to convert the United States into an alien-nation. Their presence made White citizens feel alienated because these racial Others could purportedly convert Whites into a numerical minority by the year 2050.[85] In addition, assimilation had fallen into disrepute because of its overt ethnocentric tendencies.[86] Milton Gordon was among the first to question the linear progression of assimilation. He qualified that cultural assimilation did not necessarily lead to civic assimilation or acceptance into mainstream social institutions.[87]

However, from the 1980s onward, in the corridors of institutions of higher learning, assimilation was revived once again. These academic writings by no means profess anti-immigrant politics; contrarily, their intention is to show that in spite of cultural differences—or *because* of these differences—post-1965 immigrants cope successfully with American life. Focusing on second-generation non-Whites and their success in schools (the stereotype of the "straight-A" Asian American), the prevailing academic perspective was the exact opposite of the turn of the century nationalist discourse that prescribed wholesale acculturation. The 1980s–1990s perspective posited that indiscriminate cultural assimilation was perhaps not the best possible means for social mobility in the United States. Ethnic individuals embedded in community now replaced the rational, self-interested abstract individual who had been the hero of the early-twentieth-century American success story. These ethnics succeeded because they retained ethnic networks, and "suitable" aspects of their culture such as "Confucian" family ideals.

Authors such as Margaret Gibson, Alejandro Portes, and Min Zhou described different processes of acculturation and economic outcomes for the post-1965 immigrants.[88] These non-White immigrants were seen to follow either one of the paths to assimilation:

1. They retained ethnic ties, and achieved social/economic mobility within their ethnic enclave. Immigrants and their children mobilized the social and cultural capital derived from their own ethnic groups to achieve economic success in the United States. Hence, retention of ethnicity led to positive economic and social outcomes.
2. Retention of ethnicity, however, was not uniformly advantageous. In certain cases, as with Mexican Americans in California, the preservation of ethnic characteristics led to undesirable socioeconomic outcomes because the second-generation was highly aware of discrimination against their parents, which led them to participate in a subculture that was antagonistic to mainstream values. Portes and Zhou give the example of Mexican Americans in

central California who identified with "home-country language and values, [that] brings them closer to their parents' cultural stance," thus hindering their performance in school and negatively affecting their life chances.[89]

3. Conversely, wholesale acculturation into the United States was disadvantageous for immigrants because they might get acculturated in "wrong" ways. Portes and Zhou give the example of Haitians in Miami who strongly identified as Black Americans. In this case, assimilation "is not into mainstream culture, but into the values and norms of the inner city. In the process, the resources of solidarity and mutual support within the community are dissipated."[90] Hence, second-generation youth squandered any social capital they carried with them because they picked up the wrong set of values. As a result they did not advance economically or socially.

4. The fourth case posited by assimilation theorists is a scenario where second-generation immigrant youth *selectively* retain only those aspects of their ethnic identities that can aid their success in an American world. Min Zhou opines that East Asians such as the Chinese, Koreans, Japanese, and Vietnamese whose cultures are "dominated by Confucianism, Taoism, or Buddhism selectively unpack from their cultural baggage those traits suitable to the new environment, such as two parent families, a strong work ethic, delayed gratification, and thrift."[91] If the ethnic characteristics an immigrant group "selects for display in America are approved by the mainstream, the group will generally be considered having an advantageous culture" for success in the United States.[92]

There is a strange confluence between so-called ethnic values and so-called American values. David Palumbo-Liu quotes John Brademas, president of New York University: "When I look at our Asian-American students, I am certain that much of their success is due to Confucianism. The more I see of Confucianism in action, the more I think it is the mirror image of the Protestant ethic."[93] Palumbo-Liu remarks that

[t]his happy coincidence raises the question, however, of where "Confucianism" ends and the "Protestant ethic" begins, or whether, indeed, it is possible to ascribe Asian success solely to one or the other. [T]hroughout its evocations, "Confucianism" is simultaneously envisioned as a particular product of the ancient "Orient" and a social form eerily like "our own." This produces the notion of Asians "out-whiting the whites," since "Confucianism" seems a primordial genetic disposition passed on from generation to generation and only strengthened by its transplantation in the free soil of American capitalism.[94]

5. And the fifth scenario—successful immigrants selectively retain pieces of their ethnicity, in addition to judiciously adopting only those positive

American values that will lead to success. Margaret Gibson's account of Punjabi immigrants, originally from northwestern India, in northern California first described what she termed selective assimilation. Gibson explains that second generation Punjabi immigrants achieved academic success in spite of virulent racism directed against them because they retained the desirable aspects of their parents' cultural values but also took on desirable American traits. Parents urged their children to abide by school rules, develop strong English language skills, and learn other useful skills, which Gibson deems positive American values. On the other hand, the parents pressured their children against too much contact with white peers because they might develop the negative American trait of fanatical individualism, and leave home at eighteen, begin dating, and making decisions for their lives without parental consent.[95] When one reads Gibson, one is struck by the fact that the Punjabi Americans in California seem to be hyperrational actors who know exactly which ethnic characteristics and which American ones will lead to their eventual economic success.

Retention of ethnic cultures and networks, instead of hindering the economic outcomes of immigrants as alleged at the turn of the twentieth century, is now seen to potentially facilitate the social mobility of new post-1965 immigrants. Embeddedness in a dense network of persons from one's own ethnic background facilitates becoming American. Retention of certain cultural traits provides good cultural capital. But what are these so-called good ethnic traits? If newcomers such as the Haitian immigrants in Miami display characteristics attributed to native-born African Americans (almost always negative qualities), or if immigrants take on an antagonistic stance toward white America as do the Mexican Americans in California in the example above, they have no chance of success. The aspects of non-White cultures that must be retained have to meet the standards set by the 1970s white ethnic home, where ostensibly, father is always hard working, mother is always nurturing, and children always abide by parental authority.

The immigrant home as the primary site of ethnic culture and the immigrant woman as the progenitor of this culture were previously the main impediments to American acculturation and social mobility. Early social work interventions sought to discipline immigrants, especially women, in their homes. Today, instead, we see a complete reversal. The immigrant home, that venerated site of ethnic culture, is now the linchpin of immigrant success. Ethnic, private, familial practices—such as the Confucian values in east Asian American homes described by Zhou and good values fostered in Indian American homes Gibson studies—bolster public successes. *Today, being ethnic makes one a good American.* Once again, women in their roles as wives and mothers are crucial. In the early-twentieth-century immigrant women hindered Americanization, but by the late twentieth century, their labors in maintaining family and ethnic culture nurtured a whole slew of good Americans, albeit, non-White ones this time around.

Ethnic Routes to Becoming Good Americans

Indian immigrants themselves believe that their ethnicity makes them good Americans. When asked about their unique ethnic proclivities, they speak of their orientation to their marriage, regard for immediate and extended families, and their child socialization practices. They indicate that their culture is expressed in their marriages, which are life long alliances, and "in traditional role expectations for wives, in the maintenance of natal language as the medium of communication with family members, and ethnic food habits," all of which are gendered, familial responsibilities that fall more on women than men.[96] Many Indians opine their families are superior to American families. One first generation Indian American man explains:

> The social life and social structure of the Americans is terrible. The family structure, emotional attachment toward each other, moral code of behavior— they lack all these. We are so much richer. It is bad because there is no sense of having a family if you cannot keep the family intact. Whatever the Americans do, they break it up. You cannot accept the fact that breaking up a family is good. They are going into marriage, having families, having children and then breaking it up. They cannot make up their minds as to what the hell they want. They have loose morals.[97]

In addition, many Indian immigrants believe that Americans do not have strong loyalties to their immediate and extended families. An Indian American man expressed that "Indians are much more attached to their families. We visit our relatives in India which is 10,000 miles apart. But Americans wouldn't even travel 300 miles to visit their parents. We are much more family oriented."[98] They also believe they are better parents. Another first generation man expressed that American parents "do not care for [their] children. They don't set a good example. There is no sacrifice for others and less tolerance for others. Children do whatever they like to do. Parents don't care."[99]

The family, the private sphere of the home, is perceived as the node on which the Indian American community's accomplishments rest. It is familial support, parental sacrifice, and children's obedience that facilitate their success as doctors, engineers, and computer programmers. They become public success stories as model citizens precisely because their homes are purportedly bastions of virtue, where good American citizens are raised. The home and family—fundamentally built on the gendered responsibilities of raising offspring in traditional ways, coaching children but especially daughters in classical dance and other ethnic rituals, and sexual strictures more closely adhered to in the case of daughters than in sons—become the mainspring of public success. By turning to their so-called ethnic values, they become better Americans.

Seven

Not White in Public,
Not Ethnic at Home

I raise the issues of assimilation and becoming American in the previous chapter because South Asian Americans are crucially engaged in these questions themselves. The people at Apna Ghar believe they are uniquely ethnic and therefore nonassimilative in their work, yet the pressures of funding, professionalization of social work, the institutionalization of domestic violence intervention all lead their work in unexpected directions. On the other hand, the Indo American Center celebrates "ethnic culture" as a means to assimilation. These two different modes of becoming American make more sense when we locate the shelter and the Center's actions into the larger picture of assimilation in the United States.

When I first began fieldwork, I had assumed that I would observe at Apna Ghar the cultural practices that entailed Indian-ness. Apna Ghar openly stated that it was an ethnic shelter set up to deal with the culturally specific issues South Asian American women face in leaving their abusive spouses and marital families. The shelter aimed to help immigrant women come to terms with their abuse, get their lives together, and begin anew, all in culturally familiar ways. As a spin-off from their intervention in domestic violence, the shelter hoped to radicalize second-generation women regarding gender relations. Conversely, at the Indo American Center I had presumed that I would observe the ways Indian immigrants learnt to perform whiteness, or American normative-ness. The Center's statement of purpose in its information brochure declared that it wanted to help newcomers assimilate into the United States. To summarize, I presumed that at Apna Ghar I would learn about private, familial, ethnic practices; and at the Indo American Center, I would see the practices that entailed whiteness, as new immigrants were taught how to negotiate a White public world. Yet what happened was just the opposite.

Social Work at Apna Ghar

Apna Ghar purported to be a free space; that is, a kind of space in the community that exists between private homes and large public institutions, which provides the environment in which individuals are taught self-respect and learn to act with independent vision so that they may lead a life of dignity.[1] In their brochures, and in conversation Apna Ghar staff and board members maintained that their shelter was a space where battered immigrant women arrived to learn a new self-respect on the basis of their racial identities. In addition, they professed to encourage South Asian women—battered or otherwise—learn new kinds of everyday and social politics.

The workers, like the residents, sought change. They had been handed fixed scripts in their nuclear families and communities for constructing their lives as middle-class women—achieving economic success through studying medicine, engineering, or business; leading exemplary lives as good wives; raising children who would become successful ethnic citizens. But these women turned their backs on these idealized futures. They rejected the expectations their parents had for them and instead pursued "social work," hoping to make the world in which they live a better place. In my conversations with them, I realized that these young, middle-class women pushed for a world where all persons, regardless of gender, have equal opportunities in finding a safe home. They sought to shift gender paradigms within their own personal lives and in their South Asian American communities. They felt less selfish by forgoing the economic benefits of better paying jobs for which they knew they had the social capital, as well as skills. Instead, they wanted to create a "caring community" through their engagement in various social issues.

At Apna Ghar, working-class first-generation residents and middle-class second-generation workers came together. It was a space in which women with dissimilar backgrounds met and spoke about how, in spite of their differences, the gendering of their lives were analogous. Both residents and workers had similar goals of changing the world for themselves and making new communities where their lives had meaning. Yet, the women at Apna Ghar were unable to create any lasting ties. Even the workers, coming from similar class backgrounds, were unable to make community among themselves. Though working on the very specific issue of gendered violence within their South Asian American communities, they felt no common purpose, political, or emotional ties with their coworkers so alike them. Being involved in a South Asian American women's group, many said, caused a greater sense of alienation rather than empowerment.

We were unable to build community in Apna Ghar, I think, because of the ways in which the shelter conceived of ethnicity. To exemplify Apna Ghar's position, let me quote once again, Reena, a twenty-something second-generation case worker. She said of the women who arrived at the shelter:

> You know, it's really hard to change somebody's cultural perceptions. I think that's something we could work at. I mean we are a South Asian women's shelter. I remember we had this one client who was South Asian. She'd only been in the States for about a year. I had to explain to her that she's not in India anymore. She can do a lot more here than she can there. She could get a divorce. She could get a job. And she didn't have to listen to everything her family said now because they are so far away. But it's so hard to get her to stop thinking in those terms.

When the ethnic homes from which immigrant battered women emerge contain physical/emotional spousal battery, how can Apna Ghar posit a problematized ethnicity as the path one needs to traverse in order to become an American success story? Ethnicity in their eyes was the source of problematic patriarchy and women's docile dependence. Given that women were abused within nuclear families embedded in ethnic communities, the shelter pushed women to lead independent lives separate from family and community. Only by being divorced from such an ethnicity could women be truly independent. In addition, their training in social work and the prevalent models of successful independence in other American institutions led them to notions of such abstract individuality. Apna Ghar wanted immigrant women to become atomized, self-reliant individuals who could propel themselves in this new world by the dint of their own hard work and personal endeavor.

As a result, most social relations in the shelter were contractual agreements between individuals. For example, if shelter residents baby-sat each others' children, they were asked to write up a statement and sign it in the presence of a case worker indicating the days and hours child care services would be rendered, and if any money were to be exchanged for these services, then they had to indicate that as well. This statement, cosigned by both women and the caseworker, would be filed in the logbook. Also, friendships between workers and residents were actively discouraged, because we were paid employees and the battered women were "clients." Friendships went against the grain of professionalism Apna Ghar wanted to maintain.

Apna Ghar held onto a high modernist American tradition where residents were urged to forget communal belonging and embeddedness in ethnic networks. Much of the shelter's efforts went into instructing its residents on how to live in a consumer, market-driven mass culture where success is attributed to individual efforts alone. The only thing ethnic about Apna Ghar was that most of the clientele, and almost all the workers were of South Asian origins. Though social workers understood the cultural specificities of abuse, the model for survival was not held to be culturally specific. In the process of teaching immigrant women survival skills, they were taught to become American. After all, in an American world, the only way to survive was by becoming American. Child rearing, time management, cooking, and the conduct of their private lives was to be changed into ways the shelter deemed suitable for American living. Hence, I saw at Apna Ghar, women were compelled to change themselves at a deeply personal level into something that was not specifically ethnic. Examining the case of Apna Ghar only reveals how difficult it is to provide truly culturally specific social services, given the pressures of professionalization and the means for measuring success.

Social Work at the Indo American Center

Volunteers at the Indo American Center too longed for community and actively attempted to convert this longing into a concrete reality. The board of directors at the Center recognized that Indian immigrants tended to affiliate into language groups. Tamils from the South formed their own associations, Sindhis forged their own organizations, and Bengalis fraternized with each other in their Bengali associations. In addition, religion was important; Chicago had mosques, Hindu temples, and churches for Indian immigrants. The board members envisioned their Center as distinct from all these organizations. They felt that Indians needed to think of themselves as Indians first, before retiring to their temples, mosques, and churches or as specific linguistic groups such as the Telugu Association of North America or the Kannada Kuta. The Indo American Center aspired to be the representative of a singular pan-Indic community here in the United States, inclusive of all Indians, regardless of language, region of origin, and religion. They envisioned their Center as a service organization that would first develop, and then enhance, the interests of a unitary Indian American community in metropolitan Chicago.

To a degree, the Indo American Center was quite similar to the mutual aid organizations in Chicago described in preceding pages. Unlike these early-twentieth-century immigrant organizations, however, the Indo American Center was not begun as a mutual aid society but was established for the exclusive purpose of assisting the assimilation of newer, working class Indian immigrants. The Center's mission was to "promote the interests and well-being of people from India" by offering services "that would help them *assimilate* in mainstream American society culturally, socially, and emotionally."[2] Yet, the path to American assimilation was through their Indian culture. While Apna Ghar sought to remake battered women anew, separate from familial/ethnic ties, the Center held onto an idealized ethnic identity that made Indians good Americans. The Indo American Center was not nationalistic in the sense of supporting Hindu fundamentalism in India. However, the various volunteers and workers at the Center displayed nationalistic sentiments because they idealized their sending nation and families back there. This sort of Indian nationalism was not contradictory to their acceptance of or their quest for acceptance into the United States.

If Robert Park and Herbert Miller were to read the preceding paragraph, they would nod knowingly. In their 1921 study of Chicago immigrants titled *Old World Traits Transplanted*, they described the nationalistic sentiments of the eastern/southern immigrants who ran social programs in their various societies. "A number of elements enter into the nationalistic sentiments of the immigrant," they remarked. The feeling of nonparticipation in American public life motivated immigrants to become involved in ethnic organizations so that they too could be contributing, active members in a larger society. Joining these societies brought immigrants together, and here they idealized their old homes and cultures of their sending country. Two things happened simultaneously in these organizations; first, the immigrants wished to enhance their own personal status in the eyes of the larger American public, so they worked to improve the status of the entire ethnic group of which they were a part. By making the whole ethnic group acceptable, they too as individuals—so undeniably ethnic themselves—would gain acceptance in mainstream America. In the process of developing acceptability for their group and themselves, they participated in long-distance nationalism. That is, they inadvertently as well as deliberately aided the various struggles for national self-determination going on in their sending countries. Park and Miller observed—"the fact that the individual will not be respected unless his group is respected becomes thus, perhaps the most sincere source of the nationalistic movements in America. To this extent, the nationalistic movements represent an effort to participate in American life."[3]

I had begun fieldwork at the Center with the presumption that I would learn what it took to make an Indian into an American. The Center, after all, openly stated that its mission was the assimilation of Indians into the United States. Yet, assimilation was fundamentally premised on proving themselves as good ethnics who would be steadfast Americans if only given the chance. Volunteers and board members were constantly trying to show that Indians' good cultural proclivities made them worthy American citizens. The Center focused far more on defining what was an Indian, and there were numerous debates regarding authentic ethnicity. But yet, what is authentic ethnicity? At the Center I observed and participated in endless discussions regarding the boundaries of Indian culture—what is real Indian dance, what is true Indian religion, what is genuine Hinduism, and who are the legitimate representatives of this Indian culture. The question of authenticity arises for South Asian immigrants because they want to engage as full participants in American civil society. As American subjects, Indian immigrants can never be plain "Indian," but are compelled to be authentically ethnic, legitimating their existence in an imagined American community. The quest for an authentic ethnic culture is central to them becoming bona fide American subjects.

Thinking Through the Public and Private Practices of Race

Apna Ghar utilized ethnicity to garner community support and state funding, but was unable to use this very ethnicity in "rehabilitating" battered South Asian immigrant women. In contrast, the Center celebrated ethnicity as the route to becoming American. The narratives the Center put forth in describing the Indian American "community" mainly focused on their morality, propensity for hard work, and good family values, all purportedly unique ethnic characteristics, which made them good immigrants and deserving citizens of this nation. What emerges in this story I tell is that the South Asian immigrants attempted to make "American" practices the everyday, and "Indian-ness" was a ritualized display of ethnic practices for both the American public, as well as other Indians. Their ethnicity is dissected and examined in minute detail. Ethnic culture is not taken for granted anymore, but instead, as racial Others, they have to explain their colored existence into being. They can never be South Asians in a self-evident manner as they go about cultivating their ethnicity in self-conscious ways.

American-ness, on the other hand, is routine, everyday normalcy. South Asian American immigrants will often use American-ness and whiteness interchangeably, and say that is only their public lives that are structured by whiteness. Their homes, they believe, are ethnic safe havens. Yet, as we see in Apna Ghar, non-White immigrants' private, inner selves are self-disciplined in minute ways into American normalcy so that they may endure in an American world. The power in whiteness is that it remains transparent to even immigrants who do not question or examine the contents of American-ness. Because whiteness/American-ness is not considered in detail, they are unable to name it. South Asian immigrants recognize the power of whiteness because they acknowledge that it organizes their lives, but it escapes their explanatory capacities. Whiteness, though an organizing racial principle, remains clearly invisible.

It is not just for White Americans, but for non-White immigrants such as South Asian Americans as well, silence surrounds whiteness.

Multiculturalism and Whiteness

Charles Taylor observes that personal identity in late modernity does not receive "recognition a priori. It has to win it through exchange, and the attempt can fail. What has come about with the modern age is not the need for recognition but the conditions in which the attempt to be recognized can fail."[4] And, therefore, modern liberal democracies create the conditions that permit recognition, because withholding recognition is a form of oppression. Hence, we see a rise in multicultural politics. The multicultural demand is not to just let other cultures follow practices that makes their survival possible, but more crucially, multiculturalism pushes us to acknowledge other cultures' equal worth.[5] However, Taylor cautions us to be careful about how we evaluate equal worth; first, if we think another culture has nothing of value to offer, but we still endorse it, then we run the risk of being patronizing. Beneficiaries of the politics of recognition want respect and not condescension.

The second problem in evaluating equal worth is that the standards for making judgments "are those of North Atlantic civilization," which means that we appreciate only those aspects of other cultures that can be judged by predetermined standards. Therefore, Taylor says that multiculturalism's "peremptory demand for favorable judgments of worth is paradoxically—perhaps one should say tragically—homogenizing," thus making everyone the same.[6] For a truer politics of recognition he urges us to embrace difference into our value systems and broaden our visions and evaluative perspectives. Through a fusion of horizons we may make judgments of others partly through transforming our own standards. Hence, in an ideal multicultural scenario, our evaluation standards are worked out constantly as we negotiate difference around us. According to Taylor, this is the challenge of multiculturalism; we need to deal with the sense of marginalization that communities of color feel by transforming evaluative standards through interacting with Others, but crucially, "without compromising our basic political principles."[7]

Now this poses an interesting dilemma for us, especially when we frame multicultural recognition in the realm of whiteness. Here we are under multiculturalism asking for difference to be recognized and understood, yet whiteness itself remains unacknowledged and, therefore, beyond common comprehension. Not just White Americans but non-White immigrants such as South Asian Americans too admit that whiteness exists, but it lies outside their grasp. The authority of whiteness succeeds because it fails to generate the conditions that makes it possible for us to know its parameters. That is, whiteness works efficiently because it obscures its own presence, while posing as a universal according to which all other deviations are measured and explained. Multiculturalism abets the transparency of whiteness because it shines the spotlight on all those who are conceived as different, while whiteness remains the so-called neutral observer, categorizer, and judge of what is allowable difference and what is not in the national polity. In this sense, in spite of its most altruistic intentions, multiculturalism bolsters whiteness. Evaluative standards, contrary to being transformed as Taylor idealizes, remain solidly unshakeable because the normative presence of whiteness is unacknowledged. Multiculturalism fails to create the conditions under which the presence of whiteness can be recognized. Instead, such politics engender circumstances where whiteness continues to be ominously omnipresent as the universal standard but lies beyond our explanatory capacities.

Taylor's formulation of an ideal multiculturalism focuses only on dominant groups by asking that they broaden their horizons to accept subaltern groups. It is equally important to ask how communities of color engage in multicultural politics. We have, in these preceding pages, looked at multiculturalism from the standpoint of South Asian Americans. At Apna Ghar, South Asian difference is not seen as having any worth or is even seen as harmful, as the shelter attempts to train women out of all traces of ethnicity. Conversely, at the Indo American Center, in proving their culture as having equal (or more) worth, immigrant individuals engaged involuntarily in exclusionary practices. Recognition by the state and mainstream Americans is supposed to extend social citizenship to all members of a polity, but this is not how it works on the ground. Not all members are seen to possess equal worth, and they are excluded from entering as full participants in their racialized groups and, consequently, as American citizens.

Eight

The Cultural Turn in Politics and Community Organizing

Critiquing Multiculturalism

Christian Joppke is the archetype of a more conservative critique of multiculturalism. He identifies citizenship as a legal and cultural concept. As a cultural concept, citizenship refers to sets of practices citizens follow to constitute themselves as a nation. Joppke observes that nation-states are fundamentally constituted on the principle of sedentariness, that is, the fixity of a population in a geographical territory. Yet, immigrants challenge this principle of sedentariness and the idea of the geographically bound nation-state because they are transnational subjects. They profess membership in multiple time-space locations of here and there, now and then. Their sending nations still exert an influence on their psyche and everyday life, which undermines the cultural content of American citizenship, thus challenging the American nation-state. In addition, immigrants and other groups that support immigration push for multiculturalism. According to Joppke, multiculturalism challenges citizenship by undermining "the American concept of non-ethnic, politically constituted nationhood . . . in its roots orientated public exaltation of ethnic and racial identity, multiculturalism tears apart the future orientated, civic layer that had kept the fabric of an essentially 'new' nation together."[1] To summarize, immigrants are a threat to the integrity of a nation-state on two counts; they undermine state sovereignty, and they compromise citizenship through their multiple memberships and the concomitant prevalence of cultural diversity, which then fosters a multicultural agenda in politics.

Joppke's main misunderstanding of multicultural politics lies in the fact that he is empirically off the mark by ahistorically reading American nationhood as *not* having ethnic roots and positing it as solely politically constituted where all races have an equal place.[2] As a result, he does not fully appreciate that multicultural politics actually arises from a liberal political agenda bent upon increasing citizen participation in the nation's public life.

The Racialized Content of American Citizenship

Because the inclusiveness of multiculturalism is based on difference, Joppke worries that the race card is used especially by Asian Americans and Latinos and Latinas who as new additions to the polity should not complain of historical oppressions. He observes that race is not only a form of discrimination, but more important, it is a source of opportunities for these new immigrants. He has reservations about race politics because "ethnic leaders have incentives to model their immigrant constituencies as victimized clients of the state, and to clamour for affirmative-action privileges: preferential college admission, government jobs and business contract, and political representational majority minority districts." He alleges that "'Hispanics' and 'Asians' have originally been administrative categories" and do not have any basis for collective identities, for what really do these immigrants from varied countries have in common to classify them as two corresponding racial categories? The problem with multicultural education is that it "attempts to breathe life into these categories, as the panethnic production of Hispanics and Asians." Multiculturalism encourages "drawing a Fanonesque line between racial minorities and the White majority. From this perspective, the idea of common citizenship and nationhood disappears."[3] If we mistake "multicultural elite discourse" for the common immigrant's unwillingness to integrate, Joppke says we will fail to understand that ethnicity on the ground functions as it always did—as a means of adjusting to a new society. He agonizes that race politics in multiculturalism has no corresponding supporting constituencies on the ground but that only elite people of color drive such politics.

The Achilles' heel in Joppke's argument is that he idealizes citizenship in the United States as historically universal and nonracially structured. Contrarily, as discussed in detail in chapter 6, successful Americans were those who could willfully forget their past and don the cultural mantle of *White* America. The kind of whiteness manifest in the United States constitutes a particular kind of national culture, a nucleus around which an American community is imagined. It forms the core of American citizenship. The selective exclusion that we see is not peripheral to nation-state building but is central to how social order is maintained;[4] for as Rogers Smith (1996) explains, communities are ineradicably political human creations, crafted to govern and assist some people more than others. They are capable of performing vital human services, and indeed, efforts to do without them have thus far been failures. Still, they are likely to behave in partisan ways . . . in light of their dangerous tendencies, we should understand them to be imperfect human instruments and not take them as the proper objects of our full trust or ultimate allegiance.[5]

Habermas observes that legal norms extant within a society arise within a network of interactions; that is, "the process of setting normative rules for modes of behavior is open to influence by a society's political goals. For this reason, every legal system is also the expression of a particular form of life and not merely a reflection of the universal content of basic rights."[6] Hence, to understand American nationhood, in its cultural and legal forms, as transcending race and universally constituted the way Joppke does is a gross misunderstanding given the histories of slavery, Americanization programs directed toward southern and eastern European immigrants, White-only prerequisites for citizenship by naturalization, land ownership laws in California, the forcible return of American citizens of Mexican origin to Mexico, the internment of Japanese Americans during World War II, Proposition 187, tying public school funding to property taxes to the detriment of Black urban communities, to name a few so-called "nonethnic, politically constituted" American state practices. Race is the bedrock on which this nation is built, yet, some persons believe that the cultures of American citizenship have always been egalitarian until Latino/a and Asian immigrants (or rather, their elite leaders) have illiberally politicized race to selfishly meet their own particularistic needs.

Even when Joppke explicitly posits that domestic politics foster the ways in which societies are structured, he seems to see such politics as merely weakening a previously unbiased state and its previously impartial institutions that are somehow set apart, remote, from their racialized polity.[7] Contrarily, Lopez suggests that "law does not exist as a separate phenomenon distinct from society and concerned only with policing disputes, but is an integral part of society and an essential component in the social production of knowledge."[8] Lopez even goes to the extent of maintaining that our appearance, literally the racial features that we exhibit, are to a large degree determined by legal institutions because not only have rules regulated the entry of particular kinds of persons into the United States, denied or allowed them access to resources, property ownership, restricted where they live, and so forth, but also laws have determined reproductive decisions by limiting who shall marry whom.[9]

It is an error to think that liberalism in the United States arises on its own accord; that is, liberalism occurs a priori, it is somehow a given in American politics. Ideals regarding the larger collective good arise, however, because persons understand themselves as citizens and participate in social movements so that particular kinds of politics are made possible. Inhabitants of a nation, as heirs to a specific culture, decide "which traditions they want to perpetuate and which they want to discontinue, how they want to deal with their history, with one another, with nature, and so on."[10] Social movements are partially the means by which a nation's polity keeps the state liberal and inclusive. Using the example of feminists, Habermas says that they rightfully insist gender differences in life experiences and circumstances must be part of the political sphere so that disparities with respect to equal opportunity may be discussed in the open. Similarly, multicultural politics—emerging as a spin-off from the social movements of the 1950s though the 1970s—attempt to recognize that American nationhood is historically race/gender based and to include formerly excluded communities into the political process. Multiculturalism arises from a liberal democratic agenda within in the United States.

Conservative critics wring their hands because they fear that multiculturalism splinters American society; contrarily, it attempts to achieve just the opposite because its ultimate goal is inclusiveness. When we examine multiculturalism today, we see that it has been incorporated into statist discourse through school curricula, affirmative action, government contracts with minority businesses, and grants and funding for NGOs that serve minorities. It is within this context of multiculturalism that Apna Ghar and the Indo American Center exist.

Multiculturalism's Power over the
Cultural Contents of American Citizenship

In criticizing multicultural politics from a broadly left perspective, Nancy Fraser notes that it does not go far enough in producing social change. It merely provides affirmative remedies rather than transformative solutions.[11] As such, multiculturalism is inadequate for two reasons. First, it only redresses disrespect by reevaluating earlier prejudices and leaves "intact both the contents of those identities and the group differentiations that underlie them."[12] The contents of group identities, as we have seen in our empirical cases at the shelter and the Center, are not necessarily egalitarian at all times, and often, the really difficult questions of democratic participation within groups do not get addressed. In celebrating difference, multiculturalism congeals cultural practices rather than allowing for change within groups. Moreover, redistributive affirmative policies only advocate surface reallocations of existing goods to existing groups. Hence, not only do groups get reified but this form of "enfranchisement coincides with a refortification of the state as the guarantor of rights and precludes the necessary critique of the state as the protector of liberal capitalism steadily dividing the racialized labor forces it continues to exclude from those rights."[13]

Fraser notes that race, like gender, is a bivalent mode of collective identity with "a political-economic face and a cultural-valuational face." Racism is institutionalized in the cultural realm, which results in economic disadvantages for communities of color. Hence, racialized communities bear two analytically distinct kinds of injustices that require analytically different kinds of remedies; these remedies are recognition and redistribution. Fraser notes that it is not easy to pursue these two kinds of remedies simultaneously because "the logic of recognition is to valorize group specificity." On the other hand, the "logic of redistribution is to put 'race' out of business." This poses a dilemma for antiracist activists under redistribution-recognition political regimes—how can they "fight simultaneously to abolish 'race' and to valorize the cultural specificity of subordinated racialized groups?"[14]

Present-day multicultural regimes leave racial identities intact by not questioning the deep socioeconomic structures that generate inequalities. This stance not only reinforces racial differentiation but, more insidiously, according to Fraser, it marks "people of color as deficient and insatiable, as always needing more and more."[15] Thus, there is intense backlash misrecognition. Instead of a mere multicultural politics of recognition and redistribution, Fraser says we need a truly transformative politics that will do two things—first, transformative politics should aspire to deeply restructure the relations of recognition. Such restructuring would destabilize group differentiation and allow more radical race politics to emerge. Second, politics should transform the relations of production rather than simply redistribute existing goods.

While I am in general agreement with Fraser, her race theorizing leaves me with a sense of disquiet. To wipe out palliative redistributive policies so that we may mollify angry Whites' backlash misrecognition is completely missing the quest for racial justice/equality. It is true that something like affirmative action hardly begins to address racial injustices, but to do away with it just so that we may gain the favor of the majority of Whites is to engage in a dangerous politics. Such conciliatory gestures are reminiscent of what Anthony Marx's historical comparative study of South Africa, United States, and Brazil reveals; political stability in these nation-states was undermined historically by major conflicts such as British-Afrikaner tensions or North-South clashes in the United States. To diminish these conflicts, political elites tended to "strike bargains, selling out blacks and reinforcing prior racial distinctions and ideology in order to unify whites. . . . 'To bind up a nation's wounds' among whites, blacks were bound down, and the wound of race was left to fester."[16] While the British or the more liberal northern abolitionists won the South African Boer War or the American Civil War, their eventual "policies toward blacks were closer to those advocated by the defeated Afrikaners and Southerners." Any liberalism the state may have held toward Blacks was subordinate to the compulsion to unite Whites; "the strategic and ideological imperatives for a white coalition then set the terms of official racial domination."[17] Dismantling affirmative action to placate the majority of Whites, as Fraser seems to suggest, is a politics whereby communities of color are negatively targeted in a similar manner as described by Anthony Marx in his historical sociology of South Africa and the United States.

This does not mean we endorse multicultural policies—recognition and redistribution—wholesale, because upon closer examination, Lisa Lowe notes that these policies conceal racial exclusions "by recuperating dissent, conflict, and otherness through the promise of inclusion," while simultaneously maintaining "a hegemony that relies on a premature reconciliation of contradiction and persistent distractions away from the historically established incommensurability of the economic, political and cultural spheres."[18] Commenting on the civil rights struggles for recognition and redistribution, Lisa Lowe says these movements found "themselves constrained precisely by the constitutive contradiction of liberal democracy." In a nation-state built by historical exclusion of racialized groups or racially segmented labor markets that operated through slavery, contract labor, or sweatshops, the promise of inclusion through recognizing cultural difference and distributing rights accordingly does not "resolve the material inequalities of racialized exploitation."[19] Lowe observes that multiculturalism apolitically attempts to neutralize the power inherent in the racialized cultures of American citizenship "according to the discourse of pluralism, which asserts that American culture is a democratic terrain to which every variety of constituency has equal access and in which all are represented."[20]

Contrary to popular notions of equal access, the making of imagined national communities is premised on simultaneous remembering and forgetting.[21] Certain traditions—such as the enduring myth that American citizenship is open to anyone professing to uphold notions of nonsectarianism, universal rights, and the ideal of rugged individualism—are remembered again and again in reinscribing the nation. Concurrently, forgetting is central to making a national community. Histories, or official memories, are written so that we may efface past exclusions, oppressions, and exploitations to foster the ideal that the national community has always and will forever more be premised on deep, horizontal comradeship. Multiculturalism produces an imagined national community that ostensibly includes all communities of color on the basis of an

American tradition of plurality. At the same time, multiculturalism effortlessly erases past exclusions. It is a politics that "at once 'forgets' history and, in this forgetting, exacerbates a contradiction between the concentration of capital within a dominant class group and the unattended conditions of a working class increasingly made up of heterogeneous immigrants, racial, and ethnic groups."[22] Multicultural recognition and redistribution *do* grant some rights, but these political moves are incapable of redressing the wrongs wrought by a late modern capitalist and liberal political system that sustains itself through racializing its labor force and its citizenry.

Multiculturalism has the potential to reconceptualize the public sphere. Instead of asking citizens to interact with each other as if differences do not exist, multiculturalism tries to account for difference. It attempts to develop a public sphere that includes those interests and issues that "bourgeois masculinist ideology labels as 'private' and treats as inadmissible."[23] In addition, multicultural politics encourages the existence of multiple public spheres, including subaltern counterpublics; all these developments are far more amenable to democracy instead of a singular public sphere. But these counterpublics do not necessarily encourage participatory democracy within them. Instead, as I have demonstrated in my two case studies of Apna Ghar and the Indo American Center, racialized counterpublics can also silence certain members within racialized communities; we observe that working-class individuals, queers, women, and so forth can be silenced in these alternative publics as well.

Individual Responsibilities in Fostering Democracy

Since the early 1990s, a slew of studies on citizenship have attempted to rework our notions of how democracy works. These new studies, instead of focusing on the modernization of state institutions and the market as did an earlier era of modernization academics, have examined the qualities and attitudes of the citizens themselves to explain the prevalence of democracy. Citizens' civic virtues, their tolerance for difference within their national boundaries, their desire to participate in the political processes for the good of all, to hold political officials responsible, and so forth are seen to be the central virtues of citizenship, which then allow democracy to blossom. Theorists of citizenship have shifted their attention to the merits people need to hold for a viable, flourishing democracy. For example, Galston says that citizens need to have the four following civic virtues:

1. General virtues such as courage, the willingness to obey the law, and loyalty.
2. Social virtues, which are independence and tolerance.
3. Economic virtues that embody a good work ethic, delayed gratification, and adaptability to economic change.

4. Political virtues, which entail the capacity to respect the others, eagerness to engage in public discourse, and so forth.[24]

Repression in Liberal Civil Societies

These theoretical developments are also reflected in popular media accounts of democracy or our common understandings of how democracy works. All these developments lead Jeffrey Alexander to observe that civil society is a sphere of solidarity in which abstract universalism and particularistic versions of community are intertwined.[25] Alexander writes:

> Just as there is no religion that does not divide the world into the saved and the damned, there is no civil discourse that does not conceptualize the world into those who deserve inclusion and those who do not. Members of national communities firmly believe that "the world," and this notably includes their own nation, is filled with people who either do not deserve freedom and communal support or are not capable of sustaining them. . . . Members of national communities do not want to "save" such persons. They do not wish to include them, protect them, or offer them rights because they conceive them as being unworthy and amoral, as in some sense "uncivilized."[26]

Building on a Durkhiemian notion of the sacred and the profane, Alexander posits that civil society is premised on distinctive symbolic codes that provide the structured categories of pure and impure into which every member of that society is slotted. The sacred-profane binary discourse is invoked at three levels—individual motives, the kinds of relations individuals form, and the types of institutions that arise from these relationships. For example, a viable democracy depends on citizens' capacities for autonomous thinking, rational action, and political activism. Persons with these capacities have trusting relations that are straightforward. Their decisions are believed to emerge through open deliberations rather than secretive negotiations. They do not act out of greed or self-interest but instead are concerned with the larger good. The kinds of institutions that arise are rule regulated rather than arbitrary, contractual rather than fostering ascriptive loyalty, inclusive instead of exclusive.

It is not as if members in a polity are intrinsically worthy or unworthy, but others who draw on a systematic, symbolic code assign to persons the categories of either commendable citizens or enemy. Those individuals deemed passive, dependent, or irrational are believed to create relationships that are deferential, self-interested, or conspiratorial. The institutions arising from such relationships are factional, power-ridden, and driven by personality questions. Some members in a polity are considered as having counterdemocratic codes that weaken the overall integrity of liberal civil societies. Hence, Alexander concludes that "the discourse of repression is inherent in the discourse of liberty. This is the irony at the heart of the discourse of civil society."[27]

A cursory examination of newspapers, TV shows, or even some sociological writings reveal that authors often attribute counterdemocratic motives, relationships, and institutions to communities of color. People of color are not hard working and, therefore, deplete the nation's wealth and goodwill through dependence on welfare; they are passionate peoples driven by irrational motives and easily prone to rioting; their home life is such that it channels them into crime; they have strange cultural practices that foster secretive behavior; their families are hierarchical and, therefore, their men are far more patriarchal and their women more downtrodden, thus making both sexes rather unsuitable for a liberal democracy such as the United States; or they illiberally politicize race for their own particularistic gains.

It is within this context of (White) multiculturalism and inherent repression in liberal civil societies that we need to place the kinds of social work that we see in Apna Ghar and the Indo-American Center. Multiculturalism, Nira Yuval-Davis writes in a 1999 essay, gives racialized communities the task of cultivating government to help retain their differences.[28] Two questions arise—why do racialized communities want to retain cultural differences and why does government want to assist them in maintaining differences? It is not just as if the state has an inherent need to maintain difference, but in its liberal commitment to recognize diversity, it creates by-laws, rules, regulations, grants, and so forth that allow racialized communities to thrive. Therefore, the question to ask is why do these communities hold on to distinction?

In our case, Indian Americans are cast out, cultural exiles in both India and the United States. They can never be plain Americans or plain South Asians. Prior to the entrenchment of the recognition in American politics they would have had no platform from which to speak, but today, within a multicultural context, their ethnicity allows them a location from which they speak and act. Therefore, they seek ethnic authenticity to gain validity. The quest for authentic ethnicity, however, is fraught with problems. First, even as ethnicity is a base from which Indian Americans present their authentic selves, it is also a limiting space for them. Under multiculturalism the process of ethnicization is both their empowerment and marginalization simultaneously. The process of becoming ethnic empowers them, but it also reduces them to mostly speak out as only *ethnic* citizens.

The other thing about ethnicity is that Indian-ness is a space that these particular non-Whites believe is uncolonized by mainstream United States. From this uncolonized space, they can author themselves into being and launch themselves as participating members in their new nation. Yet, to protect this space as internally coherent, they both actively and inadvertently excise dissent over the contents of Indian ethnicity. Any hint of vagueness, profanity, or cultural hybridity renders their ethnicity a vulnerable space. If they admit their ethnicity is vague, with a nebulous set of practices, with recent histories instead of ancient roots, then their ethnicity too becomes a contested location from which their truth assertions can be questioned. So instead of threatening the cultures of American citizenship, the multicultural politics extant today is far more threatening to alternative public spaces because it eradicates deliberations regarding ethnicity, thus reducing it to exclusionary practices whereby only persons deemed suitable are allowed to speak and only certain cultural artifacts are given precedence.

Reproducing Sameness Through Practicing Difference

My work shows that in the United States we are deeply ambivalent about the issue of cultural difference. In general, we perceive two kinds of cultural differences—those that threaten and those that do not. Multiculturalism is aimed at perpetuating cultural differences that do not jeopardize hegemonic American culture. The Indo American Center is replete with examples of ethnic cultural practices that add color to the public sphere but do not challenge the cultural content of American citizenship in any overt manner. Indeed, even if the ethnic rituals they engage in at the Center appear different from what we see in mainstream American spaces, the immigrants' performances tend to incorporate and exemplify the values larger society holds. That is, the elements that make up the various ethnic rituals may be exceptional, but the morals that structure their daily immigrant lives are portrayed as being identical to American values. The ethnic performances especially at the Center's Neighborhood tours in this sense are ceremonies of "rejuvenation and reaffirmation of the moral values" of the imagined American community at large.[29] The search for ethnic authenticity in the Center is not a claim of Indian-ness for its own sake, but it is a claim aimed at showing that even at their most basic ethnicized level, at what is taken to be their very ethnic essence, Indian immigrants and their families bear all the ideal qualities deemed necessary in any American. Their repeated incantations of their ostensibly superior culture not only gives them a space from which to speak in a multicultural world, but crucially, their higher culture has inured in them all the morals—pray, even more than the required minimum perhaps— that makes them superlative Americans. In a bizarre way, Indian Americans at the Center reproduce American sameness through practicing ethnic difference.

Invoking Distinction to Produce Sameness

Apna Ghar, on the other hand, signifies the breakdown of the very same colorful ethnicity that is celebrated by the Center as being full of decent values and beliefs. Ethnicity at the shelter was problematic because it reinforced patriarchy. The shelter is a site where "unliberated" women of color arrived to be free from being subjugated by their hierarchical, controlling men. Ethnicity, unlike the case of the Indo American Center, is not a seat of redemption, but instead generates social and familial dysfunctionality. Apna Ghar cannot justifiably celebrate such depraved ethnicity. The paradox of Apna Ghar is this—the shelter raises funds and grants on the basis of an authentic South Asian ethnicity, but at the same time, it cannot hold on to this ethnicity in rehabilitating South Asian battered women. The shelter no doubt offers an alternative space for women seeking to escape domestic violence, but in the name of rehabilitation, new forms of disciplines are imposed on them, training them into American-hood. They are disciplined into the cultural practices of citizenship whereby they are taught to actively construct a life through choices they make about their conduct and bear responsibility for the consequences of those choices. Their growth as autonomous individuals is promoted, divorced from familial or state dependency. They are to become self-reliant contemporary citizens of a competitive American nation. In other words, the shelter tries to convert these women into stalwart citizens who are capable of bearing the individual motives of personal responsibility and independence, who can establish social relationships that are straightforward and deliberative, thereby contributing to making strong social institutions. These are the kinds of citizens the shelter believes that American civil society will endorse, regardless of the color of their skin. The shelter, in a very different manner than the Center, invokes cultural distinction to raise funds but actively attempts to produce sameness in its women residents.

Urban Restructuring, Community Organizations, and Governance

Some people see the successive restructuring of urban governments through devolution, wherein government functions are handed over to non-profit community organizations, as growth in participatory democracy. At one level, we can optimistically view these new developments as a win-win situation where both communities of color and local governments meet their goals. Ethnic organizations are able to sustain themselves through garnering grants and funds that would otherwise be unavailable to them. And local state agencies, by entering into partnerships with organizations begun by racialized communities, can be viewed as becoming more racially liberal and facilitating the growth of participatory democracy. However, others more warily note that these developments position the third sector, occupying the innocent interstices between state and market, as a new solution to the big, inefficient government of the 1960s and 1970s. In other words, the work of governance of urban polities is being partially reorganized through the nonprofit sector, whereby community organizations govern people through taking over the function of providing social services.

Nikolas Rose describes contemporary governmentality as the plethora of activities that shape, guide, and direct the conduct of people. To govern people, he writes, "is to act upon action," which necessitates knowing what "mobilizes the domains or entities to be governed." To govern one must act upon the forces that move people, and instrumentalize these forces "in order to shape actions, processes and outcomes in desired directions." When governing modern polities we presume the freedom of the persons involved. That is, people believe that they are free individuals in their societies, and we utilize this belief they hold in governing them. Modern governance is not achieved through suppressing people, but instead their energies, desires, needs are guided into productive directions. Rose writes that "when it comes to governing human beings, it is to presuppose the freedom of the governed. To govern humans is not to crush their capacity to act, but to acknowledge it and to utilize it for one's own objectives."[30]

Looking at the new modes of urban administration, Rose says that a new era of community has dawned on us—community development, community policing, community correction, community care, and community safety. In the new architecture of government, community is infused with notions of voluntarism, charitable works, self-organized vigilance and care, and unpaid service to our fellow citizens. A multitude of sites have arisen as loci for government—prisons, clinics, schools, the marketplace, shopping malls, factories and offices, and in our case, Apna Ghar and the Indo American Center. Some people believe that the best places to learn civic virtues—the general, social, economic, and political values that Galston, for example, conceives as exemplary—are in nongovernment organizations or through voluntary work. Volunteer organizations are understood as acting like citizenship schools, where people are taught the value of giving time and effort for the common good, caring for others, and communicating with others.

While all this is perhaps true, the perversity of these developments is that in the new architecture of government community is infused with notions of voluntarism, charitable works, self-organized vigilance and care, and unpaid service to our fellow citizens.[31] Politics is now returned to society in the form of individual morality, responsibility, and ethical community, and notions of self-determination, participation, and personal accountability now pepper our governance rhetoric.[32] Indeed, in a perverse way, the personal *has* become the political. An intervening state has given way to the ideal of a facilitating state that enables schools, firms, housing estates, families, parents, and community organizations such as Apna Ghar and the Indo American Center, to act as partners in governance. It is within these changed urban economies; altered urban governments; an accommodating, culturally appropriating whiteness of a different shade; and multiculturalism that we need to locate the two South Asian American organizations, Apna Ghar and the Indo American Center.

Governing Working Class Non-White
Immigrants Through Nonprofits

From an idealized perspective—such as the one I had prior to fieldwork—Apna Ghar and the Indo American Center can be seen as South Asian niches in the Chicago landscape, free spaces, where immigrants are able to make their non-White presence felt. Free spaces can be described as "particular sorts of public spaces in the community [that] are the environments in which people are able to learn a new self-respect, a deeper and more assertive group identity, public skills, and values of cooperation and civic virtue. Put simply, free spaces are settings between private lives and large-scale institutions where ordinary citizens can act with dignity, independence and vision."[33]

Apna Ghar maintains that they are indeed such a free space where battered ethnic women arrive to learn a new self-respect, and a deeper, more assertive group identity. In addition, workers also get politicized through engaging in emotion labor. The Indo American Center too professes to be a space where Indian immigrants come together to assert their culture in the public sphere, which then gives them a sense of group worth and individual self-respect.

But instead, my case studies reveal that while both Apna Ghar and the Indo American Center hold the potential to be alternative spaces, their interventions facilitate new forms of governance whereby a partnership is posited between an enabling state and a morally responsible racialized citizenry that works on the bonds of an ostensibly natural "ethnic" community. The shelter and the Center are intermediaries between the state and working-class immigrants, birthing the process of citizenship for the new arrivals.

In popular wisdom as well as academic writings today, the retention of ethnicity is seen to make one a good American. Within this context, the ethnic home becomes a crucial site where immigrants are taught to be good Americans. At the heart of Asian Americans' model minority status lies their purportedly disciplined, hard-working families. Such familial qualities are prevalent among Asian Americans, it is believed, because of their unique ethnic proclivities. Well in line with such prevailing ideologies, the Indo American Center attempts to reproduce Indian Americans as good immigrants because of the supposedly superior values inherent in their culture. Contrary to this prevailing ideology, Apna Ghar focuses on training women out of their ethnicity. Through orders of protection and urging women to leave their abusers whether the women want to or not, the shelter tries to get women to leave "ethnic" family and, therefore, "ethnic community" behind. In addition, through minute, individual, banal ways—through parenting classes, workshops on interpersonal relations, counseling, everyday scrutiny of the shelter residents' routines and childcare practices—the shelter workers attempt to restructure the shelter residents' lives.

Though the two South Asian American organizations are doing very different things, they ultimately work toward an identical goal, and that is, producing sameness. The Indo American Center practices rituals of difference that ultimately endorse qualities valued in American citizens. The Center practices diversity to produce sameness. Apna Ghar appeals to cultural distinction to explain its existence as an ethnic space, but it trains women into sameness. Both the Center and the shelter exist in part because of multicultural developments in politics, but they do not endorse difference, they reproduce similitude.

The state does not coerce these two South Asian American organizations to act in these ways, but the shelter and the Center depend upon the state for funding, licensing, and coordination with other nonprofit groups. The shelter and the Center need to show numbers—get down to the brass tacks of providing statistics of how many persons contacted them on their hotline, how many women were provided services, how many hours of counseling they have provided, and how many persons are enrolled in their ESL classes—for future grants depend on their present successes. They streamline their work to prove their proficiency. They try to demonstrate the greatest returns on the lowest costs. In other words, they are pressed to show the "greatest bang for the buck."

In addition, the model for who is a successful abuse survivor or who is a well-assimilated immigrant is already determined, and even if these two South Asian American organizations may hold different ideals, their notions do not necessarily receive recognition in the larger schema of things. And though many individuals ask the difficult questions of what efficacy means in the shelter or the Center, there is often no time or energy to pursue these dialogues when there is work to be done. When some of workers at the shelter, for example, created friendship bonds with the residents the supervisors rightfully worried how this may affect their shelter's overall effectiveness. How did such friendships compromise the shelter's professional demeanor? Would such developments hinder the work of their institution?

And even if the volunteers and board members at the Indo American Center sought to define as broadly as possible what it means to be Indian, they were nonetheless victims of their inherited histories. They needed to envision new ways of thinking through their politics, to forge new alliances, to reimagine themselves, and conceive of where they wanted to go. Indeed, almost all individuals at the Center were incredibly committed to a new politics, but to get to that new place, they needed to understand where they come from. They cannot unproblematically freeze their personal stories, histories, and communities into sets of narratives inherited in India or imparted to them in the United States. Instead they need to understand the extent to which they have to be creative in recasting their pasts to make new futures. But the issue was that if the Center cast its constituencies more broadly, if it is more cosmopolitan in its acceptance of difference, it would have to work harder and much more concertedly to build a broad-based but tight-knit racial community. Yet, given that budgets are shrinking, the pool of volunteers is dwindling, and the number of working class immigrants needing assistance is burgeoning, the Center has no option but to focus its energies on how to raise money and get more volunteers. Therefore, to increase efficacy, the Center is pushed into defining its constituencies far more narrowly than it might ideally want to do so.

The case studies of Apna Ghar and the Indo American Center show that despite the rhetoric of multiculturalism, or perhaps more accurately *because* of it, incorporation into the American polity is not a benign process where we all exist as separate ingredients in a salad bowl, to use the current analogy describing race in the United States; instead incorporation is still about brute disciplining processes where individuals are normalized into becoming a unified citizenry. Notions of being American have altered from the 1950s to today because of the way commodities from other cultures enter the everyday world of middle-class Americans, but normative American-ness still matters, structuring the way new immigrants get incorporated into the nation's civil body.

Notes

One   Introduction

1. Carl Sandburg, "Chicago," from *Chicago Poems* (1916; reprint, University of Illinois Press, Urbana, 1992).
2. David Harvey writes that "the display of the commodity became a central part of the spectacle, as crowds flocked to gaze at them and at each other in intimate and secure spaces . . . its undoubted commercial success rests in part on the way in which the act of buying connects to the pleasure of the spectacle in secured spaces, safe from violence or political agitation." Debord would take it further: "the spectacle is the developed modern complement of money where the totality of the commodity world appears as a whole, as a general equivalence for what the entire society can be and can do." To the degree that the spectacle becomes "the common ground of deceived gaze and of false consciousness," so it can also present itself as "an instrument of unification." David Harvey, "Flexible Accumulation through Urbanization: Reflections on 'Post–Modernism' in the American City," in *Post-Fordism: A Reader*, edited by Ash Amin (Oxford: Blackwell, 1994), 376; Guy Debord, *Society of the Spectacle* (Detroit: Black & Red, 1983) quoted in Harvey, 376.
3. Christian Joppke, "Immigration Challenges the Nation-State," in *Challenge to the Nation-State*, edited by Christian Joppke (New York: Oxford University Press, 1998) 34.
4. Harvey, "Flexible Accumulation," 363.
5. Fredric Jameson, *Postmodernism, or, The Cultural Logic of Late Capitalism* (Durham, N. C.: Duke University Press, 1991).
6. David Harvey describes the built environments of cities. The social movements of the 1960s were profitably used to encourage "the exploration of product differentiation, so the repressed market desire to acquire symbolic capital could be captured through the production of built environments." Harvey, "Flexible Accumulation," 375.

7. Thomas Frank, "Why Johnny Can't Dissent," in *Commodify Your Dissent: The Business of Culture in the New Gilded Age. Salvos from The Baffler*, edited by Thomas Frank and Matt Weiland (New York: W.W. Norton and Company, 1997), 34.

8. Bob Jessop, "Post-Fordism and the State," in *Post-Fordism: A Reader*, 263.

9. T. H. Marshall posited that citizenship comprises three types of rights, each accompanied with a set of state institutions. The first set of rights, which arose in the eighteenth century, are *civil rights* that include freedom of choice in place of residence, freedom of speech, freedom of religion, freedom to own property, and the right to equal justice. Though these rights are taken for granted today, they have been the privileges of a select few for much of history. These rights were established in most European countries by the late nineteenth century, and though the United States professed that it offered civil rights to all Americans much earlier, African Americans, Native Americans, and non-White immigrants were excluded. The institutions associated with civil rights are the various courts of justice. The second set of citizenship rights are *political rights*, which developed over the nineteenth century; they refer to the right to participate in politics, run for elections, and vote for candidates of one's choice. In most nations, universal franchise for men was established by the early twentieth century, and suffrage movements eventually helped win the vote for women. Corresponding institutions are senates, parliaments, and local governments. The last assortment of citizenship rights are *social rights*, which grew during the twentieth century. The institutions most closely connected with it are the educational system and social services. Marshall, *Citizenship, and Social Class* (Westport, Conn.: Greenwood Press, 1973).

10. Charles Tilly, *Citizenship, Identity and Social History* (Cambridge: Cambridge University Press, 1999).

11. Rogers Smith, *Civic Ideals: Conflicting Visions of Citizenship in U.S. History* (New Haven, Conn.: Yale University Press, 1997), 15.

12. T. H. Marshall, *Citizenship and Social Class*, 24–25.

13. Ibid., 16.

14. Michael Omi and Howard Winant, *Racial Formation in the United States*, 2nd ed. (New York: Routledge, 1994).

15. Rogers Smith, *Civic Ideals*, 6.

16. Lisa Lowe, *Immigrant Acts: On Asian American Cultural Politics* (Durham, N.C.: Duke University Press, 1996), 2.

17. Charles Taylor, "The Politics of Recognition," in *Multiculturalism and "The Politics of Recognition,"* edited by Amy Gutman (Princeton, N.J.: Princeton University Press, 1994) 26.

18. Margit Mayer, "Post-Fordist City Politics," in *Post-Fordism: A Reader*, 320.

19. Ibid., 325.

20. Ibid., 328.

21. Harvey, "Flexible Accumulation," 366.

22. Mayer, "Post-Fordist City Politics," 320.

23. These developments had caused much concern about the separation of the church and the state prior to our current anxieties about Bush's self-described crusade against "terrorists" who are invariably Muslim in faith. The lack of the separation of the church and state and the nonsecular nature of American politics is only highlighted during these times of imminent war.

24. California has four domestic violence service organizations–Aasra, Maitri, Narika, and Sahara. Sawera is located in Oregon. Texas has Saheli and Daya. Apna Ghar and Ham Dard are in Chicago. Maryland, Virginia, and Washington D.C. have ASHA (Asian Women's Self Help). In addition, Samhati serves only Maryland. SEWAA (Service and Education for Women Against Abuse) is located in Philadelphia. Manavi serves both Massachusetts and New Jersey. Connecticut has Sneha and Shamokami. New York has Sakhi, Workers' Awaz, AIWA, Bangladeshi Mahila Samiti, Muslim Women's Committee, and Sikh Women's Association. For more information on various service providers, see the website sawweb@umiacs.umd.edu.

   Manavi is the oldest South Asian women's group against domestic violence. It was started in 1985 by a group of Indian American women who were active in the mainstream women's movement but felt excluded as women of color. Manavi began as a consciousness-raising group but very quickly became involved with domestic violence in Indian American homes (Shamita Das Dasgupta in an interview with Luvina Melwani). Melwani, "Shamita Das Dasgupta: Justice in Action," *Little India* 5, no. 3 (1995): 25.

25. For example, the South Asian Lesbian and Gay Association (SALGA) was not allowed to march in the New York India Day Parade by the Federation of Indian Associations (FIA) in 1992. The New York City Human Rights Commission intervened, and the FIA yielded. The next year, the FIA stipulated that SALGA could participate in the parade but only if they did not carry signs declaring their sexualities. SALGA refused. In 1994, Sakhi invited SALGA to march along with its volunteers. The parade organizers were displeased with Sakhi and banned them from the 1995 parade. Along with Sakhi and SALGA, South Asian AIDS Action (SAAA), the Lease Drivers' Coalition (union of South Asian cab drivers), and Yaar (a South Asian civil rights and education organization) were banned. At the parade on August 20, 1995, more than 100 South Asian activists protested their exclusion from the 15th Annual India Day Parade in New York City. See Purvi Shah, "Redefining the Home: How Community Elites Silence Feminist Activism," in *Dragon Ladies: Asian American Feminists Breathe Fire*, edited by Sonia Shah, 46–56 (Boston: South End Press, 1997).

26. Anannya Bhattacharjee, "The Habit of Ex-Nomination: Nation, Women, and the Indian Immigrants Bourgeoisie," *Public Culture* 5, no. 1 (fall 1992): 19–44.

27. Some Indian Americans refuse to believe that abuse can occur in middle-class Indian American families. They assume that because we are away from the patriarchal extended families prevalent in India, women's liberation and autonomy is heightened in the United States. See Shamita Das Dasgupta and Sujata Warrier, "In the Footsteps of 'Arundati,'" *Violence Against Women* 2, no. 3 (1996): 238–258.

28. Caitrin Lynch, "Nation, Woman, and the Indian Immigrant Bourgeoisie: An Alternative Formulation," *Public Culture* 17 (1994): 425–437. Lynch writes in response to Anannya Bhattacharjee's earlier extremely well known 1992 article, "The Habit of Ex-Nomination," wherein she writes about Sakhi in New York City. In its earlier years, Sakhi was a more radical feminist group; in addition to providing domestic violence services, it advocated freedom in sexual expression through its support for SALGA. This radicalism made the Federation of Indian Associations jittery and they banned Sakhi and SALGA from participating in Indian independence parades in New York. Lynch may have a point because the conservative FIA itself has begun establishing services for battered women. Aasra in the San Francisco Bay area is one such FIA-sponsored group.

29. Indian Americans deny the occurrence of domestic violence in their communities; they "perceive wife abuse as a lower class phenomenon that coexists with poor educational levels, economic impoverishment, and women's lack of autonomy. Because the Indian American community in this country is highly educated and skilled, community members believe that wife beating can not occur among its members." Das Dasgupta and Warrier, "In the Footsteps of 'Arundati,'" 240.

30. The motives for such information are always interest me; why are such comparisons important? What ways do they want me to answer, and what kinds of answers are these questions looking for?

31. This letter, dated July 3, 1997, was Sakhi's response to our protest from Chingari at Madison, Wisconsin.

32. The concept of free spaces, used in sociological literature on collective action, has been variously termed protected spaces, safe places, spatial preserves, havens, sequestered social sites, and spheres of cultural autonomy. Francesca Polletta, "'Free Spaces' in Collective Action," *Theory and Society* 28, no. 1 (1999): 1–37.

33. Ibid.

34. Sayantini Dasgupta, "Thoughts from a Feminist ABCD," *India Currents* 6, no. 12 (1993): 26.

35. Amita Vasudeva, "Journal Entry," in *Our Feet Walk The Sky*, edited by Women of the South Asian Diaspora Collective (San Francisco: Aunt Lute Books, 1993), 132–133.

36. Ibid., 132. Vasudeva's main purpose is to show that she is both Indian and American, the latter term tellingly used interchangeably with *White*. While Vasudeva previously felt that such a location was laden with contradictions, she says that she has now come to terms with a fragmentary existence. Many, of whom Dasgupta and Vasudeva are just two, use *White* and *American* as if the two words are synonymous. I want to note that this is *not* because they are unaware of the presence of other minorities, but it is because they recognize that American society is structured by whiteness. They are not being racist in saying White = American; they understand that the American norm is White, and if they want to become American, they too have to become White. All these essays, personal conversations, and writings indicate that White practices are not restricted to White people alone, but instead conceivably, form a repertoire of social practices that go into making immigrants American.

37. Ibid.

38. R. Radhakrishnan, "Is the Ethnic 'Authentic' in the Diaspora?" in *The State of Asian America: Activism and Resistance in the 1990s*, edited by Karin Aguilar-San Juan, (Boston: South End Press, 1994), 223.

39. This book is certainly not unique in this aspect. Two exemplary accounts of Indians in Chicago are Jean Bacon's *Life Lines: Community, Family, and Assimilation Among Asian Indian Immigrants* (New York: Oxford University Press, 1996); and Padma Rangaswamy's *Namaste America: Indian Immigrants in an American Metropolis* (University Park: Pennsylvania State University Press, 2000). Through informal interviews, Bacon details interactions between family members to explicate how new generations of members are initiated into community. Rangaswamy offers exhaustive information on the Chicago Indian American community itself.

Two   Finding Our Home in This World

All the names I use in this book are pseudonyms. I also do not reveal the exact years I worked at the shelter to further protect individuals' identities.

1. I did not interview Janet, the White executive director. Neither do I explore her racial politics, nor her interactions with workers or clients. The reason is that I focus solely on Indian Americans. What is interesting is that the board of directors hired her, not a South Asian American, as an executive director. Even though I asked, I was not able to get an answer for this decision.
2. From the Apna Ghar information brochure (not dated).
3. Lee Ann Hoff, *Battered Women as Survivors* (New York: Routledge, 1990), 7.
4. I did not want to turn on the tape recorder and gather survival narratives for sociological analyses and academic writing. Most stories of battery were shared in confidentiality and not for the purpose of being reproduced in articles and books.
5. Susan Brison, "Outliving Oneself: Trauma, Memory, and Personal Identity," in *Feminists Rethink The Self*, edited by Diane Tietjens Meyers (Boulder, Colo.: Westview Press, 1997), 12.
6. Denise Riley, *"Am I That Name?" Feminism and the Category of "Women" in History* (Minneapolis: University of Minnesota Press, 1988).
7. Likewise, lynching of Black male bodies and homophobic attacks are other instances where individuals are victimized precisely because of the social meanings ascribed to their bodies.
8. Brison, "Outliving Oneself," 18.
9. Ibid.
10. Ibid., 14.
11. A Jewish survivor of the Nazi death camps remarks of the violence perpetrated on her, "One can be alive after Sobibor without having survived Sobibor." Lawrence Langer, ed., *Admitting the Holocaust* (New York: Oxford University Press, 1995), quoted in Brison, "Outliving Oneself," 12.
12. Judith Herman, *Trauma and Recovery* (New York: Basic Books, 1992), 34, quoted in Brison, "Outliving Oneself," 14.
13. Brison. "Outliving Oneself," 17.
14. Jonathan Shay, *Achilles in Vietnam: Combat Trauma and Undoing of Character* (New York: Atheneum, 1994), 174, quoted in Brison, "Outliving Oneself," 17.
15. Brison, "Outliving Oneself," 23.
16. Ibid., 25.
17. Ibid., 28.
18. Ibid., 12.
19. Giles explores the notion of "home" among Portuguese women in Toronto. The home is inextricably tied to these women's identities. The home is a contradictory phenomenon because it constrains women, but it is also a location that provides avenues of escape and freedom. Home is a gendered location "from which Portuguese women begin to describe, defend or justify themselves and their acts." Wenona Giles, "Remembering The Portuguese Household in Toronto: Culture, Contradictions, and Resistance," *Women's Studies International Forum* 20, no. 3 (1997): 387–396.

20. Etter-Lewis says that Black women's identities are inseparable from that of the larger group identity and cannot be situated on only a gendered understanding. Likewise, Indian American women's identities cannot be separate from the larger community. Their sense of self is intricately tied to that of the larger group. See article by G. Etter-Lewis, "Black Women's Life Stories: Reclaiming Self in Narrative Texts," in *Women's Words: The Feminist Practice of Oral History*, edited by Sherna Berger Gluck and Daphne Patai (New York: Routledge, 1991), 43–58.

21. Upon reading these lines, one can assume that I deem domestic abuse as constituted only by physical violence. Contrarily, I recognize that verbal abuse, belittling, and other such controlling behavior is also abusive, but I do not write about it because, during the time I worked there, Apna Ghar deemed only physical violence as *true* domestic violence.

22. Excerpts from tape recorded interview.

23. Sangeeta Gupta writes, "Indian American men in their late 20s prefer women who are 20–22 years old as they are not as 'outspoken' nor do they express their needs and expectations clearly . . . men preferred young girls to mature women whose personalities are stronger and more developed. This viewpoint was confirmed by several men who openly stated that younger women (20–22) did not expect as much in a relationship and are 'easier to impress.'" Sangeeta R. Gupta, "Walking On The Edge: Indian-American Women Speak Out On Dating and Marriage," in *Emerging Voices: South Asian American Women Redefine Self, Family, and Community*, edited by Sangeeta R. Gupta (Walnut Creek, Calif.: AltaMira Press), 120–145.

24. Michael Strube and Linda Barbour, 1983. "The Decision to Leave an Abusive Relationship: Economic Dependence and Psychological Commitment," *Journal of Marriage and the Family* 45, no. 4 (November 1983): 785–793.

25. D. K. Snyder and L. A. Fruchtman, "Differential Patterns of Wife Abuse: A Data Based Typology," *Journal of Consulting and Clinical Psychology* 49 (1980): 878–885.

26. Stroube and Barbour, "The Decision to Leave."

27. Anannya Bhattacharjee. "A Slippery Path: Organizing Resistance to Violence Against Women," in *Dragon Ladies*, 29–45.

28. Donileen R. Loseke, *The Battered Woman and Shelters: The Social Construction of Wife Abuse* (Albany, N.Y.: SUNY Press, 1992), 96.

29. Ibid., 115. [Emphasis in original]

30. Das Dasgupta and Warrier found that women remain with their abusers because of their perception that good mothers put their needs aside in order to keep families intact. "The presence of a father, abusive or not, was regarded as essential to the proper upbringing of children. Gurpreet, a mother of two had survived beatings for more than a decade, justified her decision to remain with her husband, 'For children, I will sacrifice all. I can't take the children away from [their] security.' Mala echoed her sentiments, 'Parents must be there for children always and do what is best. I have sacrificed all my life and stayed in this abusive relationship for my children's sake.'" Das Dasgupta and Warrier, "In the Footsteps of 'Arundati,'" 251.

31. Das Dasgupta and Warrier say that the women they worked with worried about being looked down on if their abuse became common knowledge; "Mumtaz said, 'You know our community. Who will believe me? Everyone will say there is something wrong with me.' Thus when Mumtaz felt she could take the beatings no longer and had to move out of her home, she severed all her ties with her Asian Indian

friends and the community itself. She isolated herself, believing that no one from her culture would condone her decision to break up with her spouse, and thus would judge her adversely. Kanak and Parul both maintained that if they ever spoke about their abuse to others, the community would label them as 'too Westernized' and, therefore, traitors to the culture." Das Dasgupta and Warrier, "In the Footsteps of 'Arundati,'" 251.

32. PROWRA ended federal entitlement to welfare for poor women and their families. Each state will now have a distinct welfare program, with different eligibility criteria. However, minimal federal standards apply. The *Welfare Reform Network News* notes that "a state may stop accepting applications for assistance when it has exhausted the funds allotted to assistance. The end of entitlement status of welfare has implications for battered women, who may be forced to return to a violent relationship if they are unable to find and retain jobs to support themselves and their children" (*Welfare Reform Network News*, March 31, 1997). States can also set time limits of less than five years, restricting women's abilities to make and implement safe choices for themselves and their families. Legal immigrants who entered the United States after August 22, 1996, are not eligible for public benefits for five years after entering the country. The Balanced Budget Act of 1997 restored SSI benefits to legal immigrants who were receiving SSI as of August 22, 1997, and expanded eligibility to legal immigrants who were in the country on that day but became disabled in the future. This 1997 Act did not restore Food Stamps to immigrants, and states have the option to prohibit immigrants from receiving TANF and Medicaid. An excellent source of information on the impact of welfare reform on Asian immigrants is Lynn H. Fujiwara, "The Impact of Welfare Reform on Asian Immigrant Communities," *Social Justice* 25, no. 1 (spring 1998): 82–104. Kaplan states that the Attorney General has issued some provisions that give immigrants access to services and assistance "necessary for the protection of life and safety." Victims of domestic violence fall under this category. April Kaplan "Domestic Violence and Welfare Reform" (1998), available from http://www.welfareinfo.org/aprildomestic. Accessed December 2000.

33. Nahar Alam, "Domestic Workers Do Their Homework," *Samar* (summer/fall 1997): 15–20.

34. The Samar Collective. "One Big Happy Community? Class Issues Within South Asian American Homes." *Samar* (winter 1994): 10–15.

35. Nahar Alam, "Domestic Workers Do Their Homework," 15.

36. Elizabeth Ewen, *Immigrant Women in the Land of Dollars: Life and Culture on the Lower East Side, 1890–1925* (New York: Monthly Review Press, 1985), 14.

37. Ibid., 15.

38. Uma Narayan, "'Mail-order' Brides: Immigrant Women, Domestic Violence and Immigration Law," *Hypatia* 10, no. 1 (1995): 104–120.

39. Michelle J. Anderson, "A License to Abuse: The Impact of Conditional Status of Female Immigrants," *The Yale Law Journal* 102, no. 6 (1993): 1401–1421.

40. Narayan, "'Mail-order' Brides," 109.

41. For more on VAWA, see Johanna Shargel, "In Defense of the Civil Rights Remedy of the Violence Against Women Act," *The Yale Law Journal* 106, no. 6 (1997): 1849–1883; also see Stephen M. Pincus and David N. Rosen, "Fighting Back: Filing Suit Under the Violence Against Women Act," *Trial* 33, no. 12 (1997): 20–27.

42. Zygmunt Bauman sums up the conditions for community in our worlds today. He says, "gone are most of the steady and solidly dug-in orientation points which suggested a social setting that was more durable, more secure and more reliable than the timespan of an individual life. Gone is the certainty that 'we will meet again', that we will be meeting repeatedly and for a very long time to come—and that therefore society can be presumed to have a long memory and what we do to each other today will come to comfort us or grieve us in the future; that what we do to each other has more than episodic significance, since the consequences of our actions will stay with us long after the actions have apparently ended—surviving in the minds and deeds of witnesses who are not going to vanish." Bauman, *Community: Seeking Safety in an Insecure World* (Cambridge, England: Polity, 2001): 47–48.

Three   Workers at Apna Ghar

1. Of the 166 second-generation individuals interviewed, thirty-eight men and thirty women were training to be doctors; twenty-five men and sixteen women were training to become engineers; thirty-two men and twenty-five women were in business-related fields. Priya Agarwal, "Doctor or Engineer? Career Choices Among Second-Generation Indian Americans," *The Indian American* (March 1993): 24–26.
2. Anupy Singla writes that South Asian students feel "the pressure of being channeled into traditional careers of medicine or engineering. Non-traditional careers such as politics, international relations, and international development, they [feel], were still looked upon as aberrations and open to questions such as, 'What can you do with that kind of career?' and 'thank God someone else in the family has decided to become a doctor.'" Anupy Singla, "Prospects for South Asian Unity in a New World Order," *The Indian American* (March 1993): 15–17.
3. Loseke, *Battered Woman and Shelters*.
4. These policies at the shelter had to do with the politics of the shelter supervisor and executive director under whom we worked at that time. If the shelter were under the direction of individuals with different politics, it may have been run differently.
5. Ibid., 123. [Emphasis in original]
6. Freedberg examines the feminine ethic of care intrinsic to women's gendered development and the profession of social work. She says that the tension between personalized concern and scientific professionalism creates an uneasy tension. Sharon Freedberg, "The Feminine Ethic of Care and the Professionalization of Social Work." *Social Work* 38, no. 5 (September 1993): 535–580.
7. Arlie Russell Hochschild, *The Managed Heart: Commercialization of Human Feeling* (Berkeley: University of California Press, 1983).
8. See Amy Wharton, "The Psychosocial Consequences of Emotional Labor," *The Annals of American Political and Social Science* 561 (January 1999): 158–176.
9. Hochschild, *Managed Heart*, 7.
10. Chodorow says that gendered socialization leads to a feminine ethic of care. The mother is the primary care giver, and the girl child identifies with the gender of her mother; she grows up, defining herself as the primary nurturer in relationships within the family and outside of it. See Nancy Chodorow, *The Reproduction Of Mothering: Psychoanalysis And The Sociology Of Gender* (Berkeley: University of California Press, 1978).

11. Sandra Lee Bartky, "Sympathy and Solidarity: On a Tight Rope with Scheler," in *Feminists Rethink The Self*, edited by Diane Tietjens Meyers (Boulder, Colo.: Westview Press, 1997), 193.

12. Bartky quotes Elizabeth Spelman: "I must try enter imaginatively into the worlds of others. Imagination isn't enough, but it is necessary. Indeed, it is a crucial starting point: because I have not experienced what the other has, so unless I can imagine her having pain or her having pleasure I can't be moved to try to help put an end to her pain or to understand what her pleasures are. Against all odds I must try to think and feel my way into her world." Spelman, *Inessential Woman: Problems of Exclusion in Feminist Theory* (Boston: Beacon Press, 1989), quoted in Bartky, "Sympathy and Solidarity," 179.

13. Bartky, "Sympathy and Solidarity," 179.

14. Ibid.

15. In theorizing intersubjectivity, Bartky turns to Max Scheler's *The Nature of Sympathy*. According to Scheler, there are four kinds of sympathy, the first of which is "true fellow feeling," the second and third are narrow and lacking in moral base, and the final form of "fellow feeling" is genuine. The first true form of fellow feeling is one where both individuals share the exact same feelings because of the exact same cause. An example of this may be the loss parents feel over the death of their child. The second fellow feeling, translated as "emotional infection" by Bartky, has no moral base according to Scheler. These are feelings that we get from being in a crowd of people; for example, I am infected with gaiety upon entering a party. The laughter and enjoyment of others rubs off on me. Such fellow feelings are irrational because we do not consciously direct our feelings. Emotional infection is like an avalanche "so easily carried beyond the intentions of every one of its members and does things for which no one acknowledges either the will or the responsibility." Scheler's *The Nature of Sympathy*, trans. by Peter Heath, with a general introduction by W. Stark (Hamden, Conn.: Archon Books, 1970), quoted in Bartky, "Sympathy and Solidarity, 182.

    Scheler believes people become animals by associating themselves with crowds instead of cultivating individual spiritual independence. Bartky observes that Scheler does not understand that mass protests have a moral basis. We go to mass rallies so that we may be emotionally infected by each other as we fight for a common cause. We can be infected "by a sense of power emanating from the human mass we make together; moreover, the physical presence of each pledges silently to the others our continued support—and in this way we reduce out fear of isolation and defeat." Bartky, 183–184. The third form of fellow feeling is "emotional identification," where I feel so deeply with the other that my own self disappears into her self. Such fellow feeling also lacks moral worth because it works directly against the unique individuality of each person.

16. Ibid., 186.

17. Ibid.

18. Ibid., 184.

19. Ibid., 188.

20. Freudenberger is given credit for having picked the phrase "burn-out" from its colloquial reference to the chronic effects of drug abuse and used it instead to describe the psychological state of volunteers who worked in alternative health care agencies.

H. L. Freudenberger, "Staff Burnout," *Journal of Social Issues* 30 (1974): 159–165; "The Staff Burnout Syndrome in Alternative Institutions, *Psychotherapy: Theory Research & Practice* 12 (1975): 73–82. This definition is from H. L. Freudenberger and G. Richelson, *Burnout: The High Cost of High Achievement* (Garden City, N.Y.: Anchor Press, 1980); and C. Maslach and S. E. Jackson, *Maslach Burnout Inventory*, Research Ed. (Palo Alto, Calif.: Consulting Psychologists Press, 1981), quoted in Marie Soderfeldt, Bjorn Soderfeldt, and Lars-Erik Warg, "Burnout in Social Work," *Social Work* 40, no. 5 (1995): 638–650.

21. Susan Stall and Randy Stoecker, "Community Organizing or Organizing Community? Gender and the Crafts of Empowerment," *Gender & Society* 12, no. 6 (1988): 741.

22. Francis Fox Piven and Richard Cloward, *Poor People's Movements: Why They Succeed and How They Fail* (New York: Pantheon Books, 1977).

23. Vijay Agnew , "Tensions in Providing Services to South Asian Victims of Wife Abuse in Toronto," in *Violence Against Women* 4, no. 2 (1998): 163.

24. Ibid., 160.

Four   The Indo American Center

1. Mrs. Shetty, a member of the board of directors at the Indo American Center, explains the role of the Center. [Emphasis is mine] All the following statements by the various board members were written down, and they were able to carefully articulate their goals for the Center, their idealism in community work, and why the provision of such "social services" was a vital component in Indians' acceptance into the United States.

2. 1997 mission statement of the Indo American Center.

3. In the United States today, there are numerous anti-immigration organizations. FAIR, Federation for American Immigration Reform, for example, wants to set a ceiling on immigration. The belief is that immigrants take what rightfully belongs to other Americans, such as jobs, or go on welfare, that is, usurp taxpayers' hard-earned money. Another organization, the Rockford Institute states, "immigrants are a threat to U.S. cultural norms. Immigrants cannot comprehend certain intangible notions of U.S. politics, art, literature, religious morality, and work ethic." Other groups such as Zero Population Growth, Californians for Population Stabilization, the Sierra Club, and Negative Population Growth believe that immigrants contribute to overpopulation and, hence, deplete natural resources in the United States. For a description of various anti-immigration outfits, see Rita Simon, "Old Minorities, New Immigrants: Aspirations, Hopes, and Fears," *The Annals of American Political and Social Science* 530 (November 1993): 61–73.

4. Neighborhood tours can be seen as a process of museumizing Devon Avenue. Stephen Greenblatt observes that museums function "partly by design and partly in spite of themselves, as monuments to the fragility of cultures, to the fall of sustaining institutions and noble houses, the collapse of rituals, the evacuation of myths, the destructive effects of warfare, neglect, and corrosive doubt." Stephen Greenblatt, "Resonance and Wonder," *Exhibiting Cultures: The Poetics and Politics of Museum Display*, edited by Ivan Karp and Steven D. Lavine (Washington, D.C.: Smithsonian Institution Press, 1991), 43–44. Or, Regina Bendix cynically observes that displays such as the Neighborhood Tours are possible because individuals "have been suffi-

ciently savvy to alienate themselves far enough from their traditions to market them." Bendix, *In Search of Authenticity: The Formation of Folklore Studies* (Madison: University of Wisconsin Press, 1997), 8. Neither is true, however, because the Center wants to convey a sense of a lived culture, extending into the present, structuring the immigrants' ethnic selves and the ways in which they live here in the United States. Moreover, the Indian immigrants at the Center are not interested in marketing their traditions, so much as redefining a singular ethnic culture for themselves as well as their White public.

5. I take this phrase from Micaela di Leonardo's book title, *Exotics At Home: Anthropologies, Others, and American Modernity* (Chicago: University of Chicago Press, 1998).

6. The 1965 Immigration Act is commonly understood as a reaction to the Cold War; Mrs. Nayar indicates that the shortage of scientists, doctors, and so forth led to the passage of the 1965 Act, which encouraged the active recruitment of Third World professionals into the United States. However, the 1965 Act was primarily directed at family reunification. First and second preference was for the spouse, unmarried sons, and daughters of citizens and permanent residents. Third preference was for professionals, scientists, and artists of exceptional ability, and only 10 percent of these high-skilled immigrants were to be allowed within any year. It is interesting that an act primarily directed at family reunification is commonly misunderstood to be a "skilled labor recruitment" act.

7. Simone de Beauvoir writes, "Even if each woman dresses in conformity with her status, a game is still being played: artifice, like art, belongs to the realm of the imaginary. It is not only that girdle, brassier, hair-dye, make-up disguise body and face; but that the least sophisticated of women, once she is "dressed," does not present *herself* to observation; she is, like the picture or the statue, or the actor on the stage, an agent through whom is suggested someone not there; that is, the character she represents, but is not. It is this identification with something unreal, fixed, perfect as the hero of a novel, as a portrait or a bust, that gratifies her; she strives to identify herself with this figure and thus to seem to herself to be stabilized, justified in her splendor." From Simone de Beauvoir *The Second Sex*, trans. by H. M. Parshley (New York: Knopf, 1953), quoted in Erving Goffman, *The Presentation of Self in Everyday Life* (New York: Anchor Books, 1959), 57–58.

8. Greenblatt, "Resonance and Wonder."

9. Svetlana Alpers, "The Museum as a Way of Seeing," in *Exhibiting Cultures*, 25–41. She notes when objects "are severed from the ritual site, the invitation to look attentively remains and in certain aspects may even be enhanced." The museum effect, she posits, is just another way of seeing; "rather than trying to overcome it, one might as well try to work with it," 27.

10. Greenblatt defines resonance as "the power of the displayed object to reach beyond its formal boundaries to a larger world, to evoke in the viewer the complex, dynamic cultural forces from which it has emerged and for which it may be taken by a viewer to stand." By wonder he means "the power of the displayed object to stop the viewer in his or her tracks, to convey an arresting sense of uniqueness, to evoke an exalted attention." Greenblatt, "Resonance and Wonder," 42. The displayed objects at the Center evoke wonder, rather than a sense of resonance.

11. James Boon writes that museums make him sad "because of what they reveal about representation . . . so resembling and reassembling of the world, the museum-world

of fragments: fragments wrested from their pasts and elsewheres to be exhibited and categorized, only to yield instead, through their juxtaposition, aphorisms of coincidence." James A. Boon, "Why Museums Make Me Sad," *Exhibiting Cultures*, 255–277.

12. Uma Narayan, *Dislocating Cultures: Identities, Traditions, and Third World Feminism* (New York: Routledge, 1997): 132.

13. Goffman, *Presentation of Self*, 112.

14. Goffman writes that a single discrepant note can upset the entire tone of a performance. Hence "a certain bureaucratization of the spirit is expected so that we can be relied upon to give a perfectly homogenous performance at every appointed time." Goffman, *Presentation of Self*, 56.

15. In 2 A.D., Bharat-muni ostensibly wrote the *Natyashastra*, and hence sadir's new appellation, Bharat Natyam. Ironically, in separating it from the *devadasis* in temples, Bharat Natyam got further "brahminized." See Avanti Meduri, "Bharatha Natyam, What Are You?" *Asian Theatre Journal* 5 (1988): 1–21.

16. Pallabi Chakravorty, "Hegemony, Dance and Nation: The Construction of the Classical Dance in India," *South Asia* 21 (1998), 117.

17. The Academies "underlined the central government at Delhi as the official patron of Indian cultural heritage. But, the national institutions, not surprisingly, promoted the gurukul system (or hereditary lineage system), that authorized the male traditional families, or the gharanas, as the true bearers of authentic tradition. The upper-middle-class and middle-class women bowed to this modern patriarchal structure as a necessary step in their recognition and legitimization as classical dancers." Chakraborty, "Hegemony, Dance and Nation," 117.

18. Aparna Rayaprol, *Negotiating Identities: Women in the Indian Diaspora* (New Delhi: Oxford University Press, 1997), 71–72. Rayaprol wants to illustrate how immigrant women take a far more active, public role than commonly recognized. She sees women as powerful agents ordering their lives in ways they deem appropriate. Taking children to dance classes, participation in temple committees, and so forth are seen as empowering acts. Rayaprol, however, does not sufficiently recognize that these activities are directed toward the propagation of an "Indian" culture here in the United States. By enacting these social tasks, women follow gendered rules of conduct, reproduce ascribed gender norms, and reinscribe their gendering as culture bearers.

19. Ibid., 78.

20. Ibid., 122.

21. An immigrant mother explained to Rayaprol, "Every Sunday when I take my daughter for the dance class my son comes along but plays football outside." Rayaprol writes of one young man who wanted to learn Bharat Natyam, but his parents dissuaded him and decided "his time was better spent taking tennis lessons." In spite of the strict gendering of cultural pursuits, one young man in her study learnt the classical dance *Kuchipudi*; "this nonconformity disturbed the boy's parents, but as his father . . . said, 'we have learnt to live with it.'" Rayaprol, *Negotiating Identities*, 78, 122.

22. Approximately 500 films are made in Bollywood each year. In 1985, an average of 13 million Indians watched these films daily, and an average of 100 million movie tickets were sold all over India every week that year. From Sunita Sunder Mukhi, "'Underneath My Blouse Beats My Indian Heart': Sexuality, Nationalism and Indian

Womanhood in the United States," in *A Patchwork Shawl: Chronicles of South Asian Women in America*, edited by Shamita Das Dasgupta (New Brunswick, N.J.: Rutgers University Press, 1998), 186–205.
23. Ibid., 188.
24. Ibid., 193.
25. Goffman, *Presentation of Self*, 35.
26. Ibid., 35.
27. I borrow the phrase "authentic insider" from Uma Narayan, *Dislocating Cultures*, 144.
28. Lata Mani shows that Indian tradition is a product of colonialism. British colonialists, in casting around for a coherent legal system to govern their Indian subjects, looked toward religion partially because they believed that Hindus blindly follow religion and, therefore, would not question authority legitimated by Hinduism. Unable to figure out what precisely is Hinduism, they privileged Brahmanic texts because scriptures were seen as the source of authenticity. However, the scriptures were not the basis of law in precolonial India, and Mani notes this "British 'brahmanising tendency' which ignored the laws enforced by caste *sabhas* associations, and focused exclusively on brahmanic texts for the formulation of 'Hindu' law." Mani, "Contentious Traditions: The Debate On *Sati* in Colonial India," *Recasting Women: Essays in Colonial History*, edited by Kumkum Sangari and Sudesh Vaid (New Brunswick, N.J.: Rutgers University Press, 1989), 114. There is no single text on Hinduism; so the oldest texts were deemed the truest representations and took precedence over newer ones. In addition, the British hired Brahmins to interpret these texts, thus enfranchising them as emissaries of Hinduism. Whenever these Brahmin court employees used the example of "local custom" their exegesis were thrown out as inaccurate; and though these court employees premised their readings of the texts by saying "to the best of my knowledge," their interpretations were taken as incontrovertible truths. Hence, the particular form of Hinduism we see today has far more recent origins than acknowledged. The Brahmanic texts on which Hinduism today is based might be ancient, but the widespread understanding of these texts as the sole representatives of Hinduism is a relatively new phenomenon.
29. Uma Chakravarti, "Whatever Happened To The Vedic *Dasi*? Orientalism, Nationalism, and a Script for the Past," in *Recasting Women*, 27–87; Partha Chatterjee, *The Nation and its Fragments* (Princeton, N.J.: Princeton University Press, 1993); Lata Mani, "Contentious Traditions."
30. David Lelyveld describes how Maharashtrian Brahmins reformulated classical music in India in the early twentieth century "as a reassertion of Hindu culture, opposed not only to the British but also to Muslims, and as Brahman authority over lower-status communities." Lelyveld, "Upon the Subdominant: Administering Music on All-India Radio," *Consuming Modernity: Public Culture in a South Asian World*, edited by Carol Breckenridge (Minneapolis: University of Minnesota Press, 1995), 56. Dr. B. V. Keskar, Minister of Information and Broadcasting in newly independent India (1950–1962), was highly influential in formulating the musical ideologies of the All India Radio. Keskar believed that Indian music had deteriorated because of the British and Muslims, who as rulers in earlier centuries, "had appropriated and distorted the ancient art, turning it into the secret craft of exclusive lineages . . . ignorant of Sanskrit, divorced it from the religious context of Hindu civilization. Furthermore, they had bifurcated the unity of Indian music by creating a 'Hindustani'

variant as against the still safely Hindu 'Carnatic' one. . . . In Muslim hands music was no longer 'spiritual;' it has become merely 'erotic,' the special preserve of 'dancing girls, prostitutes and their circle of pimps.' Respectable Hindus had turned away from this corruption with understandable disgust" (55). Lelyveld writes that Keskar was among the new generation of Brahmins who felt the study of music was central to good education. They attempted to purge Islamic influences from this renewed musical tradition. The rise of popular film songs, however, weakened these attempts at constructing a national culture. With its preponderant use of Urdu words, rhythm and melody from western popular music, and avoidance of Sanskrit, Bollywood offered an oppositional culture—albeit commercial—to the national cultural policy (189–214).

31. Bendix, *In Search of Authenticity*, 9.
32. Goffman, *Presentation of Self*, 48.
33. *Desi* is a Hindi word that refers to any individual who originates from the subcontinent.
34. Again, there is a conflation between Hindu and Indian that rolls so easily off the tongue that the two very disparate categories seem like one.
35. Fanon, in *The Wretched of the Earth* (1961), argues that the way in which colonialism worked was that the colonizers imposed their images of the colonized on the subjugated peoples. To obtain freedom, the colonized must first rid themselves of these deprecatory self-images, and reimagine themselves anew before they can struggle for freedom. Frantz Fanon, *The Wretched of the Earth* (New York: Grove Press, 1961).
36. Shireen J. Jejeebhoy, "Addressing Women's Reproductive Health Needs: Priorities for the Family Welfare Program," *Economic and Political Weekly* (March 1–8, 1997): 475–484.
37. Narayan notes pungently, "I have sometimes wondered with wry amusement whether 'Third World individuals' were assumed to have a kind of 'knowledge by osmosis' about everything pertaining to 'their culture' or to that internally complex entity, the 'Third World.' I am less amused when I wonder whether the part of my work that pertains to 'Third World issues' might seem like 'automatic knowledge' seeping from my Third World pores, rather than the results of intellectual and political effort!" Narayan, *Dislocating Cultures*, 145.

Five   The Politics of Cultural Authenticity

1. In a fantastical scenario in *Satanic Verses*, Rushdie describes how immigrants in Britain turn into animals. Saladin Chamcha, one of the protagonists, becomes a goat-like shaitan. Another character, a male model from Bombay who changes into a man-tiger, explains, "[T]here's a woman over there . . . who is now mostly water buffalo. There are businessmen from Nigeria who have grown sturdy tails. There is a group of holiday makers from Senegal who were doing no more than changing planes when they were turned into slippery snakes." The man-tiger composes itself and then continues with anger, "[S]ome of us aren't going to stand for it. We're going to bust out of here before they turn us into anything worse. Every night I feel a different piece of me beginning to change." When Saladin Chamcha asks how Third World immigrants become animals, the man-tiger explains, "They describe us . . . that's all. They have the power of description, and we succumb to the pictures

they construct." Salman Rushdie, *The Satanic Verses,* Dover, Del.: The Consortium: Inc., 1992), 168.

2. Kamala Visweshwaran, "Predicaments of the Hyphen," In *Our Feet Walk The Sky.* She writes, "Certainly the question, 'Where are you from?' is never an innocent one. Yet not all subjects have equal difficulty in replying. To pose a question of origin is to subtly pose a question of return, to challenge not only temporally, but geographically, one's place in the present. For someone who is neither fully Indian nor wholly American, is a question which provokes a sudden failure of confidence, the fear of never replying adequately," 301.

3. Marshall Berman, *The Politics of Authenticity: Radical Individualism and the Emergence of Modern Society* (New York, Atheneum, 1970); Robert Bellah et al., *Habits of the Heart: Individualism and Commitment in American Life* (Berkeley: University of California, 1985); di Leonardo, *Exotics At Home.*

4. Bendix, *In Search of Authenticity,* 8.

5. Alessandro Ferrara, *Reflective Authenticity: Rethinking the Project of Modernity* (New York: Routledge, 1998), 53. [Emphasis in original]

6. Stuart Zane Charme, *Vulgarity and Authenticity: Dimensions of Otherness in the World of Jean-Paul Sartre* (Amherst, Mass.: University of Massachusetts Press, 1991), 6.

7. Ibid., 8. Di Leonardo would critique this escape from modernity "through the immersion in the lives of those Others considered organically whole by virtue of their distance, in time and/or space, from the etiolated world of Western logic and progress." She describes how, in the early twentieth century, Americans turned to "medieval Europeans, South Sea islanders, southwestern Native Americans—even the impoverished southeastern Europeans resident in northern industrial cities" to salvage their alienated, modern souls. These Others to American self-hood "were the grist for the antimodernism mill of the Gilded Age and Progressive Era." Leonardo, *Exotics At Home,* 2–3. Sartre's desire to become the symbolic outsider through apprenticing himself to those cast outside French culture is precisely such a move.

8. Bendix, *In Search of Authenticity,* 16.

9. Ibid., 17.

10. Berman, *Politics of Authenticity,* xix.

11. Ibid., 325.

12. Ferrara, *Reflective Authenticity,* 57.

13. Ken Plummer, *Telling Sexual Stories: Power, Change and Social Worlds* (London: Routledge, 1995).

14. Robert Park and Herbert Miller, *Old World Traits Transplanted* (New York: Harpers and Brothers Publishers, 1921), 48). [Emphasis is mine]

15. R. Radhakrishnan writes, "Her naturalization into American citizenship simultaneously minoritizes her identity. She is now reborn as an ethnic minority American citizen. Is this empowerment, or marginalization? This new American citizen must think of her Indian self as an ethnic self that defers to her nationalized American status. The culturally and politically hegemonic Indian identity is now a mere qualifier: 'ethnic.'" Radhakrishnan, "Is the Ethnic 'Authentic,'" 222.

16. This is especially the case for Muslims Indians who are often asked why don't they go to Pakistan. Since the Pakistan-India partition, many Indians presume that India is for Hindus and Pakistan is for Muslims.

17. Radhakrishnan, "Is the Ethnic 'Authentic,'" 224–225.

18. Salman Rushdie writes that nomads "are as rootless as the dunes, or rather rooted in the knowledge that the journeying itself is home. Whereas the migrant can do without the journey altogether; it's no more a necessary evil; the point is to arrive." Rushdie, *Satanic Verses*, 94.
19. Ibid., 69.
20. Goffman, *Presentation of Self*, 57.
21. See Radhakrishnan, "Is the Ethnic 'Authentic,'" 228.
22. Ibid., 229.
23. Ruth Frankenberg, *White Women, Race Matters* (Minneapolis: University of Minnesota Press, 1993) 6.
24. Pierre Bourdieu. *The Logic of Practice* (Stanford, Calif.: Stanford University Press. 1990), 54.
25. Pierre Bourdieu. *Outline of a Theory in Practice* (New York: Cambridge University Press, 1977), 80.
26. Frankenberg says that "whites are the nondefined definers of other people. Or, to put it another way, whiteness comes as an unmarked or neutral category, whereas other cultures are specifically marked 'cultural.'" Ruth Frankenberg, *White Women, Race Matters* (Minneapolis: University of Minnesota Press, 1993), 197.
27. Patricia Williams, *The Alchemy of Race and Rights: Diary of a Law Professor* (Cambridge, Mass.: Harvard University Press, 1991).
28. Ibid., 88–89.
29. Ian F. Haney Lopez, *White By Law: The Legal Construction of Race* (New York: New York University Press, 1996), 23.
30. Ibid., 158.
31. Ibid., 187.
32. Ibid., 30.
33. Ibid., 28. Lopez observes that whiteness is tied to goodness, whereas blackness is tied to all that's bad. He quotes from Frantz Fanon's *Black Skin, White Masks*: "In Europe, the black man is the symbol of Evil. . . . The torturer is the black man. Satan is black, one talks of shadows, when one is dirty one is black—whether one is thinking of physical dirtiness or of moral dirtiness. It would be astonishing, if the trouble were taken to bring them all together, to see the vast number of expressions that make the black man the equivalent of sin. In Europe, whether concretely or symbolically, the black man stands for the bad side of character. . . . Blackness, darkness, shadow, shades, right, the labyrinths of the earth, abysmal depths, blacken someone's reputation; and on the other side, the bright side of innocence, the white dove of peace, magical heavenly light." Fanon quoted in Lopez, *White By Law* (New York: Grove Weidenoeld, 1967), 173–174.
34. Williams writes that American culture "does not make all selves or I's the servants of others, but only some. Thus some I's are defined as 'your servant,' some as 'your master.' The struggle for the self becomes not a true mirroring of self-in-other, but a hierarchically inspired series of distortions, where some serve without ever being served; some master with no sense of what it is to be mastered; and almost everyone hides from the fact of this vernacular domination by clinging to the legally official definition of an I meaning 'your equal.'" Williams, *Alchemy of Race and Rights*, 63.
35. In antebellum America, the Irish were seen as an intermediate race between Black and White. However, the Irish were incorporated into whiteness through

their support of slavery. The conventional understanding is that slavery made it possible to extend citizenship privileges to the Irish "by providing another group for them to stand on," but instead the reverse is true; "the assimilation of the Irish into the White race made it possible to maintain slavery." Noel Ignatiav, *How the Irish Became White* (New York: Routledge, 1995), 69. The proslavery Democratic Party abetted the assimilation of the Irish into whiteness by taking an antinativist/proimmigrant stance. "Nativism lost out not to the vision of a nonracial society, but to a society polarized between white and black. Part of the project of rejecting nativism was to establish an acceptable standard of 'white behavior'" (76).

36. Berman, *Politics of Authenticity*; Bellah et al., *Habits of the Heart.*

37. Todd Boyd notes that whiteness is represented in its entirety, spanning "the spectrum of good and evil, high and low." Contrarily, African Americans are represented monolithically. He urges media critics to focus on "media institutions that deny a more informed representation of African American culture" in its diverse existence. "The complexities of cultural identity," he says, "are too difficult to be reduced to the redundant question of being 'Black enough.'" Boyd, *Am I Black Enough For You? Popular Culture From the 'Hood and Beyond* (Bloomington: Indiana University Press, 1997), 22–23. Boyd observes of media representations of "gangsta" culture—"considering that excess sells in general, the more excessive the African American image, the stronger the likelihood it will be accepted. The politics of negotiated identity, focusing on excess, dominates the representation of contemporary Black popular culture" (5). Rap emerges out of the violence of urban poverty, but its marketing launches young, economically/politically marginalized musicians into economic success, necessitating one to "remain true to one's cultural identity while existing in the mainstream. This is what is meant when rappers says, 'Keep it real.' Authenticity becomes a central issue" (14). Boyd identifies authenticity as a space that "is defined by those who use their complete disregard for the dictates of society and overall nonconformity to strengthen their cultural articulation" (15). While Boyd celebrates Black authenticity as an oppositional politics, I am far more skeptical of authenticity.

38. Bendix, *In Search of Authenticity*, 17.

39. Kalpana Prakash, personal communication (2001). Kalpana Prakash is an artist living in Madison, Wisconsin. Our interactions—my viewing her work and her reading my words—drove us to ask similar questions regarding ethnic authenticity.

40. Uma Narayan says that when Third World feminists enter American academia, they "enter the discursive spaces of mainstream Western academic contexts, they enter a field of Preoccupations where a variety of concerns about inclusion, diversity, and multiculturalism are already being played out." Third World feminists find that locations are already built in for them, which works to their disadvantage because "these locations work to shape our entrance, influence what is expected of us, and give us a place that often also *puts us in our place.*" Narayan, *Dislocating Cultures*, 123. [Emphasis is mine] Third World feminists are often asked to give lectures or participate in panels on issues that address the "Third World" even though they may be very qualified to speak about *Roe vs. Wade*, for example. Persons of color "routinely get cast as Native Informants while being denied auditions for other roles they could play just as well" (145)

Six   Becoming American

1. Eric Hobsbawm and Terence Ranger, eds., *The Invention of Tradition* (Cambridge: Cambridge University Press, 1983).
2. American civic identity is often idealized as structured on the belief that "mankind is endowed with unalienable rights which no laws may abrogate or nullify; that among unalienable rights of humankind are life, liberty, and the pursuit of happiness." Winthrop Talbot, "Americanism," in *Americanization: Principles of Americanism, Essentials of Americanization, Technic of Race–Assimilation, Annotated Bibliography*, edited by Winthrop Talbot (New York: H.W. Wilson Company, 1917), 1. To become an American, all one needed to do was commit themselves "to the political ideology centered on the abstract ideals of liberty, equality, and republicanism. [The] universalist ideological character of American nationality" is believed to be open to "anyone who willed to become an American." Philip Gleason, "American Identity and Americanization," *Harvard Encyclopedia of American Ethnic Groups* (Cambridge, Mass.: Harvard University Press, 1980), 32.
3. Gary Gerstle, *American Crucible: Race and Nation in the Twentieth Century* (Princeton, N.J.: Princeton University Press, 2001.
4. In addition to some of the highest rates of immigration, the early twentieth century saw a new kind of America. A majority of Americans, who led preindustrial cultural lives, encountered a rapidly urbanizing, industrializing nation, and the commodification of everyday living. Weyl writes in 1904 that "when we compare the America of today with the America of half a century ago, certain differences stand out sharply." Persons of his era had lost "their earlier frugal simplicity, and [had] become extravagant and competitively lavish. We have, in short, created a new type of American who lives in the city, reads newspapers and even books, bathes frequently, travels occasionally; a man, fluent intellectually and physically restless, ready but not profound, intent upon success, but not without idealism, but somewhat disillusioned, pleasure-loving, hard working, humorous." Walter E. Weyl, "New Americans," in *Americanization*, 100.
5. See Philip Gleason, "Americans All: World War II and the Shaping of American Identity," In *American Immigration and Ethnicity: Americanization, Social Control, and Philanthropy*, edited by George E. Pozzetta (New York: Garland Publishing Inc., 1991), 113–148.
6. Smith, *Civic Ideals*.
7. W.E.B. DuBois. "The Negro in the United States," in *Americanization*, 119.
8. In addition to the disenfranchisement of Blacks, only some immigrants were considered suitable raw material for American incorporation. In 1917, John R. Commons, University of Wisconsin-Madison economist, explained there were superior races and inferior races. A superior race arrived from a "medieval" civilization, but upon introduction to American modern civilization, these persons absorbed "the spirit and method of American institutions as any Caucasian." Commons, "Amalgamation and Assimilation," in *Americanization*, 108–109. Commons continues that temperate zones were such that "man in his struggle for existence developed the qualities of mind and will—the ingenuity, self-reliance, self-control, strenuous exertion, and will power—which make him befitting the modern industrial civilization" (109–110). He includes Chinese immigrants in the category of allowable immigrants

because they come from a medieval but superior civilization. Persons from tropical zones, on the other hand, were unsuitable for Americanization because the character attributes of creativity, independence, self-discipline, and the ethic of hard work were poorly developed in them. These qualities were weak because the environmental conditions of tropical countries made life easy; "nature lavishes food and winks at the neglect of clothing and shelter." As a result, "ignorance, and superstition, and physical prowess and sexual passion have an equal chance [of existence] with intelligence, foresight, thrift and self-control" (110). All one needed to do with individuals belonging to temperate zone races to make them eligible for modern American civilization was to catch them young, but "this much can not be said for the children of the tropical zone. Amalgamation"—which John Commons defined as race mixing that gives rise to a "common stock,"—"is their only door to assimilation. Frederick Douglass, Booker Washington, Professor Du Bois are an honor to any race, but they are mulattoes" (110).

9. Huebner, "The Americanization of the Immigrant," *The Annals of The American Academy of Political and Social Science* 27 (May 1906; reprinted in *Americanization*, 174).
10. Talbot, "Americanism," 1.
11. Benedict Anderson, *Imagined Communities* (London: Verso, 1983): 61–63.
12. Huebner, "Americanization of the Immigrant," 175–176.
13. Hobsbawm, *The Invention Of Traditions*, 280.
14. Huebner, "Americanization of the Immigrant," 176.
15. For example, English language lessons at the International Harvester Company were devoted to worker discipline. One lesson read:
    I hear the whistle. I must hurry.
    I hear the five minute whistle.
    It is time to go to the shop.
    I take my check from the gate board
    and hang it on the department board.
    I change my clothes and get ready to work.
    The starting whistle blows.
    I eat my lunch.
    It is forbidden to eat until then.
    The whistle blows at five minutes of starting time.
    I get ready to go to work.
    I work until the whistle blows to quit.
    I leave my place nice and clean.
    I put all my clothes in my locker.
    I go home.
    The Harvester World 3 (March 1912): 31, quoted in Gern Korman, "Americanization at the Factory Gate," in *American Immigration and Ethnicity*, 154.
16. Stephen Mayer, "Adapting the Immigrant to the Line: Americanization in the Ford Factory, 1914–1921," *In American Immigration and Ethnicity*, 253–268.
17. Quoted in Mayer, "Adapting the Immigrant to the Line," 260.
18. Huebner, "Americanization of the Immigrant," 178.
19. Morris Knowles, "Housing and Americanization," In *Americanization*, 259–60.
20. Helen Varick Boswell, "Promoting Americanization," in *Americanization*, 298.

21. Ibid., 299. [Emphasis in original]
22. In Topeka, Kansas, one agency taught Mexican immigrant women "American" methods of laundry. Sophonisba P. Breckinridge, *New Homes For Old* (New York: Harper and Brothers Publishing, 1921), 289.
23. Ibid., 288.
24. Ewen, *Immigrant Women in the Land of Dollars*, 85.
25. Ibid.
26. Horace Kallen, "Democracy Versus Melting-Pot: A Study of American Nationality," *The Nation* 100, no. 2590 (1915): 190–194; and 100, no. 2591 (1915): 217–220; reprinted in *Theories of Ethnicity: A Classical Reader*, edited by Werner Sollors (New York: New York University Press, 1996), 88.
27. Robert Carlson, "Americanization as an Early Twentieth-Century Adult Education Movement," in *American Immigration and Ethnicity*, 452–453.
28. Woodrow Wilson, "The Meaning of Citizenship: An Address to Newly Naturalized Citizens, Philadelphia, May 10, 1915," In *Americanization*, 79.
29. Randolph Bourne, "Trans-national America," *Atlantic Monthly* 118 (July 1916): 86–97; reprinted in *Theories of Ethnicity*, 93–108.
30. Korman, "Americanization at the Factory Gate," 150–173.
31. Carlson, "Americanization as an Early Twentieth-Century Adult Education Movement," 62–86.
32. Frances Kellor quoted in Carlson, "Americanization as an Early Twentieth-Century Adult Education Movement," 72.
33. The National Conference on Immigration and Americanization, *Immigrants in America Review* 2 (April 1916): 38–46; reprinted in *Americanization*, 279.
34. Carlson, "Americanization as an Early Twentieth-Century Adult Education Movement," 77–78.
35. Isaac B. Berkson, *Theories of Americanization: A Critical Study* (New York: Teachers College Bureau of Publications, 1920), 70.
36. Quoted in Carlson, "Americanization as an Early Twentieth-Century Adult Education Movement," 79.
37. Alfred Shultz, *Race or Mongrel* (Boston: Little, Brown, 1908), quoted in Matthew Frye Jacobson, *Whiteness of a Different Color* (Cambridge, Mass.: Harvard University Press, 1998), 5.
38. Ibid.
39. Lothrop Stoddard, *The Rising Tide of Color Against White World Supremacy* (New York: Charles Scribner's Sons, 1920), quoted in Jacobson, *Whiteness of a Different Color,* 96.
40. Stoddard, *Reforging America* (New York: Charles Scribner's Sons, 1927) quoted in Jacobson, *Whiteness of a Different Color,* 98.
41. Gleason, "Americans All," 113–148.
42. See Ibid.
43. In addition, in reaction to Nazi Germany's genocide, the word *race* in liberal circles was looked with suspicion. Thus Ashley Montagu writes in his *Race: Man's Most Dangerous Myth* (1942) that race had taken on an exaggerated emotional content and should be dropped entirely. Yet, race still came through the back door because Montagu replaced the word *race* with the *divisions* of mankind, namely, Negroid, Australoid, Caucasian, and Mongoloid, based on professed differences in phenotype. Or, Ruth Benedict's *Races of Mankind* "included a tricolored world map whose three

broad regions corresponded to 'Caucasian,' 'Mongoloid,' and 'Negroid' areas." Jacobson, *Whiteness of a Different Color*, 101–103. What we see is that European immigrants, those "Others" in early 20th century United States, were now included within the "Caucasian" family unlike the "colored" African Americans, Chinese, or Japanese who stood outside the circle of whiteness.

44. Park and Miller, *Old World Traits Transplanted*, 47.
45. Ibid., 48.
46. Ewen, Immigrant Women in the Land of Dollars, 205.
47. Park and Miller, *Old World Traits Transplanted*, 129.
48. By 1921, the Carniolian Slovenian Catholic Union organized in Joliet, Illinois, in 1894, had 17,000 members, a capital of $650,000, and had paid $1,376,135.32 in benefits to members. The most popular Italian mutual aid society, the *Unione Siciliana*, had 28 lodges; monthly fees varied from 30 to 60 cents. Sick benefits ranged from $8 to $12 per week; a death benefit of $1000 was paid to aggrieved families. Park and Miller, *Old World Traits Transplanted*, 124–132.
49. Breckinridge, *New Homes for Old*, 193.
50. Park and Miller note that immigrants held extravagant funerals. They quote a letter from Thomas I. Thomas and Florian Znaniecki. A Polish worker died from a gruesome factory accident, and the members of the Polish mutual aid society comforted the deceased immigrant's family back in Poland with descriptions of the funeral costs. The letter follows:

    ". . . now I inform you, dearest parents, and you my brothers, that Konstanty, you son, and your brother and mine, my brothers, is no longer alive. It killed him in the foundry, it tore him to eight parts, it tore his head away and crushed his chest to a mass and it broke his arms. But I beg you, dear parents, don't weep and don't grieve, God willed it so and did it so. It killed him on April 20th, in the morning, and he was buried on April 22nd. He was buried beautifully. His funeral cost $225, and the casket $60. Now when we win some [money] by law from the Company we will buy a place and transfer him, that he may lie quietly. We will surround him with a fence and put a cross, stone, or iron upon his grave."

    Thomas and Znaniecki, "The Polish Peasant," in *Europe and North America: A Monograph of an Immigrant Group*, 5 vols. (Chicago: University of Chicago Press, 1918–1920), quoted in Park and Miller, *Old World Traits Transplanted,* 125.
51. Breckinridge, *New Homes for Old*, 219.
52. Ibid., 191.
53. The Constitution of the National Croatian Society quoted in Breckinridge, *New Homes for Old*, 196. The Society's anti-Semitism is blatantly apparent.
54. Ibid., 187–221.
55. Ibid., 209–211.
56. Ibid., 212.
57. Ibid., 214–215.
58. Park and Miller, *Old World Traits Transplanted*, 306.
59. Ewen, *Immigrant Women in the Land of Dollars*, 15.
60. Breckinridge, *New Homes for Old*, 211.
61. Bellah et al., *Habits of the Heart*, 276. Micaela di Leonardo takes issue with the unencumbered self that Bellah et al. posit. She remarks, "[I]f we shift the focus to include

all Americans, both as agents and as objects of the cultural construction of the self, we perceive instead an American landscape littered with images of very cumbered selves." Di Leonardo, *Exotics at Home*, 80. She continues, "I suggest not only that there are multiple inventions of tradition in American life and many versions of the self, but also that all invented traditions, as anthropologist Frederick Barth noted in 1969 concerning ethnicity, are historically contingent and constructed on the boundaries of group membership" (81). Di Leonardo is right, but I want to draw from Bellah et al. that the unencumbered self is the *mythic norm* in American national community. And while multiple invented American traditions exist simultaneously, the national imaginary has been fired by this peculiarly American modernist tradition.

62. Bellah et al., *Habits of the Heart*, 157.

63. Ibid., 156.

64. Ibid., 282.

65. See Richard Schaefer, *Racial And Ethnic Groups* (Aldon-Wesley Education Publishers: New York, 1998). Schaefer qutoes Hansen who said that "what the son wishes to forget, the grandson wishes to remember" (from Marcus Lee Hansen, "The Third Generation in America," *Commentary* 14 [November 1952]: 493–500). Goering found that ethnicity is more important to the third generation than immigrants themselves. John Goering, "The Emergence of Ethnic Interests: A Case of Serendipity," *Social Forces* 48 (March 1971): 379–384.

66. Mary Waters, *Ethnic Options: Choosing Identities in America* (Berkeley: University of California Press, 1990), 15).

67. Di Leonardo writes that "white ethnicity suddenly became a topic of key concern. Across the nation, moribund ethnic voluntary associations revived and countless new ones formed. Popular books celebrating white ethnic experience, such as the second edition of Nathan Glazer and Daniel Patrick Moynihan's *Beyond the Melting Pot*, Michael Novak's *Rise of Unmeltable Ethnics*, Andrew *Greenly's Why Can't They Be Like Us?*, and Richard Gambino's *Blood of My Blood*, became best-sellers." Di Leonardo, *Exotics at Home*, 89.

68. Ibid., 91. The 1950s–1960s social movements all more or less sought greater right and attempted to convert the American state into a more moral entity through making it accountable to its citizenry. These new social movements were often directed at the full realization of individual rights for all persons, and not just White, middle-class men. Overall, they did not challenge the ideals of an essential American identity, so much as attempting to make the American community more broadly inclusive and egalitarian. Black Power and Brown Power movements, however, challenged the very foundations of the imagined American community.

69. Micaela di Leonardo says these claims were unsubstantiated, because, for example, at the height of white ethnic revival, "California's prototypical Italian-American community, San Francisco's North Beach, had more than 90 percent Chinese residents, and California's Italian-American population was in reality scattered far and wide across the state's urban, suburban, and rural areas. Di Leonardo, *Exotics at Home*, 89–90.

70. Waters, *Ethnic Options*, 160.

71. Ibid., 157

72. Ibid., 155–168.

73. di Leonardo, *Exotics at Home*, 93.

74. Marshall Berman, *All That Is Solid Melts Into Air: The Experience of Modernity* (New York: Penguin Books, 1982), 332.
75. Ibid., 332.
76. Ibid., 335.
77. Paul Krugman makes this observation in "For Richer: How the Permissive Capitalism of the Boom Destroyed American Equality," *New York Times Magazine*, October 20, 2002.
78. Ibid., 66.
79. Ibid., 64.
80. di Leonardo, *Exotics at Home*, 109.
81. Ibid., 109.
82. Simon says that Americans in general are skeptical of immigrants. The belief, especially strong among conservative groups such as Federation for American Immigration Reform and the Rockford Institute is that "immigrants cannot comprehend certain intangible notions of U.S. politics, art, literature, religious morality, and work ethic." Rita Simon, "Old Minorities, New Immigrants," 62.
83. George Lipsitz, *The Possessive Investment In Whiteness: How White People Profit From Identity Politics* (Philadelphia: Temple University Press, 1998).
84. Ibid.
85. This is Joppke's summarization of Peter Brimelow's 1995 *Alien-Nation*. Christian Joppke, ed., *Immigration and the Nation-State: The United States, Germany, and Great Britain* (New York: Oxford University Press, 1999), 55.
86. Nathan Glazer, "Is Assimilation Dead?" *Annals of the American Political and Social Sciences* 530 (November 1993): 122–136; Richard Alba and Victor Nee, "Rethinking Assimilation Theory for a New Era of Immigration," *International Migration Review* 31 (winter 1997): 826–872.
87. Milton Gordon, *Assimilation In American Life: The Role of Race, Religion, and National Origins* (New York: Oxford University Press, 1964).
88. Alejandro Portes and Jozef Borocz, "Contemporary Immigration: Theoretical Perspectives on Its Determinants and Modes of Incorporation," *International Migration Review* 23, no. 3 (1989): 606–630; Alejandro Portes and Min Zhou, "The New Second Generation: Segmented Assimilation and Its Variants Among Post-1965 Immigrant Youth," *Annals of the American Academy of Political and Social Science* 530 (1993): 74–98; Min Zhou, "Segmented Assimilation: Issues, Controversies, and Recent Research on the New Second Generation," *International Migration Review* 31 (winter 1997): 975–1008.
89. Portes and Zhou, "New Second Generation," 74–98.
90. Ibid., 89.
91. Min Zhou, "Segmented Assimilation," 994.
92. Ibid.
93. Quoted in David Palumbo-Liu, *Asian/American: Historical Crossings of a Racial Frontier* (Stanford, Calif.: Stanford University Press: 1999), 193.
94. Ibid., 197.
95. Margaret Gibson, *Accommodation Without Assimilation: Sikh Immigrants in an American High School* (Ithaca, N.Y.: Cornell University Press, 1989).
96. Sathi S. Dasgupta, *On The Trail Of An Uncertain Dream: Indian Immigrant Experience in America* (New York: AMS Press, 1989), 192.

97. Ibid., 73.
98. Ibid., 72.
99. Ibid., 76.

Seven   Not White in Public, Not Ethnic at Home

1. Polletta, "'Free Spaces.'"
2. 1997 mission statement of the Indo American Center. [Emphasis is mine]
3. Park and Miller, *Old World Traits Transplanted*, 143–144.
4. Charles Taylor, "The Politics of Recognition," 34–35.
5. Ibid., 64.
6. Ibid., 71.
7. Ibid., 63.

Eight   The Cultural Turn in Politics and Community Organizing

1. Christian Joppke, *Immigration and the Nation State*; "Immigration Challenges the Nation-State," 34.
2. Rogers Smith notes that liberals point "to a cosmopolitan world order in which memberships in particular political communities would have little or no importance. However, appealing such a cosmopolitan vision may be . . . advocates of liberal democratic principles still cannot be safely blind to the fact that for the foreseeable future, politicians proposing a just, democratic regime to govern all the world's people are not likely to compete for power successfully against those offering more particularist political visions." Smith, *Civic Ideals*, 9. The question to ask, says Smith, is how liberal democratic principles can be used without sacrificing the idealism they embody for the political expediency of nation building. Historically, Americanist civil ideals are believed to have produced a universalism among its citizenry, but this has invariably been truer for eastern and Southern Europeans. Those deemed non-White have been written out of the American social contract. Smith observes that successful American political actors "have not been pure liberals, democratic republicans, or ascriptive Americanists, but have instead combined politically potent elements of all three views" (6).
3. Joppke, *Immigration and the Nation-State,* 185.
4. For an excellent historical account of race in the making of South Africa, Brazil, and the United States, see Anthony Marx, *Making Race and Nation: A Comparison of the United States, South Africa, and Brazil* (New York: Cambridge University Press, 1998), 3.
5. Smith, *Civic Ideals*, 11.
6. Jurgen Habermas. "Struggles for Recognition in the Democratic Constitutional State," in *Multiculturalism,* 124.
7. Joppke notes that the sovereignty of liberal western democracies, such as the United States, are restrained by the internal challenges they face. Liberal legal systems and domestic client and constitutional politics explain "the generosity and expansiveness of Western states towards immigrants than the vague reference to a global economy and an international human rights regime. The sovereignty of states regarding immigration control is more internally than externally restricted." Joppke, "Immigration Challenges the Nation-State," 20.

8. Lopez, *White by Law*, 123.
9. Ibid., 14–15.
10. Habermas, "Struggles for Recognition," 124.
11. Nancy Fraser, *Justice Interruptus: Critical Reflections on the "Postsocialist" Condition* (New York: Routledge, 1997).
12. Ibid., 24.
13. Lowe, *Immigrant Acts*, 25.
14. Fraser, *Justice Interruptus*, 22.
15. Ibid., 30.
16. Marx, *Making Race and Nation*, 2.
17. Ibid., 10–17.
18. Lowe, *Immigrant Acts*, 86.
19. Ibid., 25.
20. Ibid., 86.
21. See Benedict Anderson's *Imagined Communities* (1983); or Michael Billig's *Banal Nationalism* (London: SAGE Publications, 1995).
22. Lowe, *Immigrant Acts*, 86.
23. Fraser, *Justice Interruptus*, 92.
24. Galston, *Liberal Purposes: Goods, Virtues, and Duties in a Liberal State* (Cambridge, Cambridge University Press, 1991).
25. Jeffrey Alexander, "Citizen and Enemy as Symbolic Classification: On the Polarizing Discourse on Civil Society," in *Cultivating Differences: Symbolic Boundaries and the Making of Inequality*, edited by Michele Lamont and Marcel Fournier (Chicago: University of Chicago Press, 1992), 289–308.
26. Ibid., 291.
27. Ibid., 301.
28. Nira Yuval-Davis, "Ethnicity, Gender Relations, and Multiculturalism," *Race, Identity, and Citizenship: A Reader*, edited by Rodolfo D. Torres, Louis F. Miron, and Jonathan X. Inda (Oxford: Blackwell Publishers, 1999).
29. Goffman, *Presentation of Self*, 35.
30. Nikolas Rose, *The Powers of Freedom: Re-framing Political Thought* (Cambridge, N.Y.: Cambridge University Press, 1999), 4. He builds from Foucault's essay on governmentality.
31. Ibid., 171.
32. Ibid., 174–175.
33. Evans and Boyte quoted in Polletta, "'Free Spaces' in Collective Action," 5.

Bibliography

Abraham, Margaret. *Speaking the Unspeakable: Marital Violence among South Asian Immigrants in the United States*. New Brunswick, N.J.: Rutgers University Press, 2000.

Agarwal, Priya. "Doctor or Engineer? Career Choices among Second-Generation Indian Americans." *The Indian American* (March 1993): 24–26.

Agnew, Vijay. *In Search of a Safe Place: Abused Women and Culturally Sensitive Services*. Toronto: University of Toronto Press, 1998.

———. "Tensions in Providing Services to South Asian Victims of Wife Abuse in Toronto." *Violence Against Women* 4, no. 2 (1998): 153–179.

Alam, Nahar. "Domestic Workers Do Their Homework." *Samar* (summer/fall 1997): 15–20.

Alba, Richard, and Victor Nee. "Rethinking Assimilation: Theory for a New Era of Immigration." *International Migration Review* 31 (winter 1997): 826–872.

Alexander, Jeffrey. "Citizen and Enemy as Symbolic Classification: On the Polarizing Discourse of Civil Society." In *Cultivating Differences: Symbolic Boundaries and The Making of Inequality*, edited by Michele Lamont and Marcel Fournier, 289–308. Chicago: University of Chicago Press, 1992.

Alexander, Meena. *The Shock of Arrival: Reflections on the Post-colonial Experience*. Boston: South End Press, 1996.

Alpers, Svetlana. "The Museum as a Way of Seeing." In *Exhibiting Cultures: The Poetics and Politics of Museum Display*, edited by Ivan Karp and Steven D. Lavine, 25-41. Washington, D.C.: Smithsonian Institution Press, 1991.

Amott, Teresa, and Julie Matthaie. *Race, Gender and Work: A Multicultural Economic History of Women in the United States*. Boston: South End Press, 1991.

Anderson, Benedict. *Imagined Communities*. London: Verso, 1983.

Anderson, K., and D. C. Jack. "Learning to Listen: Interview Techniques and Analyses." In *Women's Words: The Feminist Practice of Oral History*, edited by Sherna Berger Gluck and Daphne Patai. New York: Routledge, 1991.

Anderson, Michelle J. "A License to Abuse: The Impact of Conditional Status on Female Immigrants." *The Yale Law Journal* 102, no. 6 (1993): 1401–1421.

Bacon, Jean. *Life Lines: Community, Family, And Assimilation Among Asian Indian Immigrants*. New York: Oxford University Press, 1996.

Bartky, Sandra Lee. "Sympathy and Solidarity: On a Tight Rope with Scheler." In *Feminists Rethink The Self*, edited by Diane Tietjens Meyers, 177–196. Boulder, Colo.: Westview Press, 1997.

Bauman, Zygmunt. *Community: Seeking Safety in an Insecure World*. Cambridge, England: Polity, 2001.

Bellah, Robert, Richard Madsen, William Sullivan, Ann Swidler, and Steven Tipton. *Habits of the Heart: Individualism and Commitment in American Life*. Berkeley: University of California, 1985.

Bendix, Regina. *In Search of Authenticity: The Formation of Folklore Studies*. Madison: University of Wisconsin Press, 1997.

Berkson, Isaac B. *Theories of Americanization: A Critical Study*. New York: Teachers College Bureau of Publications, 1920.

Berman, Marshall. *All That Is Solid Melts Into Air: The Experience of Modernity*. New York: Penguin Books, 1982.

———. *The Politics of Authenticity: Radical Individualism and the Emergence of Modern Society*. New York: Atheneum, 1970.

Bhattacharjee, Annanya. "The Habit of Ex-Nomination: Nation, Women, and the Indian Immigrants Bourgeoisie." *Public Culture* 5, no. 1 (fall 1992): 19–44.

———. "A Slippery Path: Organizing Resistance to Violence Against Women." In *Dragon Ladies: Asian American Feminists Breathe Fire*, edited by Sonia Shah, 29–45. Boston, Mass.: South End Press, 1997.

Billig, Michael. *Banal Nationalism*. London: SAGE Publications, 1995, reprint 2001.

Bonilla-Silva, Eduardo. "Re-thinking Racism: Towards a Structural Interpretation." *American Sociological Review* 62, no. 3 (1997): 465–480.

Boon, James A. "Why Museums Make Me Sad," In *Exhibiting Cultures: The Poetics and Politics of Museum Display*, edited by Ivan Karp and Steven D. Lavine, 255–277. Washington, D.C.: Smithsonian Institution Press, 1991.

Boswell, Helen Varick. "Promoting Americanization." In *Americanization: Principles of Americanism, Essentials of Americanization, Technic of Race-Assimilation, Annotated Bibliography*, edited by Winthrop Talbot. New York: H.W. Wilson Company, 1917.

Bourdieu, Pierre. "The Family as a Realized Category." *Theory, Culture, and Society* 13, no. 3 (1996): 19–26.

———. *Logic of Practice*. Stanford, Calif.: Polity, 1990.

———. *Outline of a Theory of Practice*. New York: Cambridge University Press: 1977.

Bourne, Randolph S. *Atlantic Monthly* 118 (July 1916): 86–97. Reprinted in *Theories of Ethnicity: A Classical Reader*, edited by Werner Sollors. New York: New York University Press, 1996.

Boyd, Todd. *Am I Black Enough For You? Popular Culture From the 'Hood and Beyond*. Bloomington: Indiana University Press, 1997.

Breckinridge, Sophonisba P. *New Homes For Old*. New York: Harper and Brothers Publishing, 1921.

Briggs, Vernon. *Mass Immigration and the National Interest*. Armonk, N.Y.: Sharpe, 1992.

Brison, Susan. "Outliving Oneself: Trauma, Memory, and Personal Identity," In *Feminists Rethink The Self*, edited by Diane Tietjens Meyers, 12–39. Boulder, Colo.: Westview Press, 1997.

Burawoy, Michael, Alice Burton, Ann Ferguson, and Kathryn Fox. *Ethnography Unbound: Power and Resistance in the Metropolis*. Berkeley: University of California Press, 1991.

Butler, Judith. *Bodies That Matter: On the Discursive Limits of Sex*. New York: Routledge, 1993.

California State Board of Control. *California and the Oriental: Japanese, Chinese and Hindus. Report of State Board of Control of California to Gov. Wm. D. Stephens, June 19, 1920. Rev. to January 1, 1922*. Sacramento: California State Printing Office, 1922.

Calvo, Janet M. "Spouse Based Immigration Laws: The Legacy of Coverture." In *Critical Race Feminism: A Reader*, edited by Adrien D. Wing, 380–386. New York: New York University Press, 1997.

Carlson, Robert. "Americanization as an Early Twentieth-Century Adult Education Movement." In *American Immigration and Ethnicity: Americanization, Social Control, and Philanthropy*, edited by George E. Pozzetta, 450–475. New York: Garland Publishing, 1991.

Chakravarti, Uma. "Whatever Happened To The Vedic *Dasi*? Orientalism, Nationalism, and a Script for the Past." In *Recasting Women: Essays in Colonial History*, edited by Kumkum Sangari and Sudesh Vaid, 27–87. New Brunswick, N.J.: Rutgers University Press,, 1990.

Chakravorty, Pallabi. "Hegemony, Dance and Nation: The Construction of the Classical Dance in India." *South Asia* 21 (1998): 107–120.

Charme, Stuart Zane. *Vulgarity and Authenticity: Dimensions of Otherness in the World of Jean-Paul Sartre*. Amherst, Mass.: University of Massachusetts Press, 1991.

Chatterjee, Partha. *The Nation and its Fragments*. Princeton, N.J.: Princeton University Press, 1993.

Chin, Ko-Lin. "Out-of Town Brides: International Marriage and Wife Abuse Among Chinese Immigrants." *Journal of Comparative Family Studies* 25, no. 1 (1994): 53–65.

Chodorow, Nancy. *The Reproduction Of Mothering: Psychoanalysis And The Sociology Of Gender*. Berkeley: University of California Press, 1978.

Commons, John R. "Amalgamation and Assimilation." In *Americanization: Principles of Americanism, Essentials of Americanization, Technic of Race-Assimilation, Annotated Bibliography*, edited by Winthrop Talbot. New York: H.W. Wilson Company, 1917.

Daniels, Roger. *History of Indian Immigration To The United States*. New York: Asia Society, 1989.

Dar, Huma. "The Battle Cry of an Ex-Battered Ex-Wife." In *Our Feet Walk The Sky*, edited by Women of the South Asian Diaspora Collective, 252. San Francisco: Aunt Lute Books, 1993.

Das Gupta, Monisha. "What is Indian About You? A Gendered, Transnational Approach to Ethnicity." *Gender & Society* 115 (1997): 572–596.

Dasgupta, Sathi S. *On The Trail Of An Uncertain Dream: Indian Immigrant Experience in America*. New York: AMS Press, 1989.

Dasgupta, Sayantini. "Thoughts from a Feminist ABCD." *India Currents* 6, no. 12 (1993): 26.

Dasgupta, Shamita Das, and Sayantini Dasgupta. "Astride the Lion's Back: Gender Relations in the Asian Indian Community." In *Contours of the Heart: South Asians map*

North America, edited by Sunaina Maira and Rajini Srikanth, 381–400. New York: Asian American Writers' Workshop. Distributed by Rutgers University Press, 1996.

———. "Bringing up Baby: Raising a 'Third World' Daughter in the 'First World.'" In *Dragon Ladies: Asian American Feminists Breathe Fire*, edited by Sonia Shah, 182–199. Boston: South End Press, 1997.

Dasgupta, Shamita Das, and Sujata Warrier. "In the Footsteps of 'Arundati.'" *Violence against Women* 2, no. 3 (1996): 238–258.

de Beauvoir, Simone. *The Second Sex*, trans. by H. M. Parshley. New York: Knopf, 1953.

Debord, Guy. *Society of the Spectacle*. Detroit: Black & Red, 1983.

di Leonardo, Micaela. *Exotics at Home: Anthropologies, Others, American Modernity*. Chicago: University of Chicago Press, 1998.

DuBois, W.E.B. "The Negro in the United States," 1903, Reproduced in *Americanization: Principles of Americanism, Essentials of Americanization, Technic of Race-Assimilation, Annotated Bibliography*, edited by Winthrop Talbot. New York: H.W. Wilson Company, 1917.

———. *The Souls of Black Folk*. Reprint, New York: Bantam Books, 1989.

Dutt, Ela, and Aziz Haniffa. "Three Candidates Lost, but They Have Left Their Imprint." *India Abroad* 25, no. 7 (1994): 4.

Espin, Oliva M. 1995. "'Race', Racism, and Sexuality in the Life Narratives of Immigrant Women." *Feminism and Psychology* 5, no. 2 (1994): 223–238.

Esser, Josef, and Joachim Hisrch. "The Crisis of Fordism and the Dimensions of a 'Post-Fordist' Regional and Urban Structure." In *Post-Fordism: A Reader*, edited by Ash Amin, 71–98. Oxford: Blackwell, 1994.

Etter-Lewis, G. "Black Women's Life Stories: Reclaiming Self in Narrative Texts." In *Women's Words: The Feminist Practice of Oral History*, edited by Sherna Berger Gluck and Daphne Patai, 43–58. New York: Routledge, 1991.

Ewen, Elizabeth. *Immigrant Women in the Land of Dollars: Life and Culture on the Lower East Side, 1890–1925*. New York: Monthly Review Press, 1985.

Fanon, Franz. *The Wretched of the Earth*. New York: Grove Press, 1961.

Ferrara, Alessandro. *Reflective Authenticity: Rethinking the Project of Modernity*. New York: Routledge, 1998.

Foucault, Michel. *Discipline and Punish: The Birth of the Prison,* trans. by A. Sheridan. New York: Vintage Books, 1979.

Frank, Thomas. "Why Johnny Can't Dissent." In *Commodify Your Dissent: The Business of Culture in the New Gilded Age. Salvos from The Baffler*, edited by Thomas Frank and Matt Weiland, 31–45. New York: W.W. Norton, 1997.

Frankenberg, Ruth. *White Women, Race Matters*. Minneapolis: University of Minnesota Press, 1993.

Fraser, Nancy. *Justice Interruptus: Critical Reflections on the "Postsocialist" Condition*. New York: Routledge, 1997.

Freedberg, Sharon. "The Feminine Ethic of Care and the Professionalization of Social Work." *Social Work* 38, no. 5 (September 1993): 535–540.

Freudenberger, H. L. "Staff Burnout." *Journal of Social Issues* 30 (1974): 159–165.

———. "The Staff Burnout Syndrome in Alternative Institutions. *Psychotherapy: Theory Research & Practice* 12 (1975): 73–82.

Freudenberger, H. L., and G. Richelson. *Burnout: The High Cost of High Achievement*. Garden City, N.Y.: Anchor Press, 1980.

Fujiwara, Lynn H. The Impact of Welfare Reform on Asian Immigrant Communities."
Social Justice 25, no. 1 (spring 1998): 82–104.

Galston, William A. *Liberal Purposes: Goods, Virtues, and Duties in a Liberal State*. Cambridge, Mass.: Cambridge University Press, 1991.

George, Usha, and Sarah Ramkisson. "Race, Gender and Class: Interlocking Oppressions in the Lives of South Asian Women in Canada." *Affilia* 12, no. 1 (1998): 102–119.

Gerstle, Gary. *American Crucible: Race and Nation in the Twentieth Century*. Princeton, N.J.: Princeton University Press, 2001.

Gibson, Margaret. *Accommodation without Assimilation: Sikh Immigrants in an American High School*. Ithaca, N.Y.: Cornell University Press, 1989.

Giddens, Anthony. *Modernity and Self-Identity: Self and Society in the Late Modern Age* Stanford, Calif.: Stanford University Press, 1991.

Giles, Wenona. "Remembering The Portuguese Household in Toronto: Culture, Contradictions, and Resistance." *Women's Studies International Forum* 20, no. 3 (1997): 387–396.

Gilligan, Carol. *In A Different Voice: Psychological Theory and Women's Development*. Cambridge, Mass.: Harvard University Press, 1982.

Gilroy, Paul. *The Black Atlantic: Modernity and Double Consciousness*, Cambridge, Mass.: Harvard University Press, 1993.

Glazer, Nathan. "Is Assimilation Dead?" *The Annals of the American Academy of Political and Social Science* 530 (November 1993): 122–136.

Gleason, Philip. "American Identity and Americanization." *Harvard Encyclopedia of American Ethnic Groups*. Cambridge, Mass.: Harvard University Press, 1980.

———. "Americans All: World War II and the Shaping of American Identity." In *American Immigration and Ethnicity: Americanization, Social Control, and Philanthropy*, edited by George E. Pozzetta, 113–148. New York: Garland Publishing Inc., 1991.

Gluck, Sherna Berger, and Daphne Patai, eds. *Women's Words: The Feminist Practice of Oral History*. New York: Routledge, 1991.

Goering, John. "The Emergence of Ethnic Interests: A Case of Serendipity," *Social Forces* 49, no. 4 (June 1971): 379–384.

Goffman, Erving. *The Presentation of Self in Everyday Life*. New York: Anchor Books, 1959.

Gordon, George A. "The Foreign-Born American Citizen." In *Americanization: Principles of Americanism, Essentials of Americanization, Technic of Race-Assimilation, Annotated Bibliography*, edited by Winthrop Talbot. New York: H.W. Wilson Company, 1917.

Gordon, Linda. *Heroes of Their Own Lives: The Politics And History of Family Violence, Boston 1880–1960*. New York. Penguin Books, 1988.

Gordon, Milton. *Assimilation In American Life: The Role of Race, Religion, and National Origins*. New York: Oxford University Press, 1964.

Greenblatt, Stephen. "Resonance and Wonder." In *Exhibiting Cultures: The Poetics and Politics of Museum Display*, edited by Ivan Karp and Steven D. Lavine, 42–56. Washington, D.C.: Smithsonian Institution Press, 1991.

Gupta, Sangeeta R. "Walking On The Edge: Indian-American Women Speak Out On Dating and Marriage." In *Emerging Voices: South Asian American Women Redefine Self, Family, and Community*, edited by Sangeeta R. Gupta, 120–145. Walnut Creek, Calif.: AltaMira Press, 1999.

Habermas, Jurgen. "Struggles for Recognition in the Democratic Constitutional State." In *Multiculturalism*, edited by Amy Gutman, 107–148. Princeton, N.J.: Princeton University Press, 1994.

Hall, Stuart. "Cultural Identity and Cinematic Representation." In *Black British Cultural Studies: A Reader*, edited by Houston Baker, Jr., Manthia Diawara, and Ruth Lindeborg. Chicago: University of Chicago Press, 1996.

Hansen, Marcus Lee. "The Third Generation in America," *Commentary* 14 [November 1952]: 493-500. Cited in Richard Schaefer, *Racial And Ethnic Groups*. New York, Aldon-Wesley Education Publishers: 1998.

Harper, Douglas. "Small N's and Community Case Studies." In *What Is A Case: Exploring the Social Foundations of Social Inquiry*, edited by Charles Ragin and Howard Becker, 139–158. New York: Cambridge University Press, 1992.

Harvey, David. "Flexible Accumulation through Urbanization: Reflections on 'Post-Modernism' in the American City." In *Post-Fordism: A Reader*, edited by Ash Amin, 381–386. Oxford: Blackwell, 1994.

Heilbrun, Carolyn. *Writing a Woman's Life*. New York: Ballantine Books, 1988.

Helweg, Arthur, and Usha Helweg. *An Immigrant Success Story: East Indians In America*. Philadelphia: University of Pennsylvania Press, 1990.

Herman, Judith. *Trauma and Recovery*. New York: Basic Books, 1992.

Himmelweit, Susan. "Caring Labor." *The Annals of the American Academy of Political and Social Science* 561, no. 1 (January 1999): 27–38.

Hobsbawm, Eric, and Terence Ranger, eds. *The Invention of Tradition*. Cambridge, N.Y.: Cambridge University Press, 1983.

Hochschild, Arlie Russell. *The Managed Heart: Commercialization of Human Feeling*. Berkeley: University of California Press, 1983.

Hoff, Lee Ann. *Battered Women as Survivors*. New York: Routledge, 1990.

Huebner, Grover. "The Americanization of the Immigrant." *The Annals of The American Academy of Political and Social Science* 27 (May 1906): 653–675. Reprinted in *Americanization: Principles of Americanism, Essentials of Americanization, Technic of Race-Assimilation, Annotated Bibliography*, edited by Winthrop Talbot. New York: H.W. Wilson Company, 1917.

Ignatiav, Noel. *How the Irish Became White*. New York: Routledge, 1995.

Jacobson, Matthew Frye. *Whiteness of a Different Color*. Cambridge, Mass.: Harvard University Press, 1998.

Jameson, Frederic. *Postmodernism, Or, the Cultural Logic of Late Capitalism*. Durham, N.C.: Duke University Press, 1991.

Jejeebhoy, Shireen J. "Addressing Women's Reproductive Health Needs: Priorities for the Family Welfare Program." *Economic and Political Weekly* (March 1–8, 1997): 475–484.

Jessop, Bob. "Post-Fordism and the State," In *Post-Fordism: A Reader*, edited by Ash Amin, 251–279. Oxford: Blackwell, 1994.

Johnson, Lesley. "'As housewives we are worms': Women, Modernity and the Home Question." *Cultural Studies* 10, no. 3 (1996): 449–463.

Jones, Jacqueline. *Labor of Love, Labor of Sorrow: Black Women, Work, and the Family From Slavery to the Present*. New York: Basic Books, 1985.

Joppke, Christian. "Immigration Challenges the Nation-State." In *Challenge to the Nation-States: Immigration in Western Europe and the United States*, edited by Christian Joppke, 1-18. New York: Oxford University Press, 1998.

———. *Immigration and the Nation-State: The United States, Germany, and Great Britain.* New York: Oxford University Press, 1999.

Kallen, Horace M. "Democracy Versus Melting-Pot: A Study of American Nationality." *The Nation* 100, no. 2590 (1915): 190–194; and 100, no. 2591 (1915): 217–220. Reprinted in *Theories of Ethnicity: A Classical Reader*, edited by Werner Sollors. New York: New York University Press, 1996.

Kaplan, April. "Domestic Violence and Welfare Reform," 1998. Accessed December 2000. Available from: http://www.welfareinfo.org/aprildomestic.html

Knowles, Morris. "Housing and Americanization." Reproduced in *Americanization: Principles of Americanism, Essentials of Americanization, Technic of Race-Assimilation, Annotated Bibliography*, edited by Winthrop Talbot. New York: H.W. Wilson Company, 1917.

Korman, Gern. "Americanization at the Factory Gate." In *American Immigration and Ethnicity: Americanization, Social Control, and Philanthropy*, edited by George E. Pozzetta, 113–148. New York: Garland Publishing Inc., 1991.

Krugman, Paul. "For Richer: How the Permissive Capitalism of the Boom Destroyed American Equality." *New York Times Magazine*, October 20, 2002.

Langer, Lawrence, ed. *Admitting the Holocaust.* New York: Oxford University Press, 1995.

Leonard, Karen. *Making Ethnic Choices: California's Punjabi Mexican Americans.* Philadelphia: Temple University Press, 1992.

Lelyveld, David. "Upon the Subdominant: Administering Music on All-India Radio." *Consuming Modernity: Public Culture in a South Asian World*, edited by Carol Breckenridge, 189–214. Minneapolis: University of Minnesota Press, 1995.

Lieberson, Stanley. "Small Ns and Big Conclusions: An Examination of the Reasoning in Comparative Studies Based on a Small Number of Cases." In *What Is A Case: Exploring the Social Foundations of Social Inquiry*, edited by Charles Ragin and Howard Becker, 104-118. New York: Cambridge University Press, 1992.

Lipsitz, George. *The Possessive Investment In Whiteness: How White People Profit From Identity Politics.* Philadelphia: Temple University Press. 1998.

Lofland, John, and Lyn Lofland. *Analyzing Social Settings: A Guide To Qualitative Observation and Analysis.* Belmont, Calif.: Wadsworth Publishing Company, 1995.

Lopez, Ian F. Haney. *White By Law: The Legal Construction of Race.* New York: New York University Press, 1996.

Loseke, Donileen R. *The Battered Woman and Shelters: The Social Construction of Wife Abuse.* Albany, N.Y.: SUNY Press, 1992.

Lowe, Lisa. *Immigrant Acts: On Asian American Cultural Politics.* Durham, N.C.: Duke University Press, 1996.

Lynch, Caitrin. "Nation, Woman, and The Indian Immigrant Bourgeoisie: An Alternative Formulation." *Public Culture* 7, no. 1 (1994): 425–437.

MacKinnon, Catherine. *Toward a Feminist Theory of the State.* Cambridge, Mass.: Harvard University Press, 1989.

Mani, Lata. "Contentious Traditions: The Debate On *Sati* in Colonial India." In *Recasting Women: Essays in Colonial History*, edited by Kumkum Sangari and Sudesh Vaid, 88–126. New Brunswick, N.J.: Rutgers University Press, 1989.

Marshall, T. H. *Citizenship and Social Development.* Westport, Conn.: Greenwood Press, 1973.

Maslach, C., and S. E. Jackson, *Maslach Burnout Inventory*, Research Ed. Palo Alto, Calif.: Consulting Psychologists Press, 1981.

Marx, Anthony. *Making Race and Nation: A Comparison of the United States, South Africa, and Brazil*. New York: Cambridge University Press, 1998.

Mayer, Margit. "Post-Fordist City Politics." In *Post-Fordism: A Reader*, edited by Ash Amin, 316–337. Oxford: Blackwell, 1994.

Mayer, Stephen. "Adapting the Immigrant to the Line: Americanization in the Ford Factory, 1914–1921." In *American Immigration and Ethnicity: Americanization, Social Control, and Philanthropy*, edited by George E. Pozzetta, 113-148. New York: Garland Publishing Inc., 1991.

Mazumdar, Sucheta. "Racist responses to racism: The Aryan myth and South Asians in the United States." *South Asia Bulletin* 9, no. 1 (1989): 47–55.

———. "Women, Culture and Politics: Engendering the Hindu Nation." *South Asia Bulletin* 12, no. 2 (1992): 1–24.

Meduri, Avanti. "Bharatha Natyam, What Are You?" *Asian Theatre Journal* 5 (1988): 1–21.

Melendy, Brett. *Asians in America: Filipinos, Koreans, and East Indians*. Boston: Twayne Publishers, 1977.

Melwani, Lavina. "Shamita Das Dasgupta: Justice in Action." *Little India* 5, no. 3 (1995): 25.

Meyers, Diane Tietjens, ed. *Feminists Rethink The Self*. Boulder, Colo.: Westview Press, 1997.

Min, Pyong Gap, and Rose Kim, eds. *Struggle for Ethnic Identity: Narratives by Asian American Professionals*. Walnut Creek, Calif.: AltaMira Press, 1999.

Mohanty, Chandra Talpade. "Defining Genealogies: Feminist Reflections on Being South Asian In North America." In *Our Feet Walk The Sky*, edited by Women of the South Asian Diaspora Collective, 331–358. San Francisco: Aunt Lute Books, 1993.

Mohpatra, Manindra Kumar. *Ethnicity And Political Orientations Of Affluent Ethnics: A Study Of The Overseas Indians In The United States*. Norfolk, Va.: Old Dominion University, 1978.

Muller, Max. *Lectures on the Science of Language*. Delivered at the Royal Institute of Great Britain in February, March, April, and May, 1863. New York: Schribner, Armstrong, and Co., 1874.

Narayan, Uma. *Dislocating Cultures: Identities, Traditions, and Third World Feminism*. New York: Routledge, 1997.

———. "'Male Order' Brides: Immigrant Women, Domestic Violence and Immigration Law." *Hypatia* 10, no. 1 (1995): 104–112.

The National Conference on Immigration and Americanization. *Immigrants in America Review* 2: 38–46, April 1916. Reprint, *Americanization: Principles of Americanism, Essentials of Americanization, Technic of Race-Assimilation, Annotated Bibliography*, edited by Winthrop Talbot. New York: H.W. Wilson Company, 1917.

Omi, Michael, and Howard Winant. *Racial Formation in the United States*. 2nd ed. New York: Routledge, 1994.

Padilla, Yolanda C. "Immigration Policy: Issues for Social Work." *Social Work* 42, no. 6 (1997): 595–606.

Palumbo-Liu, David. *Asian/American: Historical Crossings of a Racial Frontier*. Stanford, Calif.: Stanford University Press, 1999.

Park, Robert, and Herbert Miller. *Old World Traits Transplanted*. New York: Harpers and Brothers Publishers, 1921.

Pincus, Stephen M., and David N. Rosen. "Fighting Back: Filing Suit Under the Violence Against Women Act." *Trial* 33, no. 12 (1997): 20–27.

Piven, Francis Fox, and Richard Cloward. *Poor People's Movements: Why They Succeed and How They Fail*. New York: Pantheon Books, 1977.

Plummer, Ken. *Telling Sexual Stories: Power, Change and Social Worlds*. London: Routledge, 1995.

Polletta, Francesca. "'Free Spaces' in Collective Action." *Theory and Society* 28, no. 1 (1999): 1–37.

Portes, Alejandro, and Jozef Borocz. "Contemporary Immigration: Theoretical Perspectives on Its Determinants and Modes of Incorporation." *International Migration Review* 23, no. 3 (1989): 606–630.

Portes, Alejandro, and Min Zhou. "The New Second Generation: Segmented Assimilation and its Variants." *The Annals of the American Academy of Political and Social Science* 530 (1993): 74–96.

Purkayastha, Bandana, S. Raman, and K. Bhide. "Empowering Women: SNEHA's Multifaceted Activism." In *Dragon Ladies: Asian American Feminists Breathe Fire*, edited by Sonia Shah, 100–107. Boston: South End Press, 1997.

Radhakrishnan, R. *Diasporic Mediations: Between Home and Location*. Minneapolis: University of Minnesota Press, 1996.

———. "Is the Ethnic 'Authentic' in the Diaspora?" In *The State of Asian America: Activism and Resistance in the 1990s*, edited by Karin Aguilar-San Juan, 219–234. Boston: South End Press, 1994.

Ranganathan, Murali. "Indians Top In Education, Income." *News India* 24, no. 17 (1994): 4.

Rangaswamy, Padma. *Namaste America: Indian Immigrants in an American Metropolis*. University Park: Pennsylvania State University Press, 2000.

Rayaprol, Aparna. *Negotiating Identities: Women in the Indian Diaspora*. New Delhi: Oxford University Press, 1997.

Richie, Beth E. *Compelled to Crime: The Gender Entrapment of Battered Black Women*. New York: Routledge, 1996.

Riessman, C. K. *Narrative Analysis*. Qualitative Research Method Series, 30, Sage Publications, 1993.

Riley, Denise. *"Am I That Name?" Feminism and the Category of "Women" in History*. Minneapolis: University of Minnesota Press, 1988.

Roediger, David. *The Wages Of Whiteness: Race And The Making Of The American Working Class*. London: Verso, 1991.

Rose, Nikolas. *The Powers of Freedom: Re-framing Political Thought*. New York: Cambridge University Press, 1999.

Rudrappa, Sharmila. "Disciplining Desire in Making Home: Engendering Ethnicity in Indian Immigrant Families in the United States." In *The Second Generation*, edited by Pyong Gap Min, 85–112. Walnut Creek, Calif.: AltaMira Press, 2002.

Rumbaut, Ruben G. "Assimilation and Its Discontents." *International Migration Review* 31 (winter 1997): 923–960.

Rushdie, Salman. *The Satanic Verses*. Dover, Del.: The Consortium: Inc., 1992. (First published in 1988.)

The Samar Collective. 1994. "One Big Happy Community? Class Issues Within South Asian American Homes." *Samar* (winter 1994): 10–15.

Sandburg, Carl. "Chicago." *Chicago Poems*, 1916. Reprint, University of Illinois Press, Urbana, 1992.

Sandhu, G. S. 1995. "Indian-Americans are industrious, resourceful, and prudent." *India Worldwide* (January 31, 1995).

Sangari, Kumkum, and Sudesh Vaid, eds. *Recasting Women: Essays In Colonial History.* New Brunswick, N.J.: Rutgers University Press, 1989.

Schaefer, Richard. *Racial And Ethnic Groups.* New York: Aldon-Wesley Education Publishers, 1998.

Scheler, Max. *The Nature of Sympathy*, trans. by Peter Heath, with a general introduction by W. Stark. Hamden, Conn.: Archon Books, 1970.

Shah, Purvi. "Redefining the Home: How Community Elites Silence Feminist Activism". In *Dragon Ladies: Asian American Feminists Breathe Fire*, edited by Sonia Shah, 46–56. Boston: South End Press, 1997.

Shargel, Joanne R. "In Defense of the Civil Rights Remedy of the Violence Against Women Act." *The Yale Law Journal* 106, no. 6 (1997): 1849–1883.

Shay, Jonathan. *Achilles in Vietnam: Combat Trauma and Undoing of Character.* New York: Atheneum, 1994.

Shultz, Alfred. *Race or Mongrel.* Boston: Little, Brown, 1908.

Simon, Rita. "Old Minorities. New Immigrants: Aspirations, Hopes, and Fears." *The Annals of the American Academy of Political and Social Science* 530 (November 1993): 61–73.

Singla, Anupy. "Prospects for South Asian Unity in a New World Order." *The Indian American* (March 1993): 15–17.

Smith, Rogers. *Civic Ideals: Conflicting Visions of Citizenship in U.S. History.* New Haven, Conn.: Yale University Press, 1997.

Snyder, D. K., and L. A. Fruchtman. "Differential Patterns of Wife Abuse: A Data Based Typology." *Journal of Consulting and Clinical Psychology* 49 (1980): 878–885.

Soderfeldt, Marie, Bjorn Solderfeldt, and Lars-Erik Warg. "Burnout in Social Work." *Social Work* 40, no. 5 (1995): 638–648.

Spelman, Elizabeth. *Inessential Woman: Problems of Exclusion in Feminist Theory.* Boston: Beacon Press, 1989.

Stall, Susan, and Randy Stoecker. "Community Organizing or Organizing Community? Gender and the Crafts of Empowerment." *Gender & Society* 12, no. 6 (1998): 729–756.

Stoddard, Lothrop. *Reforging America.* New York: Charles Scribner's Sons, 1927.

———. *The Rising Tide of Color Against White World Supremacy.* New York: Charles Scribner's Sons, 1920.

Strube, Michael, and Linda Barbour. "The Decision to Leave an Abusive Relationship: Economic Dependence and Psychological Commitment." *Journal of Marriage and the Family* 45, no. 4. (November 1983): 785–793.

Sunder, Mukhi Sunita. "'Underneath My Blouse Beats My Indian Heart': Sexuality, Nationalism and Indian Womanhood in the United States." In *A Patchwork Shawl: Chronicles of South Asian Women in America*, edited by Shamita Das Dasgupta, 186–205. New Brunswick, N.J.: Rutgers University Press, 1998.

Supriya, K. E. "Confessionals, Testimonials: Women's Speech in/and Contexts of Violence." *Hypatia* 11, no. 4 (1996): 92–106.

————. "Speaking Others, Practicing Selves: Representational Practices of Battered Immigrant Women in Apna Ghar 'Our Home.'" *Women and Performance: A Journal of Feminist Theory* 7–8, no. 2 (1995): 1.

Talbot, Winthrop. "Americanism." In *Americanization: Principles of Americanism, Essentials of Americanization, Technic of Race-Assimilation, Annotated Bibliography*, edited by Winthrop Talbot. New York: H.W. Wilson Company, 1917.

Taylor, Charles. "The Politics of Recognition." In *Multiculturalism and the Politics of Recognition*, edited by Amy Gutman. Princeton, N.J.: Princeton University Press, 1994.

Thomas, Thomas I., and Florian Znaniecki. "The Polish Peasant." In *Europe and North America: A Monograph of an Immigrant Group*. 5 vols. Chicago: University of Chicago Press, 1918-1920.

Thorne, Barrie, and Marylin Yalom, eds. *Rethinking the Family: Some Feminist Questions*. Boston: Northeastern University Press, 1992.

Tilly, Charles. *Citizenship, Identity and Social History*. Cambridge: Cambridge University Press, 1999.

Uberoi, Patricia, ed. *Social Reform, Sexuality and the State*. New Delhi: Sage Publications, 1996.

Vasudeva, Amita. "Journal Entry." In *Our Feet Walk The Sky*, edited by Women of the South Asian Diaspora Collective 132–133. San Francisco: Aunt Lute Books, 1993.

Visweswaran, Kamala. "Predicaments of the Hyphen," In *Our Feet Walk The Sky*, edited by Women of the South Asian Diaspora Collective, 301–302. San Francisco: Aunt Lute Books, 1993.

Waters, Mary. *Ethnic Options: Choosing Identities in America*. Berkeley: University of California Press, 1990.

Welfare Reform Network News. March 31, 1997.

Weyl, Walter E. "New Americans." In *Americanization: Principles of Americanism, Essentials of Americanization, Technic of Race-Assimilation, Annotated Bibliography*, edited by Winthrop Talbot. New York: H.W. Wilson Company, 1917.

Wharton, Amy S. "The Psychosocial Consequences of Emotional Labor." *The Annals of the American Academy of Political and Social Science* 561 (January 1999): 158–176.

White, Evelyn C. *Chain, Chain, Change: For Black Women Dealing with Physical and Emotional Abuse*. Seattle: Wash.: The Seal Press, 1985.

Williams, Patricia. *The Alchemy of Race and Rights: Diary of a Law Professor*. Cambridge, Mass.: Harvard University Press, 1991.

Wilson, Woodrow. "The Meaning of Citizenship: An Address to Newly Naturalized Citizens, Philadelphia, May 10, 1915." Reprinted in *Americanization: Principles of Americanism, Essentials of Americanization, Technic of Race-Assimilation, Annotated Bibliography*, edited by Winthrop Talbot. New York: H.W. Wilson Company, 1917.

Yuval-Davis, Nira. 1999. "Ethnicity, Gender Relations, and Multiculturalism." *Race, Identity, and Citizenship: A Reader*, edited by Rodolfo D. Torres, Louis F. Miron, and Jonathan X. Inda, 112–125. Oxford: Blackwell Publishers, 1999.

Zavella, Patricia. *Women's Work and Chicano Families*. Ithaca, N.Y.: New York: Cornell University Press, 1987.

Zerubavel, Eviatar. "Social Memories: Steps to a Sociology of the Past," *Qualitative Sociology* 19, no. 3 (1996): 283–299.

Zhou, Min. 1997. "Segmented Assimilation: Issues, Controversies, and Recent Research on the New Second Generation." *International Migration Review* 31 (winter 1997): 975–1008.

Index

abuse, 37–39; American specificities, 49–51; narratives, 38–39, 85, 87, 89–90; perspectives, 18–19; silence, 44, 56; South Asian specificities, 42–49, 52–53, 54–57, 69; stories, 42, 70–71. *See also* domestic violence

abuse survivors at Apna Ghar, 31–74, 173–174, 192; emerging as, 37–39; South Asian immigrant women, 39–40; immigrant status, 42, 72–73

African American. *See* race

Agnew, Vijay, 98–99

Alam, Nahar, 20, 59, 201n33

alcoholism, 33–34, 42

Alexander, Jeffrey, 186–187

alienation, 144; as immigrants, 44, 130–131, 175; as workers, 83, 95–98, 172–173

Alpers, Svetlana, 205n9

American: Americanization programs, 151–153, 157–159; anxieties about Americanization, 153–155, 156–157; gendered aspects of Americanization, 67, 152–153, 163; meaning of 150–151, 159; social workers, 152–153; usage of Americanization, 149; late twentieth century modes of becoming American, 160–162, 168–170, 176–177, 188–189, 193; national identity, 150–151. *See also* assimilation; citizenship; imagined communities

Anderson, Benedict, 213n11, 219n21

anomie. *See* alienation

anti-modern, 134, 161–162, 209n7

Apna Ghar: background on, 17–21, 35–36; as free space, 21, 191; fundraising and grants, 31–32, 34–35, 98–99; institutionalization, 96–99; intervention strategies, 36–37, 51–54, 57–58, 75; parenting classes, residents, 41; workers, 75–84. *See also* caseworkers

appropriation: cultural, 8, 125, 164–165; of dissent, 8, 15–16

Asian American. *See* race

recognition and redistribution, 12–13, 182–185; white prerequisites, 112, 181. *See also* Americanization; assimilation; imagined communities

civil rights, 10, 196n9. *See also* citizenship

civil society, 5; Americanization and, 151; repression in, 186–183; 218n2; third sector in, 13–14

class: IAC Board members and, 20–21, 101–102; shelter residents, 19; shelter workers, 75–78; social workers early twentieth century, 152–153; presentations of, 112, 115; whiteness and, 163–164

colonialism, 120–121, 147, 207nn28, 30. *See also* Fanon, Frantz

communities, 6–7, 14, 16–17, 74, 105, 160, 163, 165, 169, 187; of caring, 39, 82–83; domestic violence and, 18–19, 43, 53, 56–57, 74–75; formation of, 25, 30, 105, 122–123, 135, 180–181; as free spaces, 21–22; governmentality and, 189–193; imagined, 147–150, 184–185, 188; of memory, 160. *See also* citizenship

commodity, 3–4, 8, 195n2; race and, 211n37

conformity. *See* assimilation

consumerism, 4, 7–8, 14; American identity and, 67, 158–159, 163, 164–65; shelter work and, 35, 80

cooptation, 6–7, 8, 15–16, 190–191. *See also* resistance

counseling, 35, 36, 41, 52–53, 54, 85–86

cultures: in Apna Ghar, 25, 26, 189; of citizenship, 10, 11–12; clothes,

113, 109, 118, 122, 123–124; competence, 95; differences, 188, high, 115–118; ethnic, 22–24, 40, 48–49, 107, 132–133, 137–139, 145, 157,166–168, 171–172; ethnic white, 159–161; Indian, 121, 175; national, 11–12, 147–149, 184–185; post-fordist, 7–8, 14, 164–165; representation, 101, 108–118, 122, 125, 188; Third World, 114–115; turn in politics, 12–13, 15–16, 28, 164–165, 182–185; violence and, 42, 44; white, 24, 141–142, 144, 153, 164

dance, classical Indian. *See* Bharat Natyam; Bollywood

Das Dasgupta, Shamita, 18, 200n20

Dasgupta, Sathi, 217n96

Dasgupta, Sayantini, 22

democracy: American identity and 150; contradictions in, 184, 185–188; multiculturalism and, 177; participatory, 13–14, 189–190

dependence: and American women, 49–50; emotional, 49–51, 54, 56, 71, 90; South Asian women's, 41–46. *See also* autonomy; independence

discipline, 15, 64–66, 173, 176; Americanization and, 151–153, 193; of shelter residents, 41, 84, 89–90, 189, 192; of shelter workers, 29, 82, 88–89

dignity, 12, 39, 40, 177. *See also* self

domestic violence, 36–40, 50, 52 70–71, 73; denial of, 18, 197n27, 198n29; fund-raising, 31–32, 34;

About the Author

Sharmila Rudrappa is an assistant professor in the Department of Sociology and the Center for Asian American Studies at the University of Texas at Austin.